A Road Less Travelled

Tales of the Irish Missionaries

Aidan Clerkin & Brendan Clerkin

EDITORS

with a Foreword by
President Mary McAleese

OPEN AIR

Set in 11 pt on 13.5 pt AGaramond for
OPEN AIR
An imprint of Four Courts Press
7 Malpas Street, Dublin 8, Ireland
www.fourcourtspress.ie
and in North America for
FOUR COURTS PRESS
c/o ISBS, 920 N.E. 58th Avenue, Suite 300, Portland, OR 97213.

A catalogue record for this title
is available from the British Library.

ISBN 978-1-84682-317-6

NOTE ON ROYALTIES FROM SALES OF BOOK

Royalties are being donated to Mukuru Arts & Crafts, a creative arts centre founded
on the edge of Mukuru slum in Nairobi by an Irish Mercy Sister, Lori Burns.
The illustrations in this book have been drawn by students of the centre.

Printed in England
by CPI Antony Rowe, Chippenham, Wilts.

Foreword

A Road Less Travelled gives a voice to men and women who, in exercising their mission today, are the latest link in a long and proud tradition of Irish missionaries. As President, I've had the privilege to visit Irish missionaries in a number of countries around the world and have seen at first hand the direct and positive impact many of them are having on lives within their adopted communities. It is fascinating, intriguing and inspiring to read of their vision, their lifestyles, their frustrations, their challenges and their hopes for the future, especially in these sceptical times.

The sheer diversity of work performed by Irish missionaries is such that it would be impossible to speak of a typical missionary experience. However, what they all have in common is a passionate belief in human freedom and the human dignity of each person in our world. They provide education and health care to the most disadvantaged; they speak out fearlessly on behalf of those whose voices would not otherwise be heard; they work tirelessly for peace and justice. They adapt to new languages, new cultures, new ways of life, often in some of the most impoverished or conflict-ridden parts of the world. They bring a message of hope where there is need of hope and immerse themselves in doing whatever is necessary to fulfil that need.

Ireland's sad history of poverty, famine and conflict gives us a special empathy with those experiencing these same harsh realities today and our missionaries embody the keen sense of social justice which is the hallmark of the Irish people. Our official development aid programme, Irish Aid, which targets its assistance to the world's poorest people, is inspired in many ways by the efforts of generations of Irish missionaries and stands on the foundations laid by them. Today's Irish missionaries continue in that tradition of selfless service. We can measure their contribution in terms of numbers of schools built or clinics opened but what is much more difficult to measure is the real life-enhancing impact they have on the lives of communities throughout the developing world.

Through this book, we gain a rich insight into the passion and vocation that inspires Irish religious and lay missionaries. They are well-educated, talented, driven people who chose not to live comfortable lives at home but instead to make their lives among those blighted by oppression, hunger, poverty, war or inequality. They do not act in the hope of recognition or reward but it is entirely right that we recognise the enormous contribution they have made and continue to make. Theirs is a story deserving of this telling.

Mary McAleese
President of Ireland

Contents

Appendices

Acknowledgments

There are many people whose role in the creation of this book we wish to acknowledge. Most importantly, there are the many contributors who took the time and effort to get in touch with us by post, telephone and email, and who remained available for subsequent contact. We have endeavoured to include as many of them as possible in the miscellany, and we hope this final product is a suitable reward for their efforts.

We are honoured that the President of Ireland, Mary McAleese, has taken such an interest in our project and contributed an eloquent Foreword to this collection.

Our sincere thanks also go to Denis O'Brien and his colleagues Maria Mulcahy and Andrina Moore at the Iris O'Brien Foundation for their generous support from early on.

Martin Fanning and his colleagues in Four Courts Press have been very encouraging in bringing this book to fruition. Pat Close provided sound advice and forthright opinions throughout, and we would not have gotten this far without him. Cleo Murphy helped greatly with suggestions for tidying and structuring the content. Fr Eamon Aylward supported the project from its inception and provided up-to-date information on Irish missionary activity worldwide. Paul Keenan (*Irish Catholic*) and Janet Craven (Church Mission Society Ireland) helped get the word out to missionaries past and present.

We appreciate the contributions of Seán Brady, Alan Harper, Donal Dorr, Edmund Hogan, Seán Healy, John O'Shea, Tom Arnold and Justin Kilcullen. Each of them responded positively to our request for an article to frame the main collection of stories, and took the time from their busy schedules.

A small number of pieces have been amended from articles previously published in *Africa* (edited by Martin Smith), *Far East* (Cyril Lovett) and *Dearcadh* (Eddie O'Donnell). We thank their editors for permission to use these pieces here.

The wonderful illustrations were hand-drawn – from photographs provided by Irish missionaries – by Nasa Ochieng, Alphonse Mimba, Roney Odhiambo, Oscar Mukolwe and Martin Onyango at Mukuru Arts and Crafts (a project of the Makuru Slums Development Project), under the guidance of David Redmond, in Nairobi, Kenya. Michael Higgins made the world map of current missionary activity, and our brother Conor, Chris Cullen, and Kevin McDevitt all provided notable assistance.

Our uncles, Eugene and Matthew, and aunt, Mary, unwittingly planted the seed for this book many years ago, when they told us stories as children of their lives as missionaries in South Africa, New Zealand, and Nigeria, on visits home to Ireland.

I – Brendan – am, as always, indebted to the most important person in my life, my dear wife Bríd, for her constant encouragement.

As well as those named here, many other people volunteered leads for stories, provided us with contacts, or generally helped the idea behind this book to become a reality. They know who they are. We offer each one our sincere thanks.

We would like to dedicate this book to our parents, Seámus and Pauline, for their continuous support and inspiration – with this, and with everything else.

Part One

The Irish Missionary Tradition

CHAPTER ONE

A Road Less Travelled

Go to the People
Live with them
Learn from them
Love them
Begin with what they know
Build with what they have
So that when the work is done
The People can say
We did it ourselves.

– attributed to Lao Tzu (c.4th century BC)

'Ah, sure we would never tell these types of stories in Ireland – no one would ever believe us', an Irish priest told us. He had lived for thirteen years in Mozambique. So alien to the rest of us was the world he worked in, he thought his stories about that world would strain credibility.

Many people across Ireland – north and south, Catholic and Protestant – have had relatives who went out 'on the missions' to far-away places, mostly in the developing world. There were, and are, brothers, sisters, uncles, aunts, great-uncles and great-aunts in Africa, Asia and South America. Many lived out their days there. In our own family, we have close relatives who worked in Brazil, Nigeria, South Africa and New Zealand. On their infrequent visits home they would ignite our childhood imaginations with stories of adventure, and occasionally misadventure, in exotic places. As they went on their fund-raising rounds back in Ireland the missionaries would, understandably, focus on their religious work. Sometimes they would speak modestly about their small but significant development and humanitarian projects.

It wasn't until one of us (Brendan) spent a year in rural Kenya working on a development project and became friendly with some Irish missionaries in the region, that we fully realised the richness and variety of their extraordinary lives. There he discovered the daunting challenges that they face in remote areas on a daily basis. He learned of their escapades in dangerous times, of their (often hilarious) interactions with local people, and of their enriching engagement with cultures very different from our own. He learned, too, that they have to be exceptionally versatile and pragmatic people.

A missionary from Ireland could be, of necessity, an electrician, motor-mechanic, plumber, labourer, building contractor, clerk of works, public relations officer, secretary, financial wizard, linguist, accountant, welfare worker, agricultural advisor – as well as a champion of the poor, the hungry and the homeless, and a friend of factory workers, trade unionists and politicians. Not to mention the 'day job' of being a reverend – a priest, pastor or nun. It gives a whole new meaning to the term 'multi-tasking'. Very many have served as nurses, doctors, teachers and school principals in their adopted lands, some as university professors specialising in areas as diverse as anthropology, English literature, theology and medicine.

The missionaries have never been one-dimensional people. Historically, many have achieved legendary status across a range of fields. For instance, Michał Piotr Boym, a Polish Jesuit missionary in China in the seventeenth century, was also a scientist and the author of important works on Asian fauna, flora and geography. The Congregationalist Scottish missionary, Dr David Livingstone, was also a medical doctor and an outspoken opponent of slavery and is regarded as one of the greatest explorers of Africa in the nineteenth century. Sir Garfield Todd, an Anglican missionary from New Zealand, became Prime Minister of Rhodesia (now Zimbabwe) in the 1950s, and later courageously opposed minority white rule there. Dubliner John Curtis – who played international soccer for Ireland around 1900 – spent forty-four years as a missionary in China, during which time he helped to establish universities and hospitals.

Early in the twentieth century Albert Schweitzer devoted his life as a missionary doctor to treating the sick in Lambaréné, Gabon. He was also a Lutheran theologian, musicologist and philosopher who summed up his humanitarian philosophy with the memorable line: *Do something wonderful, and people may imitate it.* He was awarded the Nobel Peace Prize in 1952. A few missionaries – the Irish-trained Mother Teresa of Calcutta and the Belgian Fr Damien of Molokai, for example – have been the subject of documentaries or feature films, and have been canonised or beatified. Most, however, work with little official recognition (nor do they seek any); this book is a salute to their selfless and invaluable work.

The most obvious association of missionary work is, of course, with religion, from the biblical imperative to evangelise. It was a call first heard in Ireland fifteen hundred years ago by the saints and scholars who left these shores in large numbers to bring Christianity and learning to continental Europe in the dark centuries after the collapse of the Roman Empire. These were the *peregrini pro Christo* – the 'pilgrims for Christ' – whose missionary endeavours between the sixth and ninth centuries defined the golden age of Celtic Christianity. They chose a life of perpetual exile and service, founding monasteries, schools, hospices and centres of learning across the continent. These were charismatic leaders like Colmcille and Columbanus, explorers like Brendan the Navigator and great scholars like the philosopher, John Scottus Eriugena. Heiric, a ninth-century Frankish hagiographer, posed the question: 'Why is it that almost the entire population of Ireland, contemptuous of the perils of the sea, has migrated to our shores with a great crowd of teachers?'

Ireland's extraordinary missionary diaspora of the twentieth century was the revival of that Irish tradition of Christian missionary outreach spanning a gap of a thousand years. Now, as then, the missionaries chose voluntary exile and work in far away places. Where the earlier monks and scholars helped shape the emerging Europe of the early Middle Ages, the recent missionaries have impacted the lives of millions in Africa, Latin America, Oceania and Asia.

The emphasis in this book is less on religion than on the life experiences and the humanitarian undertakings of Irish missionaries and volunteers across the world. It is worth remembering, too, the many lay men and women who have gone abroad as volunteers in recent decades. We had a poignant illustration of the contribution of lay people to development work during our schooldays at St Eunan's College in Letterkenny, Co. Donegal. In 1992, Niall McMenamin, a former student, graduated in construction studies and went to Africa with the Volunteer Missionary Movement. In August 1993, while helping to build a hospital for the Holy Rosary Sisters, Niall was murdered during a failed robbery at the building site. He died in Kenya, aged only twenty-three. A memorial photograph of Niall hangs in the corridors of St Eunan's to remind students of his selflessness and his social conscience. There are many more like him.

The examples of missionary life which follow illustrate the sheer diversity of the missionary experience. In Kenya, Brendan came across Irish missionaries who would have no pretensions to fame or sainthood, but who show exceptional commitment and ability. People like Br Colm O'Connell from Cork, who has trained and mentored many of the famous Kenyan middle- and long-distance Olympic runners and world champions, including Wilson Kipketer, Peter Rono, Ibrahim Hussein, Lydia Cheromei, Susan Chepkemei, and his latest record-breaking protégé, David Rudisha. Br O'Connell's success in the sporting field reminds us that it was a Marist missionary from Sligo, Br

Walfrid, who founded Glasgow Celtic FC in the 1880s to help Irish immigrants in the east end of Glasgow.

Br O'Connell and other missionary teachers have shaped many young minds in their schools, some of whom have grown to achieve fame and influence. In Kenya, for example, Fr Liam Kelly taught a younger Kalonzo Musyoka, the current vice-president of that country. Another Kenyan, Wangari Maathai, is a former government minister and became the first African woman to win the Nobel Peace Prize in 2004 for her environmental and pro-democracy work; in her youth, she was educated by Loreto nuns and was involved with the lay Legion of Mary organisation (founded in Dublin). Kenneth Kaunda, the former president of Zambia, was taught by Irish Jesuit priests, whose influence he acknowledges. Sadly, not all the alumni of missionary schools have turned out as their teachers would have wished. Fr James O'Hea, the Irish headmaster of Kutama Marist College in what is now Zimbabwe, once had high hopes for a brilliant young student of his – Robert Gabriel Mugabe.

These missionaries from Ireland have lived through turbulent periods of world history – from the dark days of colonial rule through the collapse of empires to the optimism generated by independence. They have also witnessed the rise of dictators and the descent into tyranny, civil war, famine, and other catastrophes, both man-made and natural, and many have paid the ultimate price. (Though not all missionaries served in remote, inhospitable places. Some lived and worked with no less commitment or dedication in the anglophone world: in the UK, Canada, the US, Australia and New Zealand.)

Many have shown courageous leadership in the struggle for peace and social justice in their adopted lands. One such is Clareman Fr Jim Crowe, who heads the Forum in Defence of Life in Brazil. For his efforts in combating violence in one of the most brutal *favelas* in Brazil, on the fringe of São Paulo, he was awarded the accolade of 'Brazil Person of the Year' in 2007. In a lifetime of service he has faced intimidation and harassment from authoritarian regimes, as well as severe pressure from the Vatican which disapproved of his radicalism and independent spirit.

Fr Shay Cullen, nominated on three occasions for the Nobel Peace Prize for his work in the Philippines, is another exemplar of the bravery that many less well-known missionaries have shown. A Dubliner and a human rights activist, he lives with constant threats from local mobsters and sex traffickers in the Luzon region. He has kindly contributed to this volume. Courageous people like Shay Cullen and Jim Crowe bear fearless witness to another dictum of Albert Schweitzer's: Example is not the *main* thing in influencing others; it is the *only* thing. Example is leadership.

Go today to various parts of Asia, go to Oceania, to South America, to the Caribbean, to North America and to Africa, and many communities will tell you of the leadership offered by generations of Irish missionaries. People there have long and grateful memories of those who came from afar as young men and women and who stayed for decades, enriching deprived communities with their life-long commitment, service and skills. Such people have bequeathed an enduring legacy, not just in passing on their faith, but in invaluable humanitarian and developmental successes – in the form of health care, education, and agricultural, infrastructural and employment projects.

Sr Cyril Mooney from Dublin, for example, is among a small number of foreigners to have been awarded one of India's highest civilian honours – the Padma Shri – for her leadership in running several successful, and groundbreaking, initiatives as an educationalist in India over the last half-century. Fr Charlie Burrows, an Oblate priest working in Indonesia, has been a driving force behind the construction of roads to link remote communities, the establishment of schools (primary, secondary and tertiary), and even the foundation of a network of banks to allow the – mostly Muslim – people in his area to access loans for investment in local enterprise. He was the subject of Ruán Magan's *The Nazarene*, aired in May 2011 as part of RTÉ's *Would you believe?* series.

In Malawi, Tipperary-born Br Aidan Clohessy's weighty achievements include 'an impressive network of health services for local people, including a thirty-nine-bed acute inpatient psychiatric facility, a rehabilitation and vocational training programme for those recovering from mental illness, a very successful residential addiction treatment programme, as well as counselling services and outreach clinics' (*Irish Times*, 14 December 2010). He has also established a training college for mental health nurses, counsellors and clinical officers (trained to perform routine surgeries), and devised programmes featuring music, dance, and sport for street children. It is hard to overstate the impact of projects such as these.

Another notable example is that of Fr Kieran Creagh, from Belfast, who offered his life for his South African congregation very directly in 2003 by becoming the first person in Africa to receive a trial vaccine against HIV/AIDS. Honoured as International Irish Person of the Year in 2004, Fr Creagh was later shot three times and left for dead during a burglary at his house in 2007 but, after recuperating in Ireland, returned to work later that year in a Pretoria township.

Many Irish missionaries were, and are, regarded by the local communities as having a unique empathy with the people of their adopted lands. As observed by some of the missionaries themselves, this may be partially attributable to a shared history of colonisation or an understanding born of folk memories of hardship and the Famine. The long-term commitment to the local population, with most missionaries setting down roots in their community for years – often decades – certainly facilitates enduring relationships. Working on the front line, the missionaries are often resourceful and practical characters, attempting to shape a better world in otherwise neglected areas. Whatever the reason for the special bond, it means that these men and women have been excellent ambassadors for their country. Journalist Joe Humphreys relates dozens of examples of action and commitment beyond the call of duty, and of respect earned, in the course of his evaluation of the Irish missionary movement (*God's entrepreneurs. How Irish missionaries tried to change the world*, published in 2010).

In the following pages you will read vivid personal accounts of the experiences of some of these missionaries. There are extracts from diaries, from letters home to Ireland, from memoirs unpublished and privately published, and from many narratives specially commissioned for this book. There are stories from literally all around the world, stories that are in turn moving, inspiring, amusing and, in some instances, harrowing. Some missionaries tell of being robbed, abducted, and imprisoned, of being embroiled in civil strife and of coping with the murder of colleagues.

What may be inferred from these stories is the courage, idealism and dedication of the missionaries themselves. We say 'inferred' since they are, almost as a rule, too modest to claim such attributes for themselves. All of them seem to have been endowed with a strong spirit of adventure, especially those early pioneers in the forties, fifties and sixties. After long sea voyages to distant lands they often had to take to dug-out canoes, cross perilous ravines by rope-bridge, traverse infested waterways, transfer to camel or mule, and get used to travelling long distances on foot or by ox-cart, rickety bike or motorcycle. Later, there would be overladen Land Rovers and even light aircraft. There are nuns in Kenya who pilot their own small plane on missions of mercy over the pitiless Turkana Desert. Both of us have developed a profound respect for men and women who had selflessly dedicated their lives, not just to their faith, but to a practical interpretation of their Christianity based on service to humanity.

It may be contended that early modern missionaries, particularly in the nineteenth century, played a role as uninvited cultural imperialists who, often coming in on the coat-tails of foreign administrations, helped to reinforce colonialism (Prof. Edmund Hogan's historical piece in the next chapter touches on this issue). Whatever the validity of that argument in the Age of

Empire, it is less applicable to the post-colonial period covered by the majority of contributors to this book.

Not all missionaries stayed the course on which they initially set out. Some returned home for health reasons, often victims of malaria – a particular scourge in tropical lands. Some left their orders to join the laity and get married. Sadly, just as some of their colleagues in Ireland have been engulfed in scandal in recent years, it has been alleged that some of those who went on mission committed similar shameful crimes.[1] However, the vast majority of missionaries were faithful to their extraordinary calling and were forces for good in the world. We are reminded of an elderly nun, Sr Lori Burns, encountered on the fringe of Africa's largest slum at Kibera in 2006. She was in her early eighties, and had retired from a lifetime of service as an art teacher in Nairobi. Instead of opting for a comfortable retirement back home in Ireland, she had volunteered to teach art as a therapy for young – and occasionally violent – addicts in a drugs rehabilitation centre. The artwork in this book is provided courtesy of students from her centre, who have drawn the pictures from photographs sent to us by missionaries.

With the number of Irish missionaries working abroad now in sharp decline – their average age is over seventy – there is a danger that a significant chapter in the social and religious history of Ireland will be lost or reduced to a footnote in the chronicles of the last century. This book captures the most memorable, moving, and personally significant events from our contributors' lives, chosen by themselves and told in their own manner. Each piece offers a snapshot of the lives and work of these remarkable people – Irish women and men whose desire to make a difference by treading a road 'less travelled by' (to borrow Robert Frost's phrasing) has led to a host of singular experiences. Some of those extraordinary experiences are shared in the following pages.

Preceding the missionaries' personal tales is a section on the history and the legacy of Irish missionary activity. The scholars behind these pieces offer an historical perspective on the missionaries' contributions to our society. They provide an overview and a context for the stories that constitute the main section of the book. Chapter 4, Introductions, contains an assortment of perspectives and a wide range of expertise. Tom Arnold, John O'Shea, and Justin Kilcullen (the heads of Irish NGOs Concern, GOAL and Trócaire) describe

---

1 The Murphy Report (2009) names two former missionaries – Patrick Maguire and Tom Naughton – who have been convicted of child sexual abuse, and another – 'Fr Terentius' – against whom allegations have been made. In May 2011, *Prime Time Investigates* aired a report on allegations of abuse made in mission countries against a number of Irish missionary priests.

the developmental and humanitarian contribution of Irish missionaries to the developing countries where their organisations now work. Fr Seán Healy (Social Justice Ireland) highlights some of the challenges involved in that work. Cardinal Seán Brady and Archbishop Alan Harper – the leaders of the Roman Catholic and Anglican Churches in Ireland, respectively – pay tribute to the work of the missionaries abroad and offer their thoughts on the future of the movement. Finally, Denis O'Brien (The Iris O'Brien Foundation) notes the importance of documenting their lives and work.

The chapters of personal accounts are loosely arranged to reflect the wide-ranging experience of going abroad on mission. Tales of new beginnings and culture shock, recalled through youthful eyes, are towards the front of the book. Subsequent chapters are grouped thematically or by the dominant tone of the stories – though, as the missionaries recount incidents from daily life, humour and sadness may be found in unexpected places. This miscellany of memories is offered as a record, in their own words, of some of the experiences of some truly extraordinary people – Ireland's unique diaspora of the willing.

Aidan Clerkin and Brendan Clerkin
aroadlesstravelled2011@gmail.com

CHAPTER TWO

The Modern Irish Missionary Story

Revd Dr Edmund Hogan, from Cork, holds a PhD from the National University of Ireland. Ordained into the Society of African Missions in 1969, Dr Hogan has taught in Ireland at UCC, UCD and St Patrick's College, Maynooth; at seminaries in Nigeria and Zambia; and at Tangaza College (Catholic University of East Africa) in Nairobi, Kenya. Dr Hogan has contributed numerous articles to scholarly journals, and has produced two books on missionary history. His book, *The Irish missionary movement: a historical survey, 1830–1980* (Dublin, 1990), is currently the standard work on the subject. For the past decade he has also served as archivist for the Irish Province of the Society of African Missions.

From the ninth century, which marked the concluding stages of the great early medieval Irish missionary movement to continental Europe, Ireland played virtually no part in the Church's missionary endeavour. The principal reason for this inactivity was that for most of the period the Church was preoccupied with problems of survival. Indeed, for most Irish clergy, trained on the continent from the seventeenth century, Ireland was in the true sense a 'mission country'.

It was only in the nineteenth century, when its problems had been finally overcome, that the Irish Catholic Church was again capable of looking outwards. Its gaze was directed at first towards the hundreds of thousands of Irish who were emigrating and it was to cater for these that All Hallows College was founded by John Hand in 1842. Before this foundation, the Irish diaspora was served from continental seminaries, such as the College du Saint-Esprit and the Sulpician colleges, by the religious orders and, increasingly, by Irish diocesan seminaries. St Kieran's College, Kilkenny (1782) sent priests to Newfoundland and the maritime provinces of Canada and Australia. St Patrick's College, Carlow (1793) sent priests to Australia and the Americas, while St John's College, Waterford (1807) supplied the Newfoundland mission. St Peter's College, Wexford had a strong connection with the Cape Province in South Africa. All these seminaries also supplied the English mission to varying degrees. From the 1840s, Maynooth staff members went to India, in response to a request from the Holy See, to minister to the many Irish soldiers and officials employed in the East India Company (and later in the British Raj). This mission eventually collapsed. Inexperience, lack of organised support from home and the diversion of many potential recruits to the Irish emigrant communities after the Famine were the main causes of the failure. Nonetheless, Loreto and Presentation Sisters, who accompanied the priests and could rely on their Irish convents for support, did succeed in setting down roots. Their successors are there to this day.

In modern times, Ireland's first involvement in so-called 'pagan missions' – to countries with no Irish connection – came from the Protestant Churches. 'The Irish Auxiliary' to the Society for the Propagation of the Gospel (SPG) was founded as early as 1714. Members of the 'Auxiliary' were to work in the American colonies, in South Africa, India, Japan and West Africa. Perhaps the most notable Irish SPG venture was the Dublin University Mission to Chota Nagpur (India) established in 1891. No less active was the Hibernian Church Missionary Society (CMS) founded in 1814 which, in 1885, inspired the celebrated Dublin University Fukien Mission (China). Many Irish men and women were also involved in British-based or international missionary agencies, such as the South American Missionary Society, the Church of England Zenana Missionary Society, the Bible Churchmen's Missionary Society, the Moravian Missions, the Baptist Missions and the Methodist Missionary Society. Among the home-grown agencies were the Irish Presbyterian Missions and the Mission to Lepers. The story of these Protestant missionaries has yet to be properly told. But from a glance at the evidence it seems that the scale of their involvement in the work of missions was proportionately as great as that of their Catholic counterparts.

The next phase of the movement began in the latter decades of the nineteenth century when a number of French missionary institutes (chiefly the Holy Ghost Fathers and the Society of African Missions) established themselves in Ireland in order to recruit for their missions in British colonial possessions. The promotional work of these institutes did much to heighten awareness of the great missionary movement already underway from continental Europe. It also helped to convince Irish Catholic clergy and bishops that the time had come for Ireland too to play its part. Soon Irish recruits to these institutes were making their mark on the mission fields and their achievements received wide publicity at home.

The scene was now set for the extraordinary developments of the twentieth century, manifested most clearly in the formation of five indigenous missionary institutes – the Maynooth Mission to China, the Columban Sisters, the Holy Rosary Sisters, the Medical Missionaries of Mary and St Patrick's

Missionary Society. By the early 1930s, many of the older religious orders, formerly indifferent or non-committal, had become infected by the enthusiasm and were taking on missionary commitments, to the extent that Ireland was now becoming a major partner in the Church's missionary activity.

The final phase, which commenced after the Second World War, saw the active participation of Irish laity. At first the lay volunteers went out to assist in projects organised by the established institutions, working mainly in schools and hospitals, but also assisting in the growing number of development projects. Vatican II, however, brought a growing tendency among the laity to chart their own course within the overall context of the movement. Organisations like Viatores Christi and the Volunteer Missionary Movement, and development agencies like Concern, Trócaire and Gorta, were now making their own unique contributions in line with the Church's insights into the role of laity as elaborated in the decrees of Vatican II.

The contribution of the modern Irish missionary movement to developing nations is difficult to measure in exact terms. We do know that large numbers of personnel were involved. In 1982, Ireland had a total of 5,613 priests, brothers, sisters and laity working in some eighty-six of the developing countries, as well as thousands more at home providing support services. This total includes 142 missionaries from the Protestant denominations, working in ten countries. These numbers had been building up since the early 1920s. We know also from the record of their activities that those who went abroad were not only men and women of high idealism, but were among the more creative of their generation. In the field, their impact was bound to be all the more notable because they rarely confined themselves to evangelisation in the narrow sense of that term. Almost everywhere, and from the earliest days, Irish missionaries, Catholic and Protestant, involved themselves in the work of education, in providing medical care, and in meeting a large variety of social and human needs. Perhaps the education offered was not always the most appropriate. But in a situation where the intrusion of modernity was inevitable, it did enable those at risk to cope better with the great changes taking place around them.

On the level of values, Irish missionaries have sometimes been accused of religious imperialism and cultural arrogance. But recent studies[2] have shown such judgments to be superficial, and argue that the idea that European culture could colonise African cultures is patronising to the latter. During the early years of African independence in the 1960s, this historiography viewed African

2 For example, 'African conversion to Roman Catholicism', published in the *African Ecclesial Review*, vol. 24.

culture and religion as primitive and weak, with European culture and religion as being vibrant and dominant. In fact, African culture and religions were historically very robust, surviving through and adapting, as much as was necessary, to major changes down the centuries. The encounters with Arabs along the coast of East Africa are an example. Where a major encounter of cultures took place, Africa took from the incoming culture what it needed and no more. In the encounter between African traditional religions and Christianity, the Africans took what was necessary from the latter to enable them cope with the new historical reality of colonisation. Certain features of Christianity helped Africans to cope with their changed world. Other features did not. In the early days, the missionaries may sometimes have tended to implant a Church modelled on their own experiences in Ireland. But the people among whom they worked had their own expectations of what was required, and in the event the missionaries were compelled to make important adjustments. In practice, the contact between Christianity and traditional societies was in the nature of a dialogue or dialectic. The traditional systems took from Christianity those ideas and attitudes that they found relevant to their spiritual needs and at the same time enriched Christianity with insights of their own. The best argument against the charge of religious imperialism is the fact that in the developing countries a quite distinctive model of Christianity is now emerging.

One factor which worked very much to the advantage of the missionary movement was the social background of its personnel. Both in Africa and Asia the Irish worked in societies which were predominantly rural. Drawn themselves from a largely rural background, Irish missionaries were better able to understand the attitudes and values of those societies than missionaries coming from the great urban centres of Western Europe and America. The empathy of Irish missionaries with the people was greatly assisted by their capacity for adaptation. One would not have expected this from the products of a conservative rural society. However, much like the Irish emigrants to North America and the Antipodes, the missionaries seemed to relish the freedom and opportunity accorded them in their new environment. From the very beginning, service became the keynote of their apostolate, rather than a determination to impose a new Church. And they were sufficiently open to allow the terms of this service be dictated by the people among whom they worked. Thus, their involvement in education and medical work, which characterised their contribution, was more in the nature of a response than a considered pastoral strategy. In more recent times, the involvement of Irish missionaries in the struggle against injustice and poverty must be seen as a new articulation of the same responsive attitude.

The modern Irish missionary movement was conducted at a price. During the opening decades of the century, the mortality rate among missionaries in Africa was high, especially among those who worked on the west coast in what was then known as the 'white man's grave'. Yellow fever and blackwater fever claimed many young lives. Many more returned to Ireland in broken health. In Asia, and especially in China, missionaries were frequently caught up in revolutions and political turbulence. Some were asked to give their lives and many more suffered long terms of imprisonment for their beliefs. This pattern continues down to the present day as recent testimony from Africa, Asia and from South America shows. Nonetheless, one of the characteristics of the movement has always been its resilience in the face of persecution. This willingness to take risks for the sake of God's kingdom continues to be a reality.

One of the most striking differences between the missionary movement of modern times and those of earlier centuries has been the direct involvement of women. Women played a major role from the outset of Ireland's participation. The Loreto and Presentation Sisters who went to India and those small groups of Protestant women who worked in India and China set a headline for others. Not only did Irish women join continental institutes in large numbers, but they also formed three institutes of their own. The contribution of these women, Catholic and Protestant, to upgrading the status of their sex in societies where a role of subservience was often the norm, has rarely received sufficient acknowledgment. Their role in reducing the infant mortality rate through the provision of proper maternity services and childcare can never be sufficiently emphasised. In a whole range of other apostolates, too, Irish women have been to the forefront.

The modern Irish missionary movement has done much to make Ireland aware of the difficulties experienced by developing countries. In particular, it has focused attention on the areas of poverty and injustice, providing an analysis that shows the role of developed countries in creating and prolonging these problems. The effect of this has been to stimulate a response not only from the Irish government but also – and more strikingly – from the Irish people. This has ranged from financial contributions out of all proportion to per capita income, to a willingness by significant numbers of Irish men and women to place their skills at the service of the less fortunate.

What of the movement's future? Since the 1970s, the number of Catholic priests, sisters and brothers has been declining, and the complement of students in training has reduced to a trickle. Protestant agencies have suffered a similar decline in their ranks. At the same time, the number of lay volunteers has risen slightly. But, in almost all of the countries where Irish missionaries have laboured, the leadership of the Church is now in local hands and the number of local clergy and religious grows larger from year to year. Some 'mission' Churches have reached the stage where they are in a position to send out their own emissaries of the Gospel; and already the concept of 'reverse mission' (missionaries from the new Churches going out to re-evangelise the old) has become a reality. This trend is likely to intensify. At the same time there remains work to be done by Irish missionaries in supporting the nascent Churches, in nurturing missionary vocations within these Churches and in helping them to tackle the often endemic problems of injustice, inequality and poverty. It is certain that in the future the Irish missionary movement will be much smaller but more specialised.

The future of the movement will require closer co-operation between the missionary institutes and the Irish Churches. In the past missionary agencies tended to operate at a remove and were encouraged to do so by the home Church. There was, of course, much encouragement and support, but the relationship rarely went deeper. In stressing the missionary character of all Churches and calling for a greater mutuality in the work of missions, the Second Vatican Council set new objectives. But the home Church needs to do more than provide resources. It must also become involved in the planning and policy decisions of the movement as a whole. The formation of the Irish Missionary Union in 1971, which for the first time involved the Catholic hierarchy formally in the affairs of the movement, represented a first step along this new road. The establishment of the development agency, Trócaire, two years later, confirmed the hierarchy's commitment to a more direct involvement. At a time when both the structures of the missionary movement and that of the local Irish Church are declining, meaningful co-operation is more important than ever.

CHAPTER THREE

The Legacy of Modern Irish Missionaries

Fr Donal Dorr is a member of St Patrick's Society, and has lived and worked as a missionary in several African countries. He is the author of nine books, mainly on issues of international social justice and spirituality. His present work includes facilitating workshops and working with leadership teams of religious and voluntary organisations.

INTELLECTUAL AND PRACTICAL ACHIEVEMENTS OF MODERN IRISH MISSIONARIES

We Irish missionaries are generally very practically inclined. We tend to be more interested in getting the job done than in writing to tell others about what we have done or to tell them how they ought to do it. So I find it rather embarrassing to be asked to write about our 'intellectual legacy'. However, thinking about the request has made me aware of how many Irish missionaries have made an important contribution – not so much in the academic sphere, but in what might be called the practical/intellectual sphere. I think the word 'intellectual' should be extended to apply to initiatives which are creative and which break new ground – and that is the sense in which I am using it here.

The examples I give are just those that come to mind at present, based on my own limited experience and knowledge. I'm sure there are many important items which I don't recall at present or which I simply don't know about. Please forgive my 'sins of omission'.

Medicine and health education

What first comes to my mind is the valuable contribution in the field of gynaecology made by Sr Dr Anne Ward of the Medical Missionaries of Mary (MMM). Working in a quite remote area of the eastern part of Nigeria she pioneered a type of remedial surgery for young women damaged by having a child when they were too young. Specialists from all over the world came to learn from the work she was doing in this field.

More than fifty years earlier, in the 1940s, Dr Joseph Barnes, who worked as a lay missionary with the MMMs in the eastern part of Nigeria, did pioneering work in treating the leprosy which was so widespread at the time. I have no doubt that this experience played a big part in his later development as a very well-known skin specialist.

Carmelite priest, Dr Robert McCabe, has for years been running health clinics for the local Turkana people in the desert area in the north of Kenya. When he comes home on vacation he lectures in medical schools, sharing his knowledge and experience with medical students in the College of Surgeons in Dublin and elsewhere.

In recent years, the Medical Missionaries, the Holy Rosary Sisters, the Franciscan Missionaries for Africa and many other congregations of Sisters who had been working in hospitals have moved more decisively out into even more remote areas and are doing really valuable pioneering work in public health and in health education in local communities. Many of them have also devoted time to up-skilling local midwives and are linking modern health care with the use of traditional herbal medicines; for instance, an extract of the leaves of the *neem* tree has traditionally been used to treat both malaria and scabies.

Irish missionary Sisters are the backbone of much of the work for both the treatment and prevention of HIV/AIDS in Africa. Franciscan Sister, Dr Miriam Duggan, has earned international recognition for her innovative and highly successful approach to AIDS prevention, which helped to turn the tide against AIDS in Uganda, and which she later brought to South Africa. Sr Dr Maura O'Donohue (MMM) gained international recognition as a specialist in HIV/AIDS work during the years of her work with CAFOD (Catholic Agency for Overseas Development). She also presented to the Vatican an important and alarming report on the sexual abuse of African Sisters by priests and bishops. More recently, she has devoted much of her energy to the issue of human trafficking and is now in demand as a speaker at international conferences on this topic. In this work to combat trafficking she is joined by many other returned Irish missionaries, who link up with their colleagues in 'supply countries' in the developing world (see www.aptireland.org for more information).

Fr Michael J. Kelly (SJ), former professor of education in Lusaka University, has worked as a missionary in Zambia for fifty years. Recognised internationally for his expert knowledge of the effects of AIDS and other epidemics in Africa, he is a regular speaker at major international conferences.

Ecology

A truly outstanding contribution has been made by the Columban Father, Sean McDonagh, whose post-graduate diploma and master's courses in ecology, originally based in Dalgan Park, Navan, have now moved to All Hallows College in Dublin. His very many books and articles on various aspects of environmental awareness are solidly based on scientific data, as is shown by the fact that he has been awarded a doctorate on the basis of his research. In his case, too, all this intellectual achievement is oriented towards practice. His knowledge is integral to his relentless campaigning on ecological issues as well as to the degree courses he has organised and carried through in conjunction with Professor John Feehan (UCD). And of course this commitment has led to a major shift in the vision and policies of his Columban confrères and of many of the rest of us Irish missionaries.

My Kiltegan colleague, Michael Long, having returned from mission in Africa, is deeply committed to innovative ecological work—this time in a wetland area of his local Tipperary rather than on a worldwide scale. He and his fellow-workers are safeguarding endangered species and raising the ecological awareness of the many groups of school-pupils who visit the project. Similarly, many other returned missionaries have brought home with them from the environmentally damaged areas where they have worked a deep conviction of the urgency of radical ecological initiatives.

Justice, development and liberation

Many Irish missionaries—priests, brothers, sisters, and lay missionaries – have played a key role in the widespread adoption and development of what is called the 'Psycho-Social Method'. Inspired by the work of the Brazilian educator Paulo Freire, this approach to the promotion of justice, development and liberation was developed by Anne Hope and Sally Timmel, both members of the international lay women's movement called 'The Grail'. Working with local development workers, first in Kenya and later in Zimbabwe and South Africa, they developed simple exercises which are used by local 'on-the-ground' people to study the root causes of poverty and oppression, and then to organise themselves to work for justice and liberation.

Anne, though born in South Africa, took out Irish citizenship when, during the apartheid regime, she was prevented from working in her home country. She and Sally were invited to run workshops in Kenya by Enda Byrne, a lay missionary from Dublin. The method became a foundation-stone of the work of many Irish missionaries and was applied and developed by them in the most remote rural areas. From Kenya this method has spread widely in developing countries. Some years later, the two founders spelled out the elements of this method in the four volumes of the manual, *Training for transformation*.

Sr Miriam O'Brien, a Sister of St Louis, brought the psycho-social method to Liberia where, sponsored at first by the Jesuit Refugee Service, she did quite extraordinary work for very many years, in the midst of the on-going civil war. She saw peace come to Liberia before she died tragically a couple of years ago. Some of the fruits of her work are encapsulated in the master's thesis which she wrote under the auspices of the Kimmage Development Studies Centre. Meanwhile, Enda Byrne has now been using and promoting the psycho-social method in many countries for thirty-five years. In recent years he has brought it to Serbia and Kosovo. The work in all these countries has been documented by Enda and his colleagues in dozens of official reports.

Over the past forty years, Irish missionaries in Brazil and other Latin American countries, as well as in the Philippines, have been deeply involved in liberation work. They are inspired by 'liberation theology', which provides poor and oppressed people with a Christian and biblical motivation and encouragement to challenge unjust political authorities and unjust economic systems. They were not the ones who 'invented' liberation theology and basic Christian communities, but they use these ideas and have developed them 'on the ground'. Particularly striking is the innovative work done in the poor areas all around the great cities of these countries by the Spiritans, the Holy Rosary Sisters, the Medical Missionaries of Mary, the Christian Brothers, the Redemptorists, and the Columbans, as well as by my own Kiltegan colleagues and a host of other missionaries. The late Fr David Regan (CSSp), working in Brazil, wrote an interesting book called *Church for liberation*.

The cry for justice of the late Fr Niall O'Brien, a Columban Father imprisoned in the 1980s by the Marcos regime in the Philippines, was heard worldwide, through his writing and his broadcasts. In recent years, his fellow Columban, Fr Shay Cullen, has become known all over the world and has even been nominated for the Nobel Peace Prize for his PREDA institute, which rescues Philippine children sold or trapped into sexual slavery. My fellow Kiltegan missionary, Padraig Ó Maille, played a key role in the challenging and eventual ousting of the dictatorial and repressive regime of Hastings Banda in Malawi, as is recounted in his book, *Living dangerously*.

It was Irish Spiritan missionaries who established the major relief and development agency now called Concern Worldwide; and missionaries have played a big part in its history. One thinks especially of the two Doheny brothers, Fr Mike and Fr Kevin, as well as Fr Tony Byrne and Raymond Kennedy.

Many Irish missionaries have also played a big part in the life of the Irish Church's official Catholic development agency Trócaire – working on its committees and, of course, establishing many of the significant projects which it supports. Various Irish missionaries are also involved in many of the smaller relief and development agencies.

Furthermore, missionaries have had a big involvement in the 'Debt and Development' project and in lobbying government on key development issues. Kevin O'Hara is a Kiltegan missionary working in Nigeria. Appalled by the exploitative oil-drilling of Shell in the Niger Delta, he pioneered an innovative justice-and-ecology project that challenged Shell, not only 'on the ground', but also in their corporate headquarters in London. This project is documented in the research dissertation he wrote in the Centre for Action Research in Professional Practice at the University of Bath.

Bringing it back home
Nearly thirty years ago, returned missionaries brought the psycho-social method back to Ireland and established the 'Partners in Mission' agency, later called 'Partners Training for Transformation', or simply 'Partners'. It has been staffed mainly by returned missionaries. 'Partners' has conducted hundreds of workshops, empowering people and working for justice; more recently they have applied the psycho-social method to the area of intercultural relationships and dialogue.

In 2001, Maureen Sheehy published the *Partners companion to training for transformation*. In 2007, she and two other members of the staff in 'Partners', Frank Naughton and Collette O'Regan, published the handbook, *Partners intercultural companion to training for transformation*. My own study of Catholic social teaching, published under the title, *Option for the poor*, as well my books *Integral spirituality* and *The social justice agenda*, were written specifically as background resource material for missionaries and others engaged in this kind of work for justice and liberation.

Meanwhile, Noel Bradley, who worked for years with the 'Training for Transfomation' programme in Nigeria, has continued this work since his return to Ireland, and has also published important research material on his work with isolated rural men in Co. Donegal.

The original 'Partners' programme also branched out into 'Partners in Faith', founded by returned missionaries Ciaran Earley (OMI) and Gemma McKenna. Using the psycho-social method, the programme works for the personal and social development of adults from a faith perspective, particularly in areas where there is a lot of poverty and deprivation. They have published

some creative and valuable resource material. Sadly, Ciaran died in 2008, but
the work continues.

John O'Connell worked as a Columban missionary in the Philippines
where he developed a deep commitment to empowerment of the poor. Returning to Ireland he went to work with the Traveller community and founded
the Dublin Travellers Education and Development Group. This led on to the
Pavee Point Project and the Irish Travellers Movement. Sadly, John died in
1999 at just fifty years old, but his project has continued to flourish; his initiative and inspiration has contributed to a quite dramatic transformation, where
Traveller spokespersons are now articulate and confident, and well able to hold
their own in defending the cultural rights of Travellers on TV and radio.
Equally, the late Sr Helena Brennan of the Holy Child Sisters, having returned
from Africa, did remarkable work while living with Travellers in Dublin.

Fr Sean Healy (SMA) and Sr Brigid Reynolds (SM) worked on justice
issues in northern Nigeria. After their return to Ireland they did all of us a
wonderful service as the justice spokespersons of the Conference of Religious
of Ireland (CORI). Providing well-documented research, they challenged us
all very effectively on key justice issues – to a point where the *Irish Times* suggested that they were the only real opposition to then government policies.
More recently, they have moved on to set up an independent justice agency.
Their book, *Social policy in Ireland* (2006), has become a standard textbook on
social policy in this country.

Reconciliation, interculturality, and inter-religious dialogue
Justice work has led on to reconciliation work and to the promotion of intercultural and inter-religious dialogue. I think of the Columban priest, Rufus
Hally, who was remarkably successful in promoting reconciliation between
Christians and Muslims in the southern Philippines – and who eventually gave
his life in this cause. More recently, my own colleague Fr Kieran Flynn, having returned from work in a remote part of Nigeria, has specialised in both the
theology and the practice of dialogue between Christians and Muslims, particularly in Ireland. The Columban Fr Frank Hore, having engaged in reconciliation and dialogue work between Christians and Hindus at first in Fiji, and
then in many other areas of conflict, has produced the valuable *Handbook of
intercultural resources*. Meanwhile, another Kiltegan colleague, Fr Tommy
Hayden, working with Maureen Grant, has designed and conducted valuable
workshops on interculturality for missionaries, in African countries as well as
at home in Europe.

The 'Spirasi' programme, set up in Dublin by Spiritan missionaries, offers an invaluable service to asylum-seekers and refugees, particularly in the reha-bilitation and care of survivors of torture.

Seamus Farrell worked as a missionary, first in northern Nigeria and then in South Africa. From there he has brought back to Ireland, North and South, his passionate commitment to justice and reconciliation and his expertise in these areas and in the area of authentic human development. Having been involved for some time in the 'Towards Understanding and Healing Project' at the University of Ulster, he moved on to a very innovative Northern Ireland recon-ciliation programme called 'The Junction'; and he has written important reports on it. More recently, he has branched into the area of peer mediation by pupils in schools, and has co-authored the book, *Peer mediation in primary schools.*

The lay missionary organisation, Viatores Christi, was founded in Ireland fifty years ago by members of the Legion of Mary. It quickly became an inde-pendent agency. Over the years it has trained large numbers of lay missionar-ies to work overseas. It is still very active today, and much of its vitality comes from the fact that most of the work is done by volunteers rather than by full-time staff. The other major lay missionary organisation in Ireland is VMM (Volunteer Missionary Movement). Founded more than forty years ago by Englishwoman Edwina Gately, it has flourished both in Britain and in Ireland, and is strongly represented in Ireland at present. It, too, depends very much on the work of volunteers. The fact that these two organisations have not just survived, but thrived, is a tribute to successive generations of inspired and ide-alistic Christians who, over so many years, have devoted much time and energy to recruiting, training, and supporting hundreds of lay missionaries working in difficult mission situations. On their return, many of these com-mitted people have become involved in working for justice at home, frequently playing an active role in the campaigning organisation *Comhlamh* (Irish for 'solidarity').

Third-level institutions

The Kimmage Development Studies Centre, founded in 1974 by the Spiritans, catered mainly at first for missionaries, enabling them to articulate their expe-riences and develop their understanding and skills in development work. Nowadays, it attracts development activists of all ages, religions, and cultural backgrounds from all over the world, who do valuable study and research. The Institute can be seen as a major fruit of the Irish missionary enterprise.

The Kimmage Institute of Theology and Cultures, created and staffed by a consortium of Irish missionary organisations, has made an important intel-lectual contribution in the specialised education of missionaries from home and abroad. Some years ago it became a distinct department in the Milltown Institute of Philosophy and Theology. Its staff has produced a number of significant books in its specialised field. Fr Michael McCabe (SMA), one of the former presidents of the Kimmage Institute, is a very well-known expert in the field of mission theology. He lectures internationally and has written extensively on the subject.

Religious education and spiritual guidance

Very many Irish missionaries have been involved in innovative and creative projects of devising and writing materials for formal or informal religious education. For instance, before she left Kenya, Gemma McKenna was part of a team which produced a wonderful set of textbooks widely used in second-level schools. And, at third-level, the late Fr Brian Hearne (CSSp) made an invaluable contribution through his work in the Gaba Institute in Kenya and through his publications under its auspices.

Within the past couple of years, two of my Kiltegan colleagues, Leo Traynor and Noel McGeeney, working in northern Nigeria in partnership with Moses Alokpa and Jonathan Ekhator, have designed a programme called 'Sharing Education and Learning for Life'. They have also produced a 274-page manual full of all kinds of creative exercises to enable facilitators to lead young Christians through the programme.

Needless to say, many Irish missionaries have devoted endless hours to translating the Bible and all kinds of religious education materials into local languages – and also producing grammars and dictionaries of these languages, and studies of the cultures. In recent years, large numbers of Irish missionaries have taken specialised courses in spiritual direction or 'accompaniment'. By doing this they are making a major intellectual contribution to people in developing countries who are looking for spiritual guidance in their lives.

Spiritual centres

One of the most creative developments in recent years has been the setting up by returned missionaries of new types of retreat and reflection centres. Unlike the older retreat and conference centres which have been established by various religious congregations all over Ireland, these newer centres are much more informal in both tone and style.

Three such initiatives come to my mind. 'An Tobar' is a retreat centre run by the Spiritans at Ardbraccan, Navan, where people from deprived inner-city communities and other interested people can come for various formal or informal courses or celebrations on an inexpensive cater-for-yourself basis. In

Glendalough, Fr Michael Rodgers (SPS) runs the 'Tearmann Spirituality Centre'. It is a sacred place where spiritual 'searchers' of all kinds come and spend a time of quiet reflection, with as little or as much guidance as they wish from Michael. See www.tearmann.ie.

Finally, there is the 'Slí an Chroí' centre, run by Fr Seamus Whitney, situated in a beautiful location beside the headquarters of St Patrick's Missionaries near Kiltegan, Co. Wicklow. It is a place where individuals or groups can come to nourish the spirit through silence and sharing, with no imposed agenda; and there are some interesting and imaginative courses for those who are interested. 'Slí an Chroí' also offers low-cost counselling in the Sophia Counselling Centre. See www.slisophiacentre.ie.

Conclusion

Are we entitled to call all these initiatives part of the *intellectual* legacy of Irish missionaries? I think so. Granted that not all of them are strictly in academic fields, they nevertheless add up to a major body of intelligent, imaginative, and creative achievement.

Introductions

Tom Arnold has been chief executive of Concern Worldwide since 2001. Concern is Ireland's largest NGO working in emergencies, long-term development and advocacy, with workers in thirty countries (mainly in Africa and Asia). Before joining Concern, he was assistant secretary general and chief economist in the Irish Department of Agriculture and Food, and chaired two OECD committees with responsibility for agricultural policy and markets. Mr Arnold has been appointed to a number of international bodies in recent years, including the UN Millennium Project's Hunger Task Force (2003–5) and the World Economic Forum Expert Group on poverty and hunger. In May 2006, he was appointed an alternate member of the Advisory Board of the UN's Central Emergency Response Fund (CERF). He is currently chairman of the European Food Security Group, a network of forty European NGOs working to enhance food security in developing countries.

At home, the legacy continues to be reflected
Aidan and Brendan Clerkin's initiative in assembling these 'Tales of the Irish Missionaries' is a great idea and a worthy project. The stories, some decades old, others of recent years, provide a thread of continuity in this important aspect of Irish life. The missionary tradition is deeply embedded in the Irish experience, stretching back to the first millennium. The late Daniel Murphy of Trinity College Dublin provided a wonderful narrative of part of this experience in his *History of Irish emigrant and missionary education* (Dublin, 2000).

From the sixth century onwards, Irish educators made a notable contribution to different parts of the world. The process started with the exodus of monastic educators to Europe, a tradition that continued for a number of centuries. In the sixteenth century, Irish colleges were founded in various parts of Europe, serving the needs of Irish and European students, both lay and clerical, up to the end of the eighteenth century.

The exodus of Irish educators increased with the great migrations to North America in the seventeenth century and reached flood-like proportions in the nineteenth, impelled by the major historical event of the Irish famine. The whole process of Irish people reaching out to the world attained its peak through the missionary movement from the late nineteenth century, continuing until the decline in vocations began to impact on numbers from the 1960s onwards.

The 1960s represent a period of transition. During that decade many young Irish people travelled to far-off lands as lay missionaries, some connected to the work and infrastructure of established missionary orders. With the establishment of Concern in 1968, a new organisational form and movement began which allowed Irish people to travel and contribute to other countries. The 1970s brought the establishment of Trócaire and GOAL which, along with Concern, have been among the main organisations providing opportunities for young Irish people to work in developing countries in recent decades.

These new travellers from non-governmental organisations (NGOs) were not part of the evangelical tradition but they were part of the tradition of Irish people leaving their home to contribute to the development of people in other lands and, in relating their experience to their families and communities back in Ireland, to shape the way in which Irish people looked to the rest of the world. The legacy of this long tradition is important and should be explored and understood. In my view, the legacy has been overwhelmingly positive.

It has generated goodwill towards Ireland and its people across all continents. Few small countries are as well known and identifiable by people across the world as is Ireland, even if these same people will not necessarily be able to identify where Ireland is on the map. This empire of goodwill provides modern benefits in terms of political influence and business opportunities.

The legacy has impacted on Ireland's worldview and the role the Irish state wishes to play within the world. Since Ireland entered the United Nations (UN) in 1955, it has played a distinctive and credible role, its foreign policy marked by an empathy with the concerns of the developing world. At home that legacy continues to be reflected in the ongoing generosity of the Irish people towards organisations such as Concern, Trócaire, GOAL and other smaller charities in responding to disasters and in supporting economic and social development programmes in far-off lands.

Notwithstanding the importance and longevity of the Irish missionary and giving tradition, its recognition and documentation has been relatively limited. President Mary Robinson and President Mary McAleese have each acknowledged the scale of the missionary contribution. I know how much this has meant to the missionaries, many of whom have worked for decades in their adopted communities.

Progress is also being made in documenting the experience. Ruán Magan's two-part series, *On God's mission*, aired on RTÉ in 2010, situates the missionary contribution within the longer Irish historical experience, linking it with the assertion of national independence and statehood and the broader movement of decolonisation from the mid twentieth century onwards.

This book provides another important addition to the documentation of this experience. Its great value is that it provides personal and very human perspectives which, taken together, give a rich fabric of what it has been like to work as a missionary over recent decades. I hope it will be enjoyed by many readers.

John O'Shea was born in 1944. He is the CEO of the international aid agency GOAL, which he founded in 1977. Well-known for his candid public statements on humanitarian issues, he has received the Irish People of the Year award in 1987 and 1992, and was conferred with an honorary doctorate from the University of Notre Dame (Indiana, USA) in recognition of his work.

It is to the missionaries that I have always gone to find out the real story
I was sitting in a clammy cargo plane, both relieved and heartbroken to be leaving the nightmare scenes of the past few days behind me. I was flying out of Baidoa – 200 miles north of Mogadishu, Somalia – and the epicentre of Somalia's famine in 1992. My thoughts were of the villages of moving skeletons, where the infants and adults would soon be lying together in shallow roadside graves. Before long my sadness had hardened into anger; it was difficult not to rage against a world so unmoved by such agony.

That was when the voice of the only other passenger on the plane pulled me out of my reverie. I had been told before boarding that I would be travelling back to Mogadishu with a doctor from the Arab League. But such was my state of agitation I had hardly noticed him; now I realised he was asking me something: 'Where are you from, my friend?' I told him I was Irish: 'Ah, the caring nation', he replied.

His soothing words seemed to restore my shattered spirit. As the engines of the plane roared, carrying us further towards the heavens, I felt a surge of pride and privilege to be part of a nation that had won such a rich reputation for its heroic humanitarian work. All of this had been achieved by nameless unsung heroes so many thousands of miles from where they themselves were born.

This doctor knew nothing of Ireland; but he was impressed by the work he had seen done by Irish priests and nuns, by volunteers and NGOs, all over the continent of Africa. To hear this man's endorsement meant so much, because coming from what I had just witnessed, hope was not the foremost emotion in my heart. But then why should I be surprised that a stranger should hold my countrymen in such esteem? Had I not marvelled at the insights of the priests and nuns who filled me in on the real causes of the Ethiopian famine back in 1984?

The world had been told the usual story about crop failures and drought, but as always it was the missionaries on the ground who had the inside track. Despite the low rainfall, there was food enough. It was the insurgency of the Tigrayan People's Liberation Front and the ruinous war the government of Mengistu Haile Mariam had waged against them and other such groups that was the real cause of the famine. More than a million souls perished and millions more were left destitute.

The missionaries explained the obscenity of how Mengistu squandered forty-six per cent of Ethiopia's GNP on military spending, and created the largest standing army in sub-Saharan Africa, as the crops rotted in the fields because the young men were dispatched to the war zone. Throughout the appalling and needless disaster the missionaries worked tirelessly and with great tenderness, never bowing to despair or complaining about the overwhelming odds against them. The same humanity shone in Rwanda after the genocide when the mass graves were dug, and the bulldozers were called in to expedite the process of disposing of the mountains of bodies that were now posing a serious risk to the living. All the while, the missionaries and the NGOs got on with the task, doing that which had to be done, without conferences or committee meetings. They were there to help, and help they did without fear, favour or fuss.

My friend from the Arab League had their measure. He appreciated the seam of gold that these people represent in the national identity, even if they are not recognised for the astonishing ambassadorial role they have played for this country abroad. They had the fortitude and compassion to go to places they never knew, where hardship and suffering were the only certainties, and without any guarantees that they would ever see their loved ones again. Remarkable character is required to stay positive in places where every year countless infants die on the day they are born, and where so many other children perish annually.

It has been my good fortune to work with GOAL for more than three decades. When your job is to go to disaster zones and witness the full impact of catastrophe, you need to keep focused and grounded. When tragedy strikes on a massive scale and there are mass deaths, people despair and lose heart. You need to hear the truth and not some filtered version being spun in the interests of a third party.

Over the years it is to the missionaries that I have always gone to find out the real story. Time and again it was they who had the resources and practical know-how to retrieve hopeless situations. Their expertise is assured and they work without political agenda. They are the political pawns of no government; their priority is solely to make a situation better. They do so without discrimination. In Calcutta, I have seen the daughters of some of the wealthiest families sit alongside children from the slums in schools run by the Irish nuns. There would normally be no prospect of these children ever meeting each other, such is the class system in India, but the respect for an education offered by the nuns transcends the strictest social boundaries.

I have met Irish men and women who may have spent more than forty years working in the field. Their accents were as thick as if they had only left Ireland yesterday. They all will tell you the same thing: 'Of course I miss home, but this is where I am needed, so this is where I must stay.' The main characteristic that sets them apart is the love that they have for the poor. It is an affinity that is priceless. The compassion that is the hallmark of their work is genuinely inspiring. They are so effective because they concentrate on doing what they can; not on what they would like to do, but on what is achievable.

At Arlington National Cemetery in Washington they have come in their millions over the years to pray at the tomb of the Unknown Soldier. How many Irish missionaries have fallen to malaria or a thousand other diseases over the centuries in the care of the poor? Sadly, there are no marble memorials to mark their work. But much more importantly, their devotion is reflected in the smiles of millions of African children who would not be alive today were it not for their passing through.

Revd Dr Seán Healy, director of Social Justice Ireland, has been active for more than twenty-five years on socio-economic policy issues in Ireland. Before that he worked for over ten years in Africa as a member of the Society of African Missions. He holds a PhD in sociology, and has written and contributed to more than twenty books on public social policy. Fr Healy has worked on many government task forces dealing with social and economic policy issues ranging from taxation to the labour market, from housing to poverty, from income adequacy to rural development.

Building a just society
'There is no way that that volume of surplus food has been produced in the north of Nigeria. It is simply impossible for the UN to be shipping so much

food from here to Niger.' The speaker was Joe Abba, an official in the Department of Agriculture in what was then North-Central State in Nigeria. The year was 1973. The Sahel drought was at its height and he was commenting on reports that the UN was exporting a considerable volume of food from Kaduna Airport to Niamey, the capital of Niger, to the north, in the heart of the Sahel region. His comments were made at a meeting of the Social Development Committee of the archdiocese of Kaduna of which he was a member.

I too was a member of that committee and had been involved in a large project aimed at increasing the food production in a large part of the south of the archdiocese, an area that was south of the Sahel region. We were well aware of the work the UN was doing to address the plight of people in Niger and neighbouring countries where drought had decimated their crops. However, Joe Abba was convinced that all was not as it appeared, so we decided to investigate. In due course, we discovered that much of the food being flown from Kaduna to Niamey was simply being driven back to Kaduna and re-sold to the UN. A serious racket was uncovered and stopped. The work of addressing the drought continued and much money was saved as greater care was taken to ensure that the scope for racketeers to benefit was reduced as far as possible.

That incident and others like it taught me many things that have remained with me throughout my life. For example, the importance of local involvement in developing programmes and projects was very clear. It was local people who uncovered the racket that was going on and exposed it. Local people with local knowledge must always be an essential component of any development or action to build a more just world.

Likewise, the importance of having an organised structure to address issues as they arise was also clear. The archdiocesan Social Development Committee was small and poorly resourced. But it was important to have that structure so as to address the other structures – in this case the UN and the state government – on a footing that ensured they engaged with the claims that were being made. Having a credible local organisation in place is critically important if people's experience or analysis of a situation is to be transmitted effectively, and if it is to be taken seriously and acted on by those with the capacity and authority to do so.

At another level the importance of people's values was highlighted. If local people didn't think these issues were important then the racket would have continued. Justice was an important issue for people in this situation in Nigeria, as it is an important issue for people across the world today. People from many countries had contributed to the Church's effort, and other initiatives, to address the Sahel drought. They were motivated by concern for those who were suffering, and desire for them to have a better life. Likewise, the UN was motivated by a desire to improve the plight of people in very difficult circumstances.

Justice is often misunderstood as being confined to legal issues and the law. The Scriptures have a much broader understanding of justice. They tell us that justice is a harmony that comes from being faithful to right relationships – with God, people and the land. Modern psychology acknowledges the importance of ensuring relationships are good at all levels if a person is to thrive. Justice is now seen in terms of having right relationships with God and self (the interior life), with other people (the social life), with institutions (the public life) and with the environment (the cosmic life). Justice is about right relationships.

Building on this understanding, a just society can be described as one in which human rights are respected, human dignity is protected, human development is facilitated and the environment is respected and protected. This understanding of justice as right relationships should be the basis of building a future within countries and across the world.

As our societies have grown in sophistication, the need for appropriate structures has become more urgent. While the aspiration that everyone should enjoy the good life is an essential ingredient in a just society, the good life will not happen without the deliberate establishment of structures to facilitate its development. In the past, charity, in the sense of alms-giving by individuals on an arbitrary and ad hoc basis, was seen as sufficient to ensure that everyone could cross the threshold of human dignity. Calling on the work of social historians it could be argued that charity in this sense was never an appropriate method for dealing with poverty. Certainly it is not a suitable methodology for dealing with the problems of today. As recent world disasters have graphically shown, charity and the heroic efforts of voluntary agencies cannot solve these problems on a long-term basis. Appropriate structures should be established to ensure that every person has access to the resources needed to live life with dignity.

As with justice, charity is also frequently conceived in too narrow a way. It is often seen as alms-giving alone. But this understanding of charity is far too limited. In a very striking passage in the Papal Encyclical, *Caritas in Veritate*, Pope Benedict XVI writes of both justice and charity and shows how they are integral to each other.

> Charity goes beyond justice, because to love is to give, to offer what is 'mine' to the other; but it never lacks justice, which prompts us to give

the other what is 'his', what is due to him by reason of his being or his acting. I cannot 'give' what is mine to the other, without first giving him what pertains to him in justice. If we love others with charity, then first of all we are just towards them. Not only is justice not extraneous to charity, not only is it not an alternative or parallel path to charity: justice is inseparable from charity, and intrinsic to it. Justice is the primary way of charity or, in Paul VI's words, 'the minimum measure' of it, an integral part of the love 'in deed and in truth' (1 Jn 3:18), to which Saint John exhorts us. On the one hand, charity demands justice: recognition and respect for the legitimate rights of individuals and peoples. It strives to build the earthly city according to law and justice. On the other hand, charity transcends justice and completes it in the logic of giving and forgiving. The earthly city is promoted not merely by relationships of rights and duties, but to an even greater and more fundamental extent by relationships of gratuitousness, mercy and communion. Charity always manifests God's love in human relationships as well, it gives theological and salvific value to all commitment for justice in the world.

Justice and charity understood in this way are integral; they are part of our response to the needs of our sisters and brothers. They are essential components of any strategy that seeks to face up to the challenges the world is facing at present. These range from climate change to growing inequality, from banking system failure to increasing poverty, from competition for non-renewable resources to intergenerational challenges.

Since the early 1970s, when Joe Abba made his comment and a racket was exposed, the world has become a much more complex place. The challenges to be faced are massive as the model on which world development has been built is found to be inadequate and not capable of providing the future that most people desire but so many lack. But action based on values such as justice and charity as outlined here is essential to building such a future. So too are local involvement and appropriate structures. There is an urgent need to ensure that local people are involved in providing accurate social analysis concerning their reality and in shaping the decisions that affect them. For this to happen, deliberative decision-making structures are needed. Such structures would require that decisions be based on the evidence available and the experience of those involved and not on the power of any particular group.

We are at a major moment of change in human history. The world is being reshaped very rapidly as it experiences the many economic, political, cultural, social and environmental challenges that have become so obvious to many people. What is required is the political will to harness the world's potential to build a future with the characteristics of a just society – where human rights are respected, human dignity is protected, human development is facilitated and the environment is respected and protected. That was the challenge in the 1970s. It remains the challenge.

Justin Kilcullen is director of Trócaire. An architect by profession, he worked for many years in the 1970s and 1980s in Africa and Asia. Mr Kilcullen joined Trócaire as a project officer for Africa in October 1981, and in March 1993 he was appointed director. In 2002 he was awarded the Robert Matthew Medal by the International Union of Architects for his work on human settlements. He is currently the president of Concord, the confederation of European development NGOs, representing more than 1,600 such organisations across the European Union.

Trócaire and the Irish missionary movement

Recently, Trócaire published an informal history, telling the story of our work over the past thirty-seven years. The book has captured the main events and issues with which we were engaged, and tells of the people involved, capturing their memories for the benefit of the current and future generations. In the vast majority of the stories told, at their heart you'll find an Irish missionary. The struggle to overcome the Marcos dictatorship in the Philippines in the 1980s is marked by the work of the Colomban Fathers and Fr Niall O'Brien in particular. The tremendous efforts made in El Salvador in the late 1970s and 1980s were inspired by the Irish Franciscans working there. The response to the Ethiopian famine in the mid-1980s was led by the Holy Ghost Brother, Gus O'Keeffe. I could go on. Virtually every chapter recalls another missionary whose presence in the slums or place of conflict or impoverished rural area gave Trócaire its foothold. To paraphrase Isaac Newton: If Trócaire can be decreed to be a success it is only because we have been carried on the shoulders of giants!

When Trócaire was founded in 1973 the Irish missionary movement was probably at its height. There was some concern in the Church as to what the role of this new organisation was going to be. Pope Paul VI, writing to congratulate Cardinal William Conway on the founding of Trócaire, said: 'By instituting this fund the Irish Church is giving further expression to that concern which, according to the Gospel, Christians must have for their brothers and sisters in need. It will be most praiseworthy if ... the Catholics of Ireland can also maintain a new agency that has funds available for a variety of... human needs.' How was this further expression to be defined? There was an expectation in some that the funds collected in the Lenten campaign would be channelled to missionaries directly. When this did not happen automatically some tensions arose. It took some years to clarify the new organisation's role.

Trócaire was one of a new type of Church organisation that had emerged after the Second Vatican Council. Based on the concept of a Lenten campaign, these organisations were led by lay people and were dedicated to the work of justice. The 1971 synod of bishops had said: 'Action on behalf of justice and participation in the transformation of the world appear to us as a constitutive dimension of the preaching of the Gospel ...'. Thus Trócaire's work was a further dimension to the work of evangelisation and in this way is part of the seamless mission of the church to preach the Gospel.

As Trócaire's work evolved over the first years of its activities the sense of partnership with the Irish missionary congregations – the Holy Rosary Sisters and the Medical Missionaries of Mary, the Kiltegan Fathers and Colomban Fathers and Sisters – became central to Trócaire's development, together with the relationship with so many missionaries from other orders.

On joining Trócaire in 1981 my first job was as project officer for Africa. I recall well my first field trip to Sierra Leone and Nigeria. This was my introduction to the amazing work that Irish missionaries were accomplishing on the ground. In Sierra Leone I visited the diocese of Bo where the Holy Rosary Sisters were working. There I met two missionary Sisters whom I characterise as 'mighty nuns'! I met many more like them over the years. Sr Patrick Hiney was the development coordinator for the diocese. She was responsible for an extensive programme of projects covering health, education and agriculture being implemented in villages throughout the diocese. She had endless energy. Her management skills were immense as she found funding for all the different projects from a multiplicity of donors, keeping all the records straight, the reports coming, and balancing all the different demands from throughout the diocese. The outstanding project in the diocese was at the hospital in Serabu, also run by Holy Rosary Sisters. Here Sr Dr Hilary Lyons had conceived and was implementing what would now be termed a leading-edge project on integrated health care. Sr Hilary and the Holy Rosary Sisters had put together a multi-disciplinary team of professionals, all nuns, and were working to and developing the latest thinking around primary health care. This programme became an international showcase for how integrated health care should be provided. This was the Irish missionaries at their best – building on decades of experience, investing in professional training of the nuns and marrying their expertise with the commitment of their vocation to serve the poor. It was an epiphany for me!

Over the years my colleagues and I would encounter many similar examples of missionary endeavour from which we learned so much, from the slums of some of the greatest cities of the developing world – Sao Paulo, Nairobi, Manila – to regions far removed from the centres of power and commerce such as Sr Nora McNamara's pioneering work in agriculture in Kware State in Nigeria.

A lot has changed in the three decades since those first experiences of mine. The emergence of the local Church in so many countries has seen the role of the missionaries, whose numbers have been declining, change significantly. With less demand on maintaining the institutions a growing emphasis on social and political issues emerged.

The work of justice, central to the Gospel message, became more prominent in the work of the missionaries. The emergence of Training for Transformation programmes, drawing on the Latin American experience piloted by Paolo Freire, added a new dimension to the work of many missionaries. The Delta and Deles projects, in East and West Africa respectively, saw the emergence of a new justice-focused approach to missionary work. Sr Miriam Therese O'Brien, a St Louis Sister working in Liberia and Sierra Leone with refugees from the wars in those countries, typified this approach. Sr Miriam had been chair of the projects funding committee in Trócaire in the late 1980s and early 1990s before returning to Africa to continue her missionary life. She moved with the refugees as they sought refuge in the neighbouring countries, accompanying them through their travails. Eventually, they returned to Liberia where Sr Miriam founded the DEN-L project (Development Education Network – Liberia). There she worked with communities of returned refugees, helping them to rebuild their lives and to strive for justice in the new political situation that emerged.

It is through this commitment to the work of justice that the work of missionaries and the work of Trócaire have converged over the past two decades. The context for this work has changed dramatically, both politically and socially, and within the life of the Church itself. While in Ireland the Church faces many difficulties with declining membership and vocations, it continues to flourish in Africa, Asia and Latin America. Radical adjustments have had to be made to cater for these realities.

However, the essence of the missionary tradition does live on in the work of many development workers, both volunteers and professionals, who have taken up the challenge of working for the world's poor. The impact of the work of the missionaries is still felt very forcefully. The enlightened approach of successive Irish governments to development aid is a key example. There is clear recognition that Ireland's role and influence in the developing world is as a direct result of the legacy of the missionaries.

Ireland's policies, focused on the elimination of poverty, adopting a rights-based approach, eschewing tied aid programmes and focussed on eradicating hunger, are all drawn from the courageous work and stand that Irish missionaries have taken over the decades. The NGOs too continue in this vein, so many of them owing their founding inspiration to the work of missionaries in various countries of Africa and beyond.

Let us hope that this and future generations do justice to that legacy and that we will maintain Ireland's unique position in relations between the poor and wealthy regions of the world.

Cardinal Seán Brady was born in Laragh, Co. Cavan in 1939. After studying for a degree in ancient classics, he earned a doctorate in canon law in Rome. He then taught French, commerce and Latin in St Patrick's College, Cavan. He has been the Catholic archbishop of Armagh and Primate of All Ireland since 1996, and was created cardinal in 2007.

Working in the field

The Irish did not keep the Gospels' good news to themselves for long. They were excited and stirred by the message St Patrick brought them and quickly set about spreading it at home and taking it abroad to share with others. Pope Benedict, in his recent visit to Scotland, recalled the signal missionary work of Donegal-born St Colmcille (521–597), who based himself on the Scottish island of Iona.

While Colmcille made his mark close to home, his contemporaries travelled extensively over the European mainland as pilgrims for Christ. Saint Columban (543–614), one of the greatest of Irish missionaries, founded monasteries at Annagray, Luxeuil and Fonataine and also at Bregenz in Austria. His final and crowning achievement was Bobbio. St Gall (died 630) travelled part of the way with Columban, but, when the latter crossed into Italy, St Gall stayed behind in Switzerland and founded the monastery of St Gallen. The martyred Killian's remains rest at Würzburg where he died in 689, and Fergal (died 784) is buried in Salzburg. To the present day they are revered in their adopted countries and pilgrims from Ireland and elsewhere regularly retrace their journeys and maintain the links.

It is important to remember these heroic figures who continue to inspire today's Irish men and women. When popes recall Irish saints these are the names they single out for mention and they are brought to our attention at least once each year on the Feast of All the Saints of Ireland on 6 November. We must keep in mind that it was not all giving; we did our share of taking too, best illustrated by St Malachy's (1095–1148) introduction of the Cistercians from France. He persuaded them to come from Clarevaux to settle in Mellifont, Co. Louth, and thus placed us forever in his debt.

These early Irish missionaries inspired later missionary surges. Monsignor P.J. Hamell's opus magnum, *Maynooth students and ordination index, 1795–1895*, which appeared in 1982, made ecclesiastical historians in America, Canada and Australia aware that many of their pioneer priests in the nineteenth century were Maynooth men. More recently, Maynooth men have founded and have been the driving force behind the great modern missionary movements: the Maynooth Mission to China (better known as Columbans) and the Maynooth Mission to Africa (better known as Kiltegans). Nor has Mother Mary Martin been outdone, with her founding of the magnificent Medical Missionaries of Mary.

The reports in this book from more than seventy Irish missionaries, from diverse backgrounds, who have worked in fifty different countries during the past fifty years, suggest the Irish missionary spirit is alive and active. Their gripping tales make us proud and thankful. We are enriched by this collection of stories compiled by Aidan and Brendan Clerkin and told by the missionaries themselves – there is no substitute for personal experience in the field!

There are also those who are not 'professional' missionaries – our emigrants who have taken the Gospel message to the ends of the earth. Between 1850 and 1930 four million Irish men and women emigrated to America alone and played a significant part in building the Church, not only in great American cities like New York and Philadelphia, but also in little St Patrick in rural Missouri. All our emigrants have been missionaries in their way, and they must never be forgotten.

The fruits of our missionaries' work are clear for all to see. Today, we are turning to them for help as our clergy numbers dwindle. Their response is generous and I am most grateful for that.

Archbishop Alan Harper, OBE, was born in Staffordshire, England in 1944. He moved to Northern Ireland in 1966. He is the Church of Ireland's archbishop of Armagh and Primate of All Ireland. Archbishop Harper received an OBE in 1996 for services to conservation in Northern Ireland. He and his wife Helen have four children.

Ireland's greatest export

Throughout the millennia Ireland's greatest and most precious export has been its people. Most did not leave willingly: they include people captured and sold into slavery and others forced by harsh economic circumstances to become migrants – residents in lands that seemed to offer greater hope and greater opportunity.

Others, however, departed voluntarily, moved by the Holy Spirit to share the good news of the love of God with those who had not heard or those who had simply forgotten. Theirs were peregrinations of purpose. They knew themselves set on an adventure, animated by the Spirit, which through privation and sometimes untimely death nevertheless brought glory to God. The names of some are known and celebrated: Brendan, Columba, Columbanus, Comgall, Gall spring readily to mind; yet these were but the forerunners of other, less famous but equally faithful men and women, who took the Gospel to the farthest parts of the earth as they knew it in their own day.

Over the centuries, the emphasis of mission has changed with the changing needs of the people of the world and changing insights into the contemporary context and character of mission itself. Yet eagerness on the part of men and women from Ireland to share the love of God with people throughout the world continues undiminished. Mission is about bringing people into contact with the incarnate Word of God and thus mission must always be incarnational. The imperative always was to make real in the lives of men and women a direct experience of the love of God by the offering of humble and costly service.

Nowadays, however, a mission team will be as likely to be headed by an engineer, a doctor or a teacher as by a bishop or a priest. The contemporary expression of the love of God is as likely to be articulated through works of relief, aid and care as through the work of evangelisation through preaching. Furthermore, mission is more readily seen nowadays as offered in the context of partnership with the local, indigenous Church, respectful of local priorities and responsive to locally determined agendas. Mission has become 'multilateral' as Christianity has spread throughout the nations of the earth.

A further implication of the principle of partnership is seen in the contemporary understanding of mission as the characteristic work of the whole people of God, the Church. All Christians are engaged in mission whether we leave these shores or not. Such an understanding opens the door to an understanding of mission as reciprocal: it is about both giving and receiving; it is no longer paternalistic. Love is incomplete and therefore mission is incomplete where it is not reciprocated. Thus mission now embraces as essential the concept of equality. This has not always been an easy transition for westerners to make.

St Francis of Assisi is reputed to have said: 'Preach the Word of God at all times and, if necessary, use words.' Mission is, first and foremost, proclamation through the medium of love. Our Lord himself said, 'I am come that they may have life, life in all its full abundance' (John 10:10). The fulfilment of these words is what the Church seeks to offer and enact for any who will receive the gift. Abundant life is, by definition, holistic. It requires fulfilment for the whole person, body, mind and spirit. But it is not individualistic for fullness of life is lived in community and therefore community building and community healing is also a legitimate aspect of the work of mission.

Nowadays the canopy of the tree of mission spreads further and incorporates more than traditional understandings of mission once knew. One thing has not changed, however, and that is the spirit of love, faith, sacrifice, commitment and courage that continues to mark the men and women who offer themselves for the service of God beyond the shores of this small island. The pulse of mission through the love of God beats as strong and constant in Ireland as ever it did.

Denis O'Brien is a well-known entrepreneur, and the chairman of the Iris O'Brien Foundation. He is chairman of the Haiti Action Network, was chairman of the 2003 Special Olympics, which were held in Ireland, and he sits on the board of Concern USA.

I am delighted and honoured to support Aidan and Brendan's work in documenting the enduring legacy of Irish missionaries and volunteers abroad. The stories capture the true spirit of endeavour, humanity and a real sense of being 'a man (or woman) for others'.

The work of missionaries and volunteers in essence embraces the extraordinariness of the ordinary: the need to reach out and connect with people of all races, colours, creeds and circumstances to promote and protect human life and culture. This book shines a light onto the efforts made by Irish missionaries through the years, and how this work continues to be essential in enabling and bettering the lives of others.

What this book records is the courage and steely determination of the men and women who commit their lives to helping others across the globe – from small villages in remote barren landscapes through to community groups within mega cities. Much more than a mere spiritual journey, these stories show a true triumph of human spirit to do more, to give more, to challenge the fundamental issues and to never give up. Selflessness, dedication and humility are in boundless supply in each and every story: stories sprinkled with danger and sadness fuse with stories of humour and compassion to deliver a true tribute of hope and inspiration.

While recording the history and purpose of missions past, the book is rounded out with contributions from leading figures from religious and humanitarian organisations as well as individual volunteers who continue to further champion the work of missionaries past and present. Aidan and Brendan Clerkin deserve acknowledgment for collating and documenting the stories for this book which will now serve as testament to missionaries and volunteerism past, present and future.

Denis O'Brien
Chairman, The Iris O'Brien Foundation

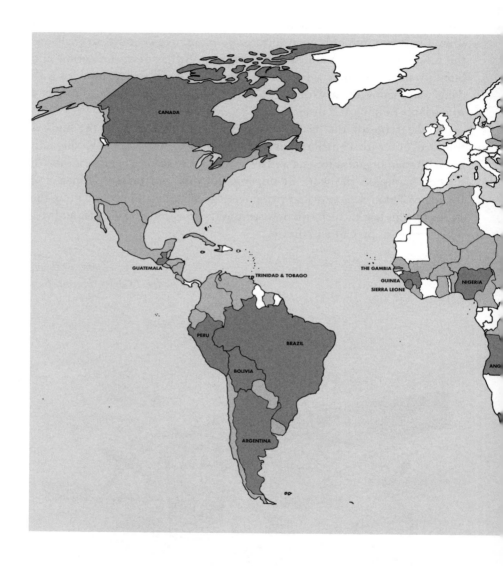

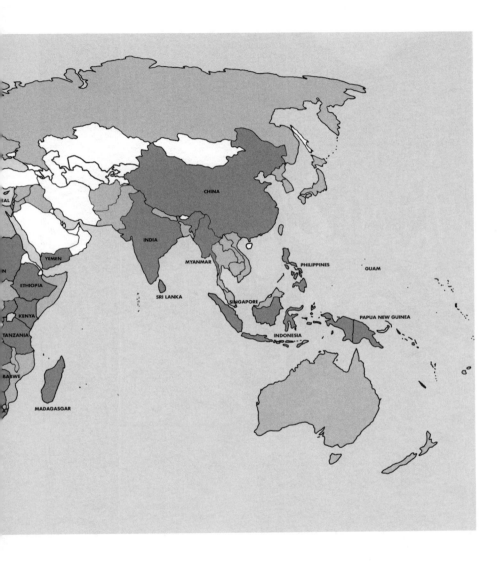

Map: countries which are represented by stories in this book are named and in dark shading. Other countries where Irish missionaries operate are in light shading.

Part Two

Tales of the Irish Missionaries

CHAPTER ONE

The Adventure Begins

Fr Brian Treacy is a Kiltegan Father from Co. Limerick who has been living in Kenya since the 1960s.

'It was all Swahili to me' (based on extracts from my diary)
It was 6 October 1965. Less than six months after my ordination as a priest, I sailed into Mombasa Port with its palm trees and its ancient buildings. I remember feeling great anxiety: *what am I doing here? What does the future hold for me? Am I crazy to be coming to this place?* I felt so inadequate, and not at all sure of myself, despite all my theological training. This fear was to stay with me for years.

I had a large tea-chest of theology books as luggage. I had supposed that they would be of great help to me in my missionary work, but truth to tell I hardly looked at one of them in the years ahead. They just didn't seem to be relevant to this new situation. I remember that first Tuesday morning in Molo, asking Brian after breakfast, 'Where do I start, or what do you want me to do?' Without saying a word he handed me a book on Swahili grammar, and said, 'This is where you start'. I was rather disappointed that I wasn't being given any real work to do. Brian said he was going off somewhere to say Mass, and he hoped to be back in a few hours.

After a while I started glancing through the grammar, but I got bored very quickly. Soon there was a knock at the door, and I shouted, 'Come in'. Nothing happened, so I shouted a bit louder. Still nothing, so I opened the door. There was an old woman outside, and I welcomed her, 'Good morning, how are ya, come on in.' She immediately started a long speech, which of course was gibberish to me, and I kept speaking English, which was gibberish to her, but there was nobody around to whom I could call for help. Eventually, she went off. I remember picking up the Swahili grammar again, now realising why I had been handed this as my first task on my first morning as a missionary priest. That was my first morning's work.

A day or two later I transferred to Nakuru town, where I stayed for the next three months. Nakuru was one huge parish at the time; the area we covered then is now about twenty parishes. It was a difficult enough time for me, as I was just beginning to study Swahili seriously, and I found it tough going. I was studying six-to-eight hours a day, but seemed to be making no progress. When I tried to use the little bit I had, the Kenyans would tell me not to worry and would reply in English, which was not what I desired at all.

I remember one day at my desk trying to figure out the meaning of some words from a basic text for six-year-old children. I couldn't even find the words in the dictionary, and I was frustrated and near despair. Luckily, Conor and Eddie came into the room, and were joking that I must have finished the whole course by this stage. I explained to them that I was about to give the whole thing up as a bad job, that I couldn't even find the words in the dictionary. Then they explained to me that Swahili words have a basic stem, and you add on little bits and pieces to it, usually at the beginning, so when going to the dictionary you have to find the basic stem-word. No wonder I couldn't find anything in the dictionary! For example: the word 'alisema', meaning 'he said' – the first 'a' is he, the 'li' is past tense, and 'sema' is the verb to say. So you would have to look up 'sema' in the dictionary.

I was about two months in Nakuru when my language studies were interrupted: I got my first bout of sickness. I really felt very ill – dreadful headache, high fever, vomiting and diarrhoea. So the doctor was called in. He told me that I had hepatitis, 'yalla jaunders'. He came back a few days later, expressing surprise that I hadn't turned yellow.

Subsequently, I got many bouts of nausea and fever but nothing too serious. It was about seven years later that I went for a tropical check-up at the MMM hospital in Drogheda. There I met the famous Dr Forbes-Brown, a veteran of East Africa, and a character. After doing all the tests, he asked me if I got malaria frequently, and I said no, I had never had it. 'Are you trying to tell me that you've never had malaria, and your blood is full of the damned thing? Have you never been sick?'

So I told him about the bout of hepatitis, and subsequent fevers. Forbes-Brown exploded: 'And what the bloody hell do you think all that was, only damned malaria of course. Damned idiot of a doctor who couldn't see that straightaway!' It all made sense to me then.

In January 1966, I was appointed to Elburgon with Bobby Kavanagh. I was slowly finding my feet as a missionary, and was becoming proficient in the Swahili language. Joe Murray, on the other hand, had a curious brand of Swahili which was unique to himself. It consisted of about fifty nouns, three or four verbs, and the third person singular past tense, which was used on all occasions. For example, Joe wanted to announce that he was going to Nakuru tomorrow, but what he would in fact say was that 'tomorrow he went to Nakuru.' Or something like, 'And then he blessed the convent', meaning 'I will now bless the new convent'. And yet everybody seemed to understand exactly what he was saying.

At this time I also began to learn a little of the Kikuyu language. I found it a much tougher proposition than Swahili, with more subtle sounds and pronunciation, but I felt that I might be able to get it eventually. By now I was increasingly confident I could communicate with the people.

We used to do a lot of home visitation late in the evening, as most people were out all day and didn't get home until nearly dark. We always got a typical African welcome: just come in, make yourself at home, and join us for supper. Everyone gathered around the fire in the middle of the floor with the three cooking stones and the cooking pot on top of the stones. The smoke was supposed to go out through the grass roof of the hut, but often the hut filled up with very acrid fumes. This was devastating for us who were not used to it. We were a great source of merriment to the kids, who watched us as we tried to bend our heads lower and lower to keep under the cloud, tears pouring down our faces.

The Kikuyu food in general was very tasty for us, as it was based very often on potatoes, vegetables, and maize. It was much easier for us to eat than the Kalenjin food, which is almost exclusively *ugali* and *sukuma wiki* – a maize mush and a kind of kale boiled very often to nothing, and then finished off with sour milk with some charcoal added. This sounds dreadful, but in fact I got to like it a lot after the initial revulsion.

It was a great experience to watch these very poor people in their daily lives, especially to observe the Kikuyu women. The way they worked – walking maybe five or six miles in the morning to their *shamba* (small field), with the baby strapped to their back, carrying the *jembe* (hoe) and a sack, chatting and laughing, and very often sewing a basket or something as they walked along. Later in the evening you would see them coming home at dusk, with huge loads on their backs – maize, potatoes, beans, peas, firewood, and the baby now tied to the breast in front or else sitting on top of the load on the back, monarch of all he or she surveyed. And the mothers still chatting and laughing, though exhausted.

After acquiring independence in 1963, it was fascinating to observe the tactics of the Africans as they made their moves to buy out the *mzungu* (European) farms. Someone would go first to the European's house, and ask the farmer how much would he sell his farm for, and the reply always was that it was not for sale, thank you.

'Yes, I know that, but what price would you be selling it for anyway?'
'But I told you that it is not for sale at all.'
'I see, thank you very much.'

A week or two later, another group would come with the same question, or the chief would be sent, or some higher officials would go or just ring up the owner and ask the price. After a year or two of this, the *mzungu* would get the message and start negotiating, and it was remarkable that in the end almost every European-owned farm was bought out by groups of Africans, the vast majority of whom were Kikuyu. One had the feeling that wise old Jomo Kenyatta was orchestrating the whole project behind the scenes. But there was virtually no trouble – it was almost always just moral and psychological pressures that persuaded them to sell out in the end.

Paul Healy, from Dalkey in Dublin, was formerly diocesan administrator in Kitui, Kenya. He is now the head of Trócaire in Asia, primarily based in Pakistan, India, and Afghanistan.

Early days in Kitui, 2002

First impressions. Akamba women on the backs of bicycles. It is the only time they rest. The remainder of the time they walk and walk and walk. Women carrying *kuni* (loads of wood for the fire). Women walking miles for relief food. Women carrying water. Women doing almost anything to survive, to get their children through school, to feed them. And faith. Faith so simple and so trusting that people will go through anything and still have a glimmer of hope about them.

I saw a group of people one day. They were shoved into the lorry like cattle, and they were singing and they were happy. They were all standing and it looked most uncomfortable and crushed. There is no room for your own personal space here. People nudge up to one another. Personal space belongs to the 'West'. It has no room here and it is not needed. The warmth of another is the norm. The 'other' is anybody. The community is so large. I am not used to it. I like the space and distance of Europe. They almost sit on top of you at times here. Smells and colours.

Fr Joe Cantwell returned to Ireland. He had been here for more than twenty years, and he just walked out the door leaving everything behind him. Pictures, television and a bottle of wine from South Africa are all there as if he was coming back tomorrow. He left the tin of biscuits and the cups on the small coffee table and the door is open to the world like the Akamba people taught him. Did he not prize any of his possessions? Does he not hold on to anything? How did he learn to do that? I am here to use his electricity and I disturb the two little opaque lizards with their big black eyes. They are the friends of missionaries. They are welcome guests to the house and spend their time eating the mosquitoes. The mosquitoes like me. They like the sweet, thick blood of an Irishman (fee-fi-fo-fum). Two attacks of malaria in the year are not so bad though and I haven't had an attack since Tanzania. Now that was a good language course in Tanzania. Loads of work and loads of space as the Americans like it. And you can learn Kiswahili.

Kikamba – the language of Kitui – is a different story. I can't get my mouth around it. I love the sound of it. I would love to speak it, but I never will. Richie Brennan, my companion in Kitui, is working here forty years and still struggles with it. That, I suppose, is the great poverty of my being here. My deepest desire is to connect and I can't speak the language. With my English or Kiswahili I will only touch the surface.

There is, however, a universal language. It is beyond my ability to describe it, but it is the language of love and compassion and being connected to people. I can see it in the eyes of some whom I have got to know. I can see it in their eyes and in their ease with me and I know I have a place there with them. I know I am accepted and loved.

Why such positive feelings in Kitui? Maybe it is because I have something to fight for. Maybe it is because I have always felt attracted to the margins of society. I love the land and I love the people and I love my chickens and trees and beans, tomatoes, onions and maize. And I love the last hour of the day. I come home and I walk around and take a final look at the farm, and I sit down and watch the sun go down and I am thankful for the day. And I think of all that has happened during the day and I think of all the people at home and the people here and I wonder if the rains tonight will knock the flowers off the bean plants and leave us with no beans. And I think of all the people that will need seed next year.

It's funny that I haven't mentioned the corruption. It is everywhere, you know, as prevalent as the AIDS virus (and there are 20,000 orphans in Kitui alone). I spend a lot of time going on about AIDS and the endemic corruption. But these are not the issues that capture me at first. It is the beauty of the people and their land and the harshness of the place when it dries up, and their courage in the face of it all and the absolute value of community. Where did our sense of community disappear to in Ireland?

Sometimes I wonder if I am any good at this job at all. And I look forward to tomorrow. I used not to be like this. But this is another day in paradise. I will get out of bed in the morning and put my feet on the floor and be thankful for my life and for the new day and I will look forward to my quiet time of prayer and to everything else that happens in the day.

I had been appointed to Nuu. Nuu is 'bleak', as Richie would say. Little food and a lot of poverty. It frightens me a bit, you know. I don't like to say it, but it does. I wonder at myself and my ability to stay with the silence and the heat and dust. How do I feel about travelling 55km on a dirt track for my second Mass? Are those twenty people worth all the sweat? And yet the joy attracts me, the sense of welcome when I arrive.

It is a big day when I arrive. Singing and dancing and laughing. And I will breathe in the warmth of their welcome and the celebration of their faith and I will go home exhausted. And, like the people here, I will spend the end of the day wondering about the crops and seed for the next rains and thanking God for the opportunity. I feel graced to be here.

Catherine O'Sullivan is a member of the Institute of the Sisters of the Infant Jesus. She has worked for fifty years in Malaysia, Peru, Northern Ireland and Bolivia. She is currently living in Coolea, Co. Cork.

Flowers in the Peruvian Desert

It was a leap year when I arrived at the airport in Lima, Peru – midnight on 29 February 1988. After scrutinising my passport at length and mumbling in Spanish under his breath, the officer ordered me to the back of the queue: '*No stay in Peru … enough money, must go back to own country.*' What was wrong? I was about to panic, when another officer came to my rescue, telling me in a friendly voice to come back *mañana* (tomorrow) to put things in order. I was soon to learn that *mañana* was the great escape word when a problem became too complicated to be solved on the spot. I myself became proficient in its use over the years!

In this case, as in many other instances, *mañana* never came and I was able to spend more than eleven uninterrupted years at my post. This was my first introduction to the way of life in Peru, a way of life that was easy-going and often chaotic, but from the chaos came acceptance, understanding and great creativity.

My destination on that first night was Collique, a sprawling village in the barren foothills of the Andes. Fortunately, I arrived under the cloak of darkness and I didn't have to face my surroundings until the next day. One shock was enough at the time. The Sisters with whom I was to share my life and mission were very welcoming, though none of them were able to speak English. It wasn't easy to wrap my tongue around the bit of Spanish I knew so I was glad to get to bed almost immediately.

Life was difficult during those early months. That first morning, when I went outside, I just couldn't take it. I went to my room and wept my eyes out. There wasn't a sign of vegetation anywhere. Huts of straw clung to the sides of rocky hills. Unfinished buildings made of concrete, with iron girders protruding from each corner, flanked the main road that was called Avenida Revolución. The walls of our house, like those of our neighbours, looked shabby and unsightly. They were left in that condition, I was told, to avoid a display of graffiti, posters and revolutionary slogans. Battered mini-buses billowed dust in all directions as they tried to weave their way around potholes that occupied more space than the surfaced road!

In my first letter I wrote: *I wonder how I will ever survive without a tree, flower or blade of grass. On the other hand, I feel a deep sense of satisfaction in that we are situated right in the midst of the people, people of all ages buzzing with activity.*

Yes, there were people everywhere – about 60,000 of them, all within walking distance. They were mainly families who had migrated from the hills, or *sierra,* supposedly in search of a better life and education for their children. The village of Collique and the six hundred other villages on the outskirts of Lima were called *Pueblos Jovenes* (Young Towns), and were at various stages of development.

One of the greatest inconveniences was the lack of running water. We had to buy a certain number of litres weekly. Yet this in itself was a life-giving experience. When the children saw the truck appearing, they shouted, *Agua! Agua!* Water! Water! Everyone rushed out in front of their houses and chatted to their hearts' content until the truck reached them. It was a celebration of community life! It was the same when the garbage collector appeared. Long before we saw it we would hear, *Basura! Basura!* Garbage! Garbage! Here was another opportunity for a friendly chitchat, as we all gathered round with our bags. However, years later, we were delighted when everyone contributed to the installation of running water which also helped to build up a good community spirit.

Of course, it took me months to make sense of it all. The local 'Faith and Joy' schools in which the Sisters worked, together with teachers who travelled many miles daily, were a great source of stability in the village. I could have taught in a well-established school but I chose to work outside the system. I felt there was a great need to journey with the villagers in search of ways of responding to other urgent and challenging needs. In time, this resulted in the promotion of initiatives to reduce some of the economic problems encountered in daily living: the education of children with special needs, care of the sick and the elderly, and the initiation of a network of basic Christian communities that were a great source of strength and unity in a situation plagued by violence.

The terrorist group, *Sendero Luminoso* (Shining Path), was very active at the time. Bus journeys were obstructed continually. It took hours to get from one place to another, and I was often caught in crossfire in the city.

My jottings at this time show how I felt: *I struggle to live, to grow, to bloom, but I feel fettered, blocked, held back. My heart aches for friends of the past. I feel wrenched by homesickness, separation and distance. Violent feelings surge within me. There is no beauty in these* cerros *(hills) – devoid of vegetation, with rocks, sand, huts and ramshackle houses. No phone calls, no newspapers, no interchange in your own language. I feel forlorn, wandering about, grappling with a new language, struggling to come to grips with local customs and practices. How will I ever survive?*

It was the bleakness of the desert surroundings that had the worst effect on me. There was no plant life anywhere except for what we kept inside in pots. One day I had placed a little desert plant outside my window. For weeks it looked stunted and miserable though I watered it continuously. It had been growing secretly, but my imprisoned mind prevented me from seeing the growth that was taking place. One morning when I looked out, the little plant had produced a beautiful flower. This had a wonderful effect on me. I realised that I too had to blossom where I was planted and that I was here in this desert to change my own way of being rather than that of the people around me. With this revelation, a great calmness came over me. I felt a surge of enthusiasm rise within me and it struck me very forcibly that I was where I always wanted to be, right in the midst of the people and being one with them in their difficulties, their hopes, their fears, their pain and their joy.

As the months went by, a great friendship with the people began to develop. With time, I discovered that the villagers were wonderful people with a great wisdom that had been hard earned from life. They were very friendly and welcomed me wholeheartedly when I visited. I spent months assimilating what was happening in the lives of these courageous and resilient people and allowed it to seep through the numbness until it became part of me. I, too, wanted to become a flower of the desert and allow my roots to access the sap that was giving life and hope to my newly-found family.

Born in 1921, Fr Kevin Longworth was a Westmeath man who played Gaelic football for Longford. In the 1940s, he set off for Nigeria, where he was to serve for most of his missionary life until he retired to Kiltegan, Co. Wicklow in 2002. He also lived in New Orleans, New York, and California, and became an American citizen. He published his memoirs, *Harvesting memories*, in 2003. Sadly, he passed away in September 2010, during the final preparation of this collection. Ar dheis Dé go raibh a anam.

Arrival in Nigeria, 15 April 1948

There were channel markers blinking in the pre-dawn light as we entered the Bonny estuary, a dreary panorama of mud flats and mangrove islands. A few canoes bobbed here and there, and with the sun rising on our starboard the grey mud flats glistened like ice on a pond. We turned and twisted among the mangroves as the gong went for breakfast. I remember there was some kind of fish on the menu and it was not too good. It tasted as if it had been fished out of that slimy mud a few days back.

I think that I put a few finishing lines to my journal, which I had been writing during the voyage. I mailed it home later. I wish I had kept it. There was nothing exotic about my entry to Nigeria, just all this mud and humidity.

Through the bush to Ekononaku

It was now the middle of May. I suppose the whitethorns were blossoming in every hedge in Ireland and exam fever was cranking up the temperatures in every college. But in Calabar the rains were beginning. There were at the time some thirty-eight bush stations in the region, and fourteen of these were practically inaccessible in the wet season. So I had no time to spare to get to them.

Calabar bush lies in a densely-forested area, stretching north eighty miles from the city of Calabar to Ogoja, and in an easterly direction seventy miles to the Cameroon border. Apart from a small section in the south, known as 'The Plantations' (since most of the town's foodstuffs are produced there), the area is sparsely populated. The hamlets and villages look as if they had been dropped by parachute into the small isolated clearings of the forest.

Each village supports about 200–300 inhabitants, mostly of the Ekoi tribe, a people up to now completely uninterested in European civilisation. The Ekoi men spend their time in the forest shooting and trapping wild boar, deer, and monkeys. The meat is dressed and preserved by a process of smoking and then taken south and sold in Calabar. The proceeds go to the village purse held by the chief. The women are responsible for the supply of fresh vegetables, collecting them from the bush – plantains, wild bananas, cocoa-yams, etc.

That May day we set out on foot, following the muddy trails through the dense forest. Very soon we came upon fresh elephant tracks – the excitement of watching out for the herd kept us all moving at a good pace! Our next encounter was an unexpected river. We came on it so suddenly and immediately my heart missed a beat. The sound of running water is always a welcome one in the bush but this time there was no sound, just a broad, smooth, deep-flowing river which, everyone saw, could not be forded. I was beginning to have visions of a night out there in the open when I saw to my right a suspension bridge slung between two tall trees. So eager was I, in fact, that I forgot all my bush etiquette and scrambled up ahead of the carriers to be first across.

There it was, forty yards of frail basket-work swinging out across the torrent! I had heard that these bridges are not very reliable and so, gripping an overhanging branch just in case, I eased myself out over the water. I hadn't gone far when I realised that this bridge was creaking more than any bridge has a right to creak. Holding tight to my branch I looked back for reassurance and was just in time to see one of the main 'cables' parting from where it joined the tree! I still cannot remember how I got back to *terra firma*. The position was really serious as we had only two hours of daylight left and could not see how to negotiate this obstacle. On top of this came the first distant rumble of thunder, heralding the approach of a storm.

Luckily, one of the carriers who had been scouting upstream returned to say he noticed a slight ripple further up which might indicate shallow water. And sure enough we found it was only a few feet deep at this particular spot. Nevertheless, fording a river is a tricky business at the best of times and I spent an anxious fifteen minutes as the loads were carried across. The water was waist high and a slip might have very unpleasant consequences. However, we all got over safely and started off on the last lap of our journey.

By now the storm had caught up with us, and the crash and roll of the thunder coupled with blinding flashes of lightning was something I shall never forget. We didn't mind the torrential rain, but the light was fading fast and there was still no sign of a house or anything to indicate a human presence. I was becoming really scared. The lightning was all around us and there was no guarantee that we were even on the right path.

Suddenly, turning the corner, we caught our first glimpse of the village. To say we were relieved was putting it mildly, because I don't think we could have gone any further. The villagers welcomed us with true African hospitality, gave us food and fixed up the rest house for our stay. For the first time since leaving Ireland, I sat at a fire and warmed myself.

Fr Vincent Boyle (SMA), originally from Belfast, spent many years in Nigeria, arriving there in 1946. The following are his recollections of the early years there, as told to Fr Peter McCawille, a colleague in the SMA.

The work in Nigeria

Lafiagi parish must have been a hundred miles square in area and in it we had fifty-two out-stations and fifty-two schools. We had no car, so we used bicycles to get around. When I went out first, in the forties, we were very much isolated and it was extremely difficult. It was very lonely in the bush. But you just had to get used to it and after a while you became completely absorbed in the people, in the house visitations, in the routines of daily life. We lived among the people and we became part of their lives.

The language didn't resemble anything I had ever learned, but I began to pick it up as I got to know people and their ways, visit the schools, attend the catechism classes and visit the houses in the evenings. I got completely caught up in the whole activity. The initial sense of isolation disappeared after a while and, just like others before me, I became part of the place.

The hardest thing was the suddenness of the transition, the 'culture shock'. All I ever knew or was used to had completely disappeared; there were no evening papers, no radio, no nothing! And you'd say to yourself: *'In the name of God, what have I done to land myself in this situation?'* But it was extraordinary how we adapted to it.

Education was very important. Bishop Kelly had set up many primary and secondary schools and training colleges. Each parish priest was a manager of a number of primary schools and the bishop was the overall proprietor. It was unbelievable what we had to do as ordinary parish priests (the place was so big everybody was a parish priest). For example, you had to pay the teachers, and that meant you had to go down to Benin City regularly to collect the salaries. At that time, there were no currency notes, only coins, and you would be travelling back with maybe £500 or £600 in coins – it was a very dangerous practice! The schools were a full-time job on their own. You had to build the schools according to government regulations; make sure that they were properly staffed; ensure that educational materials were distributed and that the teachers were doing their work; keep an eye on the buildings themselves and oversee all repairs; and fill in form after form about schools in the most remote and isolated areas.

Illness

I got very bad fevers in the beginning, in Agenebode. The nearest doctor was in Benin City, which was over a hundred miles away, and there was hardly any road. I was with Fr Tommy Murray in Uzairue at the time and we got a sick call that one of the parishioners was dying. He looked at me and I looked at him. He said, 'I've got a fever' and I replied, 'I've got a fever too!'

The dying man was about forty miles away and the only transport we had was the bicycle, so I, being the younger man, volunteered and set off with a young fellow on another bicycle. At that time, you had the midnight fast, so that didn't make matters any easier. When I finally arrived at the village, wasn't the 'dying' man out on a deck chair smoking a pipe! He said he had 'small belly ache'. He 'thought he want to go die, but he never die yet and he welcomes Fada very much'. It was I who felt like dying just there and then after the forty miles on a bicycle over hills and valleys!

I continued on down to Agenebode, and I got a terrible fever there, nearly blackwater fever. I spent about four days going in and out of consciousness. Quinine was the awful stuff you had to take, and there was a liquid form of it which was worse again. I'll never forget it. I went into a kind of coma and the young fellow with me had to put my hands into basins of cold water, as cold as you could get at any rate, and that used to bring me round. I always remember the mosquito net over my bed and, when I regained consciousness at some stage, I saw what looked like clouds over the net. It turned out to be the faces of the local people looking down at me.

In the end, someone had the sense to go to the Post Office where they sent a telegram to Bishop Kelly in Benin City. He sent word to Fr Greene in Uromi who came up with a doctor. In the meantime, Fr Tommy Murray came up to see me – he had cycled the whole way too and he was half-dead! So I anointed him and he anointed me and we were both in that state when Fr Greene and the doctor arrived. Fr Murray came out of it all right and I was brought on a mattress in the back of a pick-up truck to Uromi, to a hospital Fr Greene had built. There was a doctor there, Dr Clatworthy, and she treated me.

I spent about two weeks there, in the small house where Fr Greene lived, and all the other priests who thought I was dying came to visit me. They had a couple of 'wakes' – 'pre-wakes' might be more accurate – when all of them would be playing poker outside and every now and again Fr Greene would check on me to see if I was alright. But penicillin had just come in at the time and that's what saved my life. I had a funny feeling in the middle of it all that I was somehow 'above myself'. I read later about people in similar situations, near to death, who experienced the same thing. That was the worst sickness I ever had. Afterwards, I had reasonably good health all through the years.

I did five years on my first tour before coming home. At that time you really didn't get home until there was a replacement for you. But then the twenty-one-month tour came in later and there was no longer a question of the bishop holding you until a replacement came.

A lot of adjustments had to be made when you got home. The Irish climate, the cold and the dampness and all that, would get to you. And all the changes: some people had grown up, while others had died. But it was wonderful to be with your family again. We got a year's holiday, which I thought was ridiculous, but it was necessary because of the time we had spent in Africa.

Colonialism

Where I was living, the centre of colonial administration was in Auchi and there you had the district officer (DO), his assistant (ADO) and various offices like the sanitation office and the judiciary. The DO would see to it that law and order was kept in the area and he went around to the different chieftaincy areas to review judgments in cases that had been tried under native law and custom. We depended on them to get permission to buy land for new schools and churches and so on. Sometimes you'd run across a DO who would be troublesome and block your way, while some of the different education officers would do their best to try to push the Anglican Church rather than the Catholic Church.

At that time the administration was very Muslim-minded. Much of the army was located in the north of the country – barracks and training camps, for example. It seemed to us that the British favoured the north because they could control it more easily than the south. In the north, the Sardauna of Sokoto was like a feudal lord who had control of a vast area. So all the British had to do was approach him, win his favour, and through him they had control of the region. Down in the south, you had smaller areas with many different tribes and a multiplicity of religions (pagan, Christianity, Islam), which made things more difficult to control in times of trouble.

Independence in Nigeria kind of happened overnight and we suddenly realised we had to be careful of the degree of relationship we had with other white people in order not to be lined up with the people up on the 'big hill' – usually the coolest and best part of the town where the colonials lived. Independence, though, had little impact on the people in 'the bush' where I worked. The people really respected the priests and they identified the 'white man' priest with the early priests their parents and grandparents had told them about. These old priests had made such an impression, living there for years with them without ever getting home, that other priests afterwards were identified with them. In later years, in different areas, every priest was 'Greene' or 'Mahon' or 'Kelly'.

Sheilagh Jebb served as a nurse with the Anglican organisation CMS Ireland (Church Mission Society) in Nigeria, from 1950 to 1976. After that, she also worked in Yemen, Sudan, Sierra Leone, and The Gambia. Her father, Revd Charles W. Jebb from Ardee, Co. Louth, was a pioneering missionary in Nigeria from 1907 to 1933. She declined an OBE for her work from Queen Elizabeth II, and published her memoirs, *Going for God*, in 2008. She has lived in Bangor, Co. Down since 1992.

A nurse in Yemen

In 1976, after spending my first week in Yemen learning Arabic, I was driven out to Rada'. It was to be my home for the next three years. I soon discovered that there was no road after the first forty miles! We drove over mountains and through deep valleys full of rocks with scarcely a track to follow: no signposts, and landmarks which seemed to be duplicated all over the place. Beautiful little flat-roofed stone houses sat on every hilltop; heaps of stones removed through the centuries were piled up at the corners of fields wherever there was a piece of flat ground, and everywhere I saw walled vineyards with a few vines and pomegranate trees. I wondered how I would ever find the way when driving alone, and how I would have the nerve to negotiate the steep winding tracks up the mountains.

When I arrived in Rada' I was thrilled to meet three Glaswegian nurses, and a Danish lady with whom I would lodge. I was introduced to some of their Yemeni friends, attending the inevitable afternoon tea parties when some twenty neighbours would crowd into a small room with beautiful alabaster windows that let in light but no air. It soon became very hot.

The Yemeni women always had separate apartments from the men and were heavily veiled – except for those who worked in the fields. These women often smeared yellow grease on their faces to prevent sunburn because white skin was admired. The conversation never seemed to flag. Nearly all were illiterate.

We were frequently invited to wedding celebrations, and sometimes waited long hours with the bride late into the night only to find that the bridegroom would not appear to collect her until the next evening – and then not before midnight. There seemed to be wonderful harmony among the wives of each individual man – usually four by the time the husband was thirty years old, and the youngest wife might be fourteen. The mothers-in-law seemed to arrange which women did what work! I especially liked one beautiful woman who had been a first wife but did not bear any children, who nevertheless seemed to love whole-heartedly each child born to the 'junior wives'. She was thankful that her husband had not divorced her – as many others would have done.

All the Yemeni people called me *Sherifa*, which pleased me very much. Coincidentally, this was the exact equivalent of my Yoruba name, *Sola*, in Nigeria – meaning 'someone who is honoured'.

Fr Brendan Payne is a native of Athlone, Co. Westmeath. He was appointed to Kenya after his ordination in 1982. He is the vocations director for the Kiltegans in East Africa. He lives in Nakuru, Kenya.

First love in the Turkana Desert

Turkana Desert – where's that? That was the question many people asked when I was appointed to Turkana in north-western Kenya in 1982. I was not going alone. Gabriel Dolan, my classmate, accepted the same appointment.

After an enforced stopover in Amsterdam we eventually arrived in Nairobi, and the following day we travelled for six hours to Kitale in the Rift Valley. The journey did not feel long as everything seemed new, wonderful, different, African. We met other Kiltegan priests on the way; they looked so tanned while we seemed to be shockingly white. Another night in a different bed and then on to the town of Lodwar. The road was in bad shape and we arrived in the dark, after travelling nine hours, and had supper with the bishop, John Mahon. I still remember the view from his house the following morning. The landscape was barren, hot, shimmering, the sun beating down. It was widely accepted that the Turkana Desert was one of the toughest postings. Now I was beginning to see why.

Gabriel and I stayed in Kataboi, a small fishing village on Lake Turkana and a two-hour drive from Lodwar, for several months, learning the local tribal language. It is a hard language to learn and there was very little written in relation to its grammar. But with time and patience, sweat and tears, we managed to get a working knowledge of the language and then we were ready. I was appointed to stay at Kataboi while Gabriel went to work in Lodwar.

Everything seemed so very different. At first I kept comparing everything – weather, people, culture – to Ireland but slowly, slowly, Turkana became part of me. I did find the heat, day and night, very hard to get used to. (In 1983 it rained nine times in the whole year, and that was virtually all in the same week.) The children followed me everywhere. They nicknamed me Fr Nasadiki (a Swahili word meaning 'I believe'). Even this simple gesture of acceptance by the children meant a lot. When I attempted to speak the language, they would laugh and correct me if I made a mistake, which was often, but it was the best way of learning. The adults were more polite and would not correct me as they tried to understand what I was saying.

All missionaries have significant moments in their first 'tour' that stay with them for life. Like the first time I preached, without notes, in the Turkana language; the seventy-eight baptisms on my first Christmas Day and the 150 at Easter; the bouts of homesickness; getting malaria; the evocative rising full moon over the still waters of Lake Turkana.

Kenya slowly taught me to appreciate people over things, celebration over punctuality, and the ability to accept the many surprises, good and bad, that each day brings. I learned a lot about the culture of the Turkana people and about myself. In the desert you do not wear masks. Once that is accepted, life gets less complicated.

I appreciate that I was part of a missionary family, many of whom had laboured for years in the Turkana Desert before I arrived. On the missions I became a jack of all trades – an ambulance driver bringing the sick to hospital, a taxi driver transporting people, an undertaker burying the dead, encouraging the youth for music festivals, teaching the old and young how to swim, and providing retreats. You have to be many things to many people, but still be aware of your limitations.

I am now living in Nakuru in the Rift Valley, but Turkana will always be a part of me. It was my first love.

Revd William Odling-Smee served with the Anglican USPG in India in the 1960s. He moved there with his wife and child, and two further children were born while in India. He worked as a doctor and surgeon there for three years. He now lives in Northern Ireland.

A surgeon in southern India

I qualified as a doctor in 1959, and in 1961 my wife and I and our first child, aged nine months, went out to India with the SPG (Society for the Propagation of the Gospel, now the USPG or United SPG). We went by ship from Southampton via the Suez Canal, and landed at Bombay. We had to buy tickets and travel by train to Nandyal, a twenty-four-hour journey, and a real culture shock awaited us. Nandyal is in Andhra Pradesh in south India.

We were met at the railway station by Bishop Arthur Partridge, and were introduced to the ways of living in India, with no air conditioning, no running water, and only intermittent electricity. He and his wife were very kind and supportive. They had lived in India for twenty-five years and were expert at helping newcomers to overcome the difficulties.

There were two hospitals in the diocese, St Werburgh's in Nandyal, and St Raphael's in Giddalur. When we got our own house, I started to work in St Werburgh's with an older Indian doctor. I had had some surgical experience, and so I got all the surgery to do, and all the operative obstetrics as well. So from having only assisted at a Caesarean section in Northern Ireland, I found myself having to do them now without help. It was a scary experience.

But as we were the only medical help for this community, it was better than nothing. I found it very difficult, coming from the NHS, to ask for money, and was desperate when I realised that we might have saved a life if we had had the money for expensive antibiotics. And then there was infectious disease. I saw patients with smallpox and with tetanus, and as I watched them die I realised just how impotent we were in the face of this huge disease burden. I suppose that I am one of the few remaining doctors here who have seen and treated smallpox.

Every summer we had a cholera epidemic because the people would drink the river water without boiling it. These epidemics remain in my memory as the real drama of modern medicine. A local parish priest would come and say that there was cholera in his village, and would we come and help. So we would load up the jeep and when we got there we would be shown some very sick people. They were put outside, because if they died inside the local people believed that the whole family would die. We put needles into veins, and infused dextro-saline, and watched the patients revive, often in the space of one hour! It was all very dramatic and surreal with drip bottles hanging on trees.

After I had been in Nandyal for six months, the doctor in Giddalur went off to Australia, and the Bishop asked me to go up there and look after St Raphael's Hospital. So we went, and spent two-and-a-half very happy years there. Giddalur is quite remote, and high in the Eastern Ghats, and is a little cooler than the plains of Nandyal. For all the time that we lived there we were the only Europeans in the whole valley, but we lived like the Indians. We also became expert at sitting cross-legged on the ground and eating curry with our fingers off a plate of banana leaves.

We became very friendly with the Roman Catholic mission, which was staffed by the White Fathers. They did not have any medical facilities, and I was happy to share with them what we had. We also treated the very large Hindu community, and I got to know a number of them very well. They were gentle people, and wonderful to me. I had the privilege of being taken to temples and being present at Hindu worship, and I learned that all people are seeking after God, a notion of the Absolute, usually in ways determined by their culture, and that every seeking is as valid as the next.

While we were in Giddalur I realised that it would be effective for us to create outlying dispensaries attached to the local parish churches, and for a doctor to visit these dispensaries from time to time. So I used to spend about two days every week travelling around, and as a result I got to know the area well. I often travelled by bus, for we only had one car, and the buses, although ramshackle, were reliable. I went with two nurses and a compounder, and so we were a small team. But when the buses broke down we had to walk, and there were many volunteers willing to carry our things for a few pence. I have a lovely photograph of a little boy carrying my stethoscope.

One summer the monsoon failed, and there was starvation. I had never seen anyone die of malnutrition until then and it was a shock to realise that if we had had food a little earlier, the child that had just been brought in need not have died. We were supplied with milk powder by the UN Food Programme, and this was very useful at this time. When there was plenty of food, it was difficult to know what to do with it as milk was not normally used by the Telugus. In the heat it went off very quickly, and so yoghurt was a much more important part of their diet.

After we had been in India for three years, and produced two more children, it was time to come home. Surgery seemed to be something that I was good at, and so I decided to get a formal training as a surgeon. If I went back to India, it would be very useful to the people there, and if I stayed at home it would earn me a living. So I did my formal training, which took five years, and by then it was politically difficult to be a missionary in India.

But as I look back on those three years in India, I realise that the way I practise surgery was set in those years, and that my Christianity was also determined then. My time in India helped me realise that the Hindus were seeking to understand the ineffable idea of God as much as I was, and that basically all religion is a representation of this journey. When you realise this, you pave the way for tolerance and inclusiveness between the world's major religions.

Sr Anne Maher lived in India from 1955 to 1994, where she worked as a teacher in the Loreto schools. She has returned to Ireland, and now lives in Bray, Co. Wicklow.

Indian kaleidoscope

When I think back over thirty-nine years of life in India, the image that comes to me is a kaleidoscope – a riot of colour, sounds, tastes, smells, feelings.

People, places, journeys all crowd in, calling to be remembered and appreciated. What I say here is not a theological exposition of the purpose of mission, but a very personal reflection on my own experiences as a missionary.

I first went to India in 1955. People often ask me, 'Why did you go?' It is one of those questions which can only be answered in the language of faith. I was at school in Loreto, Crumlin, and there the foreign missions were a background matter of fact. We saw nuns who were going on the foreign missions – one who taught me French went to Mauritius, and another went to East Africa, and others still to India and South Africa. Yet when I entered, it was not explicitly with the intention of going abroad.

After completing my degree in UCD and a year teaching in school, the Mother General said to me: 'I'm sending you to India in October when the nuns from there come back.' And so it came about that I left Ireland and travelled by sea to India, which was to be home from home for the next thirty-nine years. At Dun Laoghaire Harbour there was another set of goodbyes, as the families of those who were leaving stood around in the cool wind for the final moment. I sometimes wonder who made the greater sacrifice: those who went or the ones who let them go. I often think of the many nuns who went in earlier days, knowing they would never see Ireland again. It is a very precious part of Irish spirituality. There must be many cemeteries all over the world with Irish dust.

And it is not just the first time that leaving Ireland is painful. In fact, I found that it was worse every time, and the loneliness seemed to increase with each visit. And in case you may think only women experience this, I know many men who find it equally hard. In fact I've heard one say after coming back from a holiday at home: 'I feel it's almost better not to go at all than to feel like this afterwards.' By degrees (of separation?), loneliness passes and life goes on happily again.

'Culture shock' is the phrase they use now for what I experienced when I first arrived in India. Of course, as a member of the religious order, I was entering a more or less familiar sub-culture, which probably helped. As I look now at India, it is all so much part of my system that I have almost stopped noticing the significant differences: climate, languages, food, dress, religions, social customs, the list is endless. And within the sub-continent of India, as I transferred from one state to another, there were further cultural adjustments to be made. I grew to love the colour and vibrancy of it all.

My life in India was spent working in our Loreto schools. The school system there is that the primary and secondary are a continuous school, and that after the equivalent of Leaving Cert there is a further optional two-year course where students specialise in five subjects as a preparation for university. So you are looking at schools with 1,000–2,000 students – for us, all girls. The girls are almost all non-Christians, and the staff also. There may be two Sisters working in the school, or at most four. The medium of instruction is English as that is the link language in India. With twenty-five states, seven union territories, fifteen major languages and over 800 other languages, the sub-continent needs a common medium.

My first problem was dealing with a whole new set of names: Tapati Ahluwalia, Malini Chatterjee and Zeenat Hussein replaced Mary Byrne and Teresa Murphy and Angela Sheridan. And obviously the various religions were represented: Hindus, Muslims, Sikhs, Parsees and many others.

Evangelisation through schools is a slow and imperceptible process, but very effective all the same. In terms of the numbers who become Christians it may seem a failure, but I am convinced that many of the girls who attend our schools do learn Christian values that they draw on later in life. There is no religious vacuum in most of their lives, so Christianity, though it appeals to them, does not seem necessary. However, there are some areas (mostly rural and undeveloped) where the religion is animism and where life is ruled by fear of evil in a personal and supernatural form.

The Loreto schools that I was involved in began in India in 1841 when the first group of Loreto nuns came from Ireland to Calcutta – the first nuns ever on the sub-continent. Later, the Loreto Order in India had nuns from Australia, England, Mauritius, Yugoslavia, as well as from Ireland. Indeed, Mother Teresa was an Albanian who trained with the Loreto Sisters in Dublin. With such a huge population there is naturally a great demand for schools in India, and one of our biggest problems is to keep the number of students that we admit to a fairly reasonable level. All of our schools cater not only for financially well-off families, but also for girls of very poor backgrounds, especially Christians, who might otherwise not be able to get a good education. The work I was doing was always in urban areas but we also have various types of educational and health care programmes in rural areas.

One school with a very special character is an orphanage that we run in Calcutta. There are about 400 boarders there, ranging in age from eight to seventeen years. Don't think of this school in terms of boarding schools in Ireland. It is run on a shoe-string. The accommodation and food are very basic, less than basic by Irish standards. The housework is done by the girls themselves.

Nearly all of the girls come from broken homes or are orphans and naturally, as a result, there is a high level of emotional pain in their lives. I must say though that once I had recognised this situation I found it very rewarding to watch these girls getting it all out of their system and gradually developing into happy, mature people. Many of the ones I knew as real 'problem cases' are now happily married with children of their own. The vicious circle, of children of cruel parents becoming cruel parents themselves, is broken. I have many happy and amusing memories of my years there and nothing but admiration for the nuns and teachers.

Besides Calcutta I also lived for eight years in Shillong in the north-east of India, a totally different climate, culture, and language situation. Shillong has a very matriarchal society, so the women are very assertive. I don't think I will ever forget the enthusiasm and free-ranging exchanges that took place among the laity in preparation for the many changes after Vatican II. In fact, when I reflect on my thirty-nine years in India, it is the friends that I remember more than anything else. I have often gone into a small shop early in the morning and found the owner-shopkeeper busy at his prayers in front of flowers and incense, which he doesn't interrupt to serve his customer, and he takes it for granted that I will respect this and wait for him to serve me.

There was another man whom I used to meet regularly when I was on my way to daily Mass in the parish church early in the morning. He reared pigs in the village near us and would go to the hotel up the road on his bicycle to collect left-over food in two big cans. When he saw me he would call out the Hindu morning blessing: '*Ram Ram*', and I would answer with the Christian one: '*Jesu ki barai*'. It was a happy moment for both of us. He once told me: 'I look out every day for a chance to help someone else and if the opportunity doesn't arise I spend an extra ten minutes in prayer instead. I have not passed this practice on to my children yet, but if I persevere, I will certainly teach it to them.'

As I read over what I have written I find I have mentioned mainly the positive memories, and yet no pattern is complete without its contrasts. Of course my kaleidoscope contains darkness as well as light. No one could live for long in India and not feel the heaviness that the constant presence of poverty brings. The newspapers and TV news there have the same quota of crimes and tragedies. Natural disasters – earthquakes, floods, and epidemics – are on a vaster scale with greater consequences than we are used to because of the far greater population. And there is also a growing Hindu fundamentalism that seems to be threatening the very foundations of democracy. In spite of all this, my overall feeling in regard to India is one of affection and confidence.

Fr Denis O'Neill served with the Kiltegan Fathers in Kenya from the 1950s, at a time when it was still a British colony. He now lives in his native Dublin.

First impressions, 1958

Coming from Nairobi to Kitui I was introduced to the murram road – an unpaved dirt track – and to a life of potholes. Endless bush from Thika to Kimangua village. Elspeth Huxley wrote in 1913 of the land beyond Thika whither we were heading: 'If you went on long enough you would come to mountains and forests no one had mapped and tribes whose languages no one could understand.'

People lived deep in the bush, not near the road, usually in beehive-shaped native huts. It was a vast, primitive, desolate area, a world of red earth, dust and thirst. This thirst was quenched somewhat by the Wakamba's native beer (*uki*), which the tribespeople could often be seen savouring outside their huts while perched on their distinctive, three-legged stools.

You would see women bent low under enormous loads suspended by leather straps that bit into their foreheads. There was a distinct grace with which they carried light loads, and even relatively heavy loads, on their heads. I have memories of women on the road to Mombasa carrying enormous loads, one walking along with the poise of the catwalk model while carrying on her head a forty-gallon drum as if it were a pumpkin, as well as women on their way to the market ferrying huge sacks of mangoes or bananas. Another vivid recollection was that of boys playing with bows and arrows – this was a land of hunting, and from the age of three every male was required to learn the age-old art of the hunter.

Duik duik (wild deer) were abundant. The *duik duik* were often stunned by the headlamps of the landrovers and jeeps that would fly by, full of hunters, and I remember thinking how out of place this thundering mechanical force seemed in this land of natural tranquillity. I always hoped the animals would escape, especially the young ones. They were so graceful. Unfortunately most of them would not make it. The Wakamba people cheered if you hit a *duik duik*; much of the meat they ate came from hunting. Young men would form an arc, each one with a bow-and-arrow, and gradually force the animals into an ambush. Wild birds were a constant threat to the millet that the Wakamba sowed, and I still remember the whoosh of the slings as they chased away these birds. Every rock, every elevation was manned by slingers, which called to mind the Balearic slingers of the Gallic wars.

The shyness and the happy faces of children we encountered was a joy to behold. Babies were usually carried on their mother's back, but mothers often breast-fed as they walked and talked at the local market. The markets were a magical place and provided a real occasion for socialising and recreation. Tiny children tired from walking would say: '*Mwaitu, ungue*', meaning 'Mammy, lift me up'.

The thunder of drums at night provided the heartbeat of the evening's social events; dancers would pass with what seemed like chalked faces and wearing black. When they greeted each other it was a potent expression of respect, and it was charged with such emotion and intensity that it would look alien to our Western eyes. Life was full of variety. It was a world of visiting (*Kukethanya*: going to greet). This could involve long journeys, going to greet the grandmother (*susu*), grandfather, aunt, or uncle. They had an extraordinary love of grandparents. It was so important to get to know all the names. Curiously, two people of the same name greeted with the words 'The Name'.

Thirst was a constant preoccupation of life here, and life revolved around the search for water. In barren spells, women could be seen on their way to the dry riverbed to fetch water (*kutava kiwu*); digging in the sand, waiting for the water to well up, washing their children by the river. And in times of plenty: young people jumping into the flowing rivers; children playing hop-scotch or beating the wheel; making lorries and cars from tins and bottle tops. The sandals made from tyres were called 'for shooing the squirrels' (*kulungya nduu*). The riddle games, thousands of riddles; sitting outside, on mats, on three-legged stools, on a sack, eating mangoes from a basin; women bringing home the sugar cane for children, *ndukolwe nie*, don't forget me; the importance of respect (*ndaia*) …

A myriad of creatures shared this world with the Wakamba: squirrels, lizards, flies, hornets, the terrible scorpions under the stones, millions of insects, safari ants, dung beetles. There were many terrors that roamed by night – the ubiquitous mosquito, snakes passing by on the path, even once under the fridge! On one occasion I even had to kill a cobra in the oratory in Mutito. We would often see elephants enjoying a *siesta* on the road to Mombasa, leaving us helplessly waiting for them to get a move on. Meeting giraffes crossing the road between Kavingoni and Ikanga was a common and colourful occurrence.

Interaction with an environment such as this never ended, and there was the constant fetching of firewood (*kuuuna ngu*), shelling peas (*kusyulya nzuu*), and the never-ending *kuima*, cultivating and weeding. All of these activities were carried out with the sound of singing in the air.

And funerals. In the home. The grave dug in the compound. The love of washing, washing their bodies, they said.

And men drawing the circle for a new hut, making holes for the poles, women thatching the hut, dashing on the mud, gourds (*kikuu*) all sizes, goats in the home in the morning, hens, cockcrow, hustle and bustle ... Lasting impressions.

Fr Gerry Clenaghan, of the Oblate Order, moved to work in Canada in the 1940s. For many years he was heavily involved with the 'Frontier Apostles' lay mission-ary movement. He later ministered in Alaska, where he worked with the local Inuit population, and, more recently, in California. He now lives in Dublin.

On the missions in Canada

My eighty-six years thus far have been as follows: twenty-five in Ireland, twenty-nine in Canada, two in Alaska, and thirty in the western United States. I was received into the Oblate Novitiate in Co. Limerick in 1940. During my first year in the seminary I came across *The shooting of Dan McGrew* by Robert Service. I was captivated by the tales of the Yukon and the pioneers there. During the next six years, until I was ordained in 1947, I read avidly everything I could find on the subject of fur traders, gold seekers, and missionaries. While Oblates are on every continent in more than seventy countries, and I was definitely willing to go anywhere that Rome would send me, I had a special preference for Canada.

This is where Divine Providence comes in – at my ordination, the ordain-ing prelate was Bishop Anthony Jordan, vicar apostolic of Prince Rupert, Canada! Before leaving for home with my family that day, I stopped by to pay my respects to the bishop. I mentioned to him that I was sorry not to be going to work in his missionary diocese: 133,000 square miles in extent, four times the size of Ireland! A month later, I received a call from the Irish provincial to say that I was assigned to Bishop Jordan's diocese on the west coast of British Columbia. I would be joining two classmates, Fr Ted Green and Fr Ed Ballesty, and leaving for Canada in October 1947. It would be nine years before I saw dear old Ireland again.

Fr Green and I were assigned to live at the pro-cathedral in Prince Rupert with Bishop Jordan and the pastor, Fr Jim Carroll, who was from Cavan. This was a wonderful start for two young priests. I am forever grateful for the example and guidance they gave us. Ted was parish assistant, while I was to travel to the outly-ing missions: Queen Charlotte Islands, fifty or sixty miles off the west coast, as well as north by overnight ferry to Stewart, British Columbia, and Hyder, Alaska. Fr Ballesty was at Lejac, 500 miles east of Prince Rupert. Unfortunately, his health gave out and he had to return to Ireland after just one year.

After a year in Prince Rupert – where the average rainfall is 120 inches a year – I was sent to replace Fr Ballesty at Lejac. There, I was responsible for two native missions, Stellaquo and Fort Frasier, as well as a mixed congregation at Fraser Lake. I had three Masses every Sunday morning, a round trip of about thirty miles. In those days, fasting from midnight was compulsory – not even a glass of water until I got back for breakfast at 1.30pm (wish I could do that now!). Five years later, I was pastor at Burns Lake, with Fr Ivan Mc Cormick, who was from Prince Edward Island. Ivan took care of several outlying missions. It was a privilege to minister to both Native Americans and settlers. They truly appreciated our ministry.

My next assignment was to Prince George where my good friend, Fr Carroll, was now pastor. To the north, I had a string of missions in what is known as the Rocky Mountain Trench: Summit Lake, Finlay Forks, Fort Grahame, Ingenika, and Fort Ware. Needless to say, we did not have a Mass every Sunday in each place. It was ninety miles down from Prince George to McLeod. My forty-foot riverboat, with outboard motor, was stored there.

A full day's travel took me sixty miles downriver to Finlay Forks where the Parsnip and Finlay Rivers meet to form the mighty Peace River, which flows several hundred miles north to the Yukon. From the Forks, it was five or six days upstream (160 miles) to Fort Ware, with stops along the way. This was my program from May to October. After the rivers had frozen over, I depended entirely on the kindness of local bush pilots, God bless them, to tip me off when a seat was available to bring me to visit my flock.

Noreen Foley was born in Co. Kerry. She joined the Sisters of Mercy in Tralee, trained as a teacher, and taught in Colaiste Íde in Dingle. She then moved to Kenya for ten years. On returning to Dublin in 1994 she completed postgraduate studies and worked as co-ordinator of the congregational archives. In 2006, a request came from the Mercy Sisters in Yola, Nigeria for somebody to assist, and she set out again for mission territory. Since leaving Kenya, three of her close missionary friends have been murdered – one of whom, Fr Gerry Roche (RIP), was the man who invited the Mercy Sisters there in the first place. She now lives in Mallow, Co. Cork.

From Kerry to Kenya

Ever since the missionary Sisters visited my local primary school when I was a child, with their mite boxes for 'the black babies' and their intriguing stories of Africa, I had felt a call to the missions stirring in my soul. Many years later, as a Sister of Mercy, that wonderful dream was unexpectedly realised.

At the end of August 1983, three of us bade farewell to our homes and convents in Kerry, and set out enthusiastically to face a very new challenge. Fr Gerry Roche, a Kiltegan missionary working in Kenya, had invited the Kerry Mercy Sisters to found a new mission in his parish in Kipkelion. (In December 2009, we were shocked and deeply saddened to hear that Fr Gerry had been very violently murdered in his mission in Kericho. We owe him a great debt of gratitude. *Ar dheis Dé go raibh a anam.*)

After a tremendous welcome by the Irish missionaries at Nairobi Airport, we were driven the four-hour journey to Kipkelion. Outside Nairobi, I caught my first glimpse of a sprawling shantytown – row after row of tightly packed little tin-roofed shacks with scarcely any breathing space between them. Utterly appalling living conditions. I remember staring open-mouthed in disbelief … and heard a cry somewhere deep inside me.

However, there was another side to Kenya as well. I was amazed at the number of people – many vibrantly dressed – walking along the roads. Were they going to a football match or what? I was astounded too at the speed of the over-crowded *matatus*, with so many human beings clinging to the back doors! I felt a surge of gratitude at the sight of the giraffes, zebras and other wild animals in their natural surrounds: this is *Africa*! And *I* am here!

On approaching the Kipkelion mission, the beautiful surrounding hills were strangely inviting. It was as if I was born for this moment. I noticed a little boy with a stick rolling his bicycle-wheel along the dirt road. It was like turning back the clock for me to the 1950s in Ireland. That little boy could have been my own brother! The welcome afforded us in the mission left nothing to be desired. A good Irish party followed as many missionaries gathered from far and near.

I could never overestimate the importance of the context into which we found ourselves, a missionary context with so much support at so many levels: from Kiltegans, the Volunteer Priests, the Franciscan Brothers and Sisters, the Incarnate Word Sisters from Molo… and the Sacred Heart Sisters from Kericho. The latter were remarkable for their generosity and sharing – giving us their sisal floor-mat, ironing board and spare cutlery. Later on they got a present of a sum of money and gave us half!

Next morning, waking to the familiar sound of the cocks crowing, I stepped cautiously, wary of the lizards, spiders and strange insects sharing my room and maybe my shoes. We had neither curtains nor blinds. There, peering in the window at me, were several curious, small, shiny, black faces! It was

Sunday and they were gathering for Mass. It seemed rather early to me, two hours at least!

Soon we heard singing and clapping draw near our house. The women had come to escort us in their tribal dance to the church. The people were eagerly awaiting the 'new arrivals'. The Chief and his assistant were seated in a place of honour at the top. The Mass was lively – everybody participating to the full with no inhibition. At the offertory, I was moved to see these poor people bringing up their offertory gifts – potatoes, maize, eggs, a hen, a goat! They wanted to share the little they had so generously. The Chief and local leaders assured us that our coming was a ray of hope for the people: they desperately needed a medical clinic and a secondary school for girls. Of course, these had not been built yet, but no worry. *Hakuna matata!* – All would be well!

After some time at language school in Nairobi, we returned to Kipkelion to savour life there and begin our mission. There was still no school – the foundation had fallen in with the coming of the rains. The plight of the women touched us deeply. We were appalled at the huge heavy loads they were obliged to carry and the long hours they worked – even when pregnant. We quickly realised that we were facing an uphill struggle.

'A secondary school for girls?' laughed the men. 'They know how to give birth ... to draw water and firewood ... and to work in the *shamba*. What more do they need to learn?' The promised school building had been delayed because of the rains, but undaunted, we all pulled together like a *meitheal*, drawing stones for the foundations from the quarry and the hillside – in the sweltering heat and with no clean drinking water. Eventually, in February 1984, out of a bare hillside we saw Mercy Girls' Secondary School open its welcoming doors for the first time to an eager group of girls. And a few curious goats!

At that time, I was full of enthusiasm and ready for any challenge ahead. Teaching in a new culture was daunting enough. I remember preparing one lesson in biology using the special books I had brought from home that would help me impart the scientific terms in a way the girls could understand. For them English was their third language. After a while, I asked the question: 'Do you understand?' There was a blank stare on the young faces in front of me. Then slowly one student stood up ... then all followed. What was going on? As I teased it out with some of the more 'fluent' girls, they explained the problem. They had heard the words 'do' and 'stand' ... so they did stand! I clearly had a long way to go. In a short time, I would find myself saying, 'Are you understanding me?', and they would readily respond. I had to start learning and unlearning faster than I had ever done in my life before.

And challenges galore there would be – trying to equip the new school, and providing water for its population. After a year we hit our first major crisis – most of our students left! We now became painfully aware that the girls needed a boarding school. Their huts had only one living room and a kitchen; there was no room for study, and besides, there was plenty of work to do. Some of them walked several miles to the school. They told us that they were frightened, especially when the maize was fully grown, because they could be pulled into the field at any moment and raped. While these stories deeply disturbed us, we could see no way to provide boarding facilities. It was a mission impossible for us, or so we thought.

At our social gathering on St Patrick's Day, Fr Gerry introduced me to a person who seemed particularly interested in hearing my story. Over a cup of tea, I told him all. When I had finished he asked, 'Do you know who I am?', and smiled. Of course, I didn't. To my embarrassment, I discovered that he was none other than the first secretary to the Irish ambassador. Because of that chance conversation, our new dormitories and kitchen were up and running in no time and many more much-needed facilities were added, surpassing all our expectations. The ways of God are strange.

Our Mercy Mobile Clinic had extended far out into the hills by now, providing ante-natal and post-natal care for the mothers, a preventative programme of vaccinations for the small children and a curative service for the many sick who had no place else to go. The Mobile Team provided the only reliable health service for miles around as well as a much-needed basic education in preventive care.

The clinics were a real eye-opener for us all. We saw at first hand just how much the people suffered. The sanitary conditions were appalling, hygiene was poor, and scabies was common. There was no place to wash hands, not enough water to keep the body clean. The water was brown, coming straight from the river where the animals drank and people bathed. Children were not vaccinated so child-diseases were rampant: measles would sweep over a young child overnight, and polio had left many a young person maimed for life. Ear and eye diseases were an everyday occurrence. Anaemia left the body listless and weak. Amoebic dysentery was a constant scourge and malaria an ever-present reality. Many suffered from dehydration. TB, tuberculosis, was all too evident.

Education in basic health care was badly needed. The Mobile Team's work was cut out for them. We also organised school clinics to monitor the students and provide whatever help was required. At one stage we got a supply of multivitamins from Kerry. Gradually, we noticed that the girls were refusing to take them. Word had gotten round that the new Sisters were trying to ensure that the girls remained virgins like themselves!

As another Sister joined the team later, it expanded its scope to address the critical AIDS/HIV pandemic. It took a long time for the local men to realise that this was no fabricated story – the women who gathered for their conference in Nairobi in 1985 did not come to spread a lie so as to keep the men away from their girlfriends. AIDS became a real burning issue when a beautiful young teacher began to waste and die… then another and another. Only then did they believe what the Sisters and their team had been saying over the years.

Lasting friendships were established through both the schools and clinics, thereby breaking down the cultural and religious barriers. Personally, I was deeply moved by the warm way the people welcomed me into their humble mud-huts as if I were one of their own. The basic Christian communities held the key to the vitality of the Catholic Church. I loved the days we spent together cultivating, weeding or harvesting the little church-plots, not only generating a much-needed income, but an extraordinary community spirit too. I particularly loved the harvest time, especially if the yield had been good, and joy shone on every face as we sang and worked.

Yet for all that joy I still recall the pain of loneliness – searing at times and unrelenting. But then there was the joy at an unexpected visitor to our place. And living close to nature was a truly healing experience. It was like a balm for the soul and body.

Over a period of time, and with the expertise of the Irish Franciscan Brothers, we developed the school farm. It afforded the students first-hand experience in practical aspects of agriculture and enabled them to become virtually self-reliant in food production. We planted many indigenous trees, as we knew that the desert was creeping ever closer because of over-intensive farming. Here was a new exciting venture. I had discovered my inner farmer!

I rejoiced to hear news of the birth of the newborn calf and loved the fun at the naming. I still get a surge of energy as I remember walking over the farm and seeing an eagle sitting at ease right near me on the post of the basketball pitch. I used to enjoy some moments of solitude beside a lovely pond alive with playful, frisky, frogs. I remember with sadness the day the frogs were collected because they were required for the national biology examination. Something did not feel right. It reminded me of my brother who could not kill the turkey for Christmas, because he knew her too well! For a few days, I had a terrible sense of loss, even nausea. Even then, I had some intuition that we are all connected, human and non-human.

Fr Enda Watters is a Spiritan Father who studied in UCD, Jerusalem and Chicago. He has travelled to over thirty countries, on every continent, in roles as varied as magazine editor and secretary of the Irish Missionary Union, as well as being a pioneering missionary in Brazil. He wrote about some of his experiences in his book, *Missionary memoirs*, published in 2009. Fr Watters currently lives in his hometown, Dublin.

To the end of the Earth: Papua New Guinea – 1976

We arrived early at the airport. Because of the mountainous nature of the country and the innumerable gorges and chasms, the normal, and indeed only, way to get to many of the valleys was by air. Our destination was Mt Hagen in the high hills to the north-west. Planes left for other destinations and, as each plane took off, the waiting crowd clapped.

Eventually, we took off in a Fokker Friendship. For a while we cruised along the coast over the reefs and coral islands and then we turned inland. We climbed steadily over thick forest, great volcanic gorges and wide rivers. We finally reached our destination, the great fertile valley of Mt Hagen, sur-rounded on every side by towering mountains reaching 12,500ft.

The people of this valley were unknown to the rest of the world until 1933 when some gold explorers, who were accompanied by an official of the Aus-tralian government, discovered the valley. When one considers that humans have lived in Papua New Guinea for some 27,000 years, and that much of it was unknown until the 1930s, it is understandable that it became something of a paradise for anthropologists. The research of the Pole, Bronislaw Malinowski, and Americans, Robert Redfield and Margaret Mead, is very readable and conveys a vivid picture of the life of the people they studied.

I found the air light and cool and enjoyed travelling to the different mis-sion houses in this beautiful valley. The mountains surrounding the valleys reach a great height: Mt Hagen, which gives the valley its name, is 12,354ft. Then there is Mt Jaka, 9,400ft; Mt Kubor, 14,300ft; and Black Mountain, 7,685ft. Two rivers run through the valley, the Jumants and the Waghi.

The people lived high up on the sides of the mountains, with their gardens or farms below. Smoke rising through the trees indicated farms that were out of sight. The status of the pig surprised me. Women nursed them at the breast like infants and picked lice from them. A man going to do some business would bring along a few pigs on leads like pet dogs to show that he had 'cap-ital'. Alas, when it came to great festivities roast pig was the supreme delicacy. The people also ate dogs, large birds, turtles and lizards. Their food included bananas, sugar-cane, sweet potatoes, taro roots and leaves and coconuts. For export they grew tea, coffee, cocoa beans, nutmeg and copra.

The town of Mt Hagen, capital of the valley and lying towards the south-west, had some quite modern shops. One of the fascinating things about Papua New Guinea was how one comes across the most primitive and the most modern, side-by-side. The people coming from outside the town to shop or do business were obliged to wear some leaves to cover their nakedness. I was surprised to see a large poster of Pope Paul VI displayed in a chemist's shop. At the bottom was printed: *'Have you taken your pill today?'* It was not too long after the Pope had published his famous encyclical, *Humanae Vitae*.

There was another amusing incident when I attended the funeral of a Catholic at Mt Hagen. A lorry-load of his 'pagan' friends arrived, all dressed simply in mud. Carrying their ten-foot spears they looked really fierce. The modern touch was that one of them had an umbrella tied on the top of his spear in case of rain! I might mention that there was plenty of rain and lightning in this part of the world.

The most dangerous journey by road that I made in all my travels was to one of the mission stations, Karap, which was outside the valley and involved driving over mountains 7,300ft high. The road, like other roads in Papua New Guinea, was simply a winding track scraped out on top of the escarpment, crossing over bridges made of logs. There was always the risk of falling over the edge – less than a yard away from our jeep – into a precipice. Landslides were an ever-present danger. But we enjoyed some stupendous vistas. At one point our jeep took us over the clouds and, as if airborne, we could look down on them floating in the valleys below ...

Travelling by air brought its own excitement. The day I left Kamina I had an experience that is very common in Papua New Guinea – one of frustration at the uncertainty of ever getting a plane. I was down at the airport early in the morning but no flight was going to Kerema, which was my destination. Several times more I went down when planes landed but none of them was going to where I wanted to go. When at last a plane for Kerema did arrive, I scrambled aboard very gratefully. But not for long. Apparently our pilot was new and, as he turned the plane around for take-off, a wing got caught in the branches of some bamboo trees. There was no panic. The passengers got out and helped the pilot to disentangle the plane, laughing gleefully and enjoying the situation. Once we were airborne I found myself wondering just what damage the bamboos had done to that wing. Again I reflected how extraordinary it was that some of the most primitive people in the world could take air-travel so much for granted. In their native dialect they called airplanes 'the great silver birds'.

The day I was leaving Papua New Guinea I decided to take home some souvenirs and settled for attractive tray cloths adorned with a map of the country. The shop assistant was packing them for me when I noticed something written in the corner of one: *Irish Linen, Ulster: Made in Ireland.* It seemed rather silly to bring back souvenirs of Papua New Guinea made in Ireland so I bought some local souvenirs instead.

Sr Mairéad Foley, a Mercy Sister, left Ireland in 1971 to serve in Nigeria. She now lives in Waterford.

Tending the sick – and the odd camel – in Nigeria

I arrived in Nigeria in October 1971. We touched down in Kano Airport before embarking on an internal flight to Yola. The tropical sun and balmy atmosphere as the jet set down in Kano still live on in my memory. All earth's creatures seemed to be rejoicing in the beautiful sunshine, not a cloud in the azure sky.

On arriving at Yola Airport I was met by Sr Philomena who escorted me in a Land Rover to Numan to catch the ferry to take us to the road and then to the bush path to Bare mission. The entrance to the ferry was a hive of activity – people on foot, lorries, bicycles, kit cars, animals, traders – all waiting to be accommodated for the short trip across the river. The people all seemed very relaxed and happy – no one in a great hurry! The whole experience was quite a culture shock. Language was a huge barrier, not to mention the heat. Having crossed over, we soon reached the bush path to the mission compound, where we were welcomed by Sr Emmanuel Ahearn. There was a fine church, school, health centre, house, all looking neat and tidy, with many trees and some flowering desert roses in bloom.

I was gradually introduced to the local people by Sr Emmanuel. We travelled on foot and bicycle to the nearby villages on visitation or sick call. Later we acquired a Honda 50 motorbike, which made life easier when travelling along the narrow paths. As time went by, I commenced work in the health centre, where the people walked over long distances for treatment for various illnesses: malaria, filarial (worms), snake bites and many other tropical complaints. We soon commenced an under-fives clinic and later an ante-natal clinic. Both proved very beneficial to the health of the people.

It was customary for a tribe called Fulani to travel south in the dry season in search of water for their cattle and camels. Bare was a stop on their way to the Cameroons. The Gongola River was close by and met their water requirements. They set up camp close to the health centre and attended regularly for various treatments. Once I was requested to treat one of the camels for an infected hoof. I duly commenced a course of penicillin injections and cleaned up the wound. The camel lay down while I cleaned the hoof and applied bandages! In about a week the hoof healed up well and the owner paid me in French currency and all went happily on their way south. Many of these men suffered eye injuries from the horns of the cattle, which I treated with antibiotic ointment and oral antibiotics and advised them to attend a doctor on arriving at their destination. Sadly, no ophthalmic specialists were available in our area.

My abiding memory of the people was their sense of community and care for each other when family and friends needed help. Their sense of celebration, both of liturgy and other family events, was unique. The respect and courtesy, both to each other and to us missionaries, was such a joy to experience from these people who lived such a simple lifestyle. They travelled miles through rough terrain and intense heat to receive modern medicine and treatments. Native remedies were severe and not always reliable.

At times their faith in us missionaries made me feel humble, and I thank God and the congregation for affording me the opportunity to experience such richness during my years there.

Kathleen Byrne was born in Killabeg, on the border of counties Wicklow and Carlow. Known as Sr Patricia, she served as a Good Shepherd Sister in Indonesia from 1953. Her sisters Emily and Teresa were missioned to Sri Lanka and Singapore, and Egypt and Sudan, respectively, also as Good Shepherd Sisters. All three are now back in Ireland.

Lend a helping hand
In 1953, I arrived in Indonesia as a Good Shepherd missionary, and remained there for forty-four years. Communication was my first problem, as the Sisters in my new community conversed in Dutch, and everyone else spoke Indonesian all the time. However, we had a small kindergarten school where I had the joy of sitting at the back of the class for some time each day. The children were intrigued at having an adult as a pupil and greatly enjoyed correcting my many mistakes.

The city of Jakarta has a population of around twelve million people. An American tourist aptly described the situation with his quaint remark: 'Back in America we say "wall to-wall-carpet" but here in Jakarta I would say "wall-to-wall people".' I remember the feelings I had the first night I walked home after a meeting. With great difficulty I made my way along the pavements where many homeless people had made their bed for the night. Fortunately, the climate is mostly clement, except during the rainy seasons when getting shelter would be difficult.

Most of my neighbours and friends were truly poor. One day, while reaching out to help such a family, I had an unexpected experience. Ibu Han, a mother of twelve small children and a heart patient herself, came with the sad news that her husband had just died in the nearby hospital. Her situation was all the more poignant because she felt she had no one to make all the funeral arrangements. Sr Jose and myself rose to the challenge.

First we went to the hospital, where we got the measurements for the coffin, then crossed the crowded city to the undertakers. It was late afternoon by the time the coffin was ready. Not having enough money to hire a hearse, we gladly accepted a neighbour's offer to use his van. Only half the coffin would fit in, so Sr Jose sat with her legs in the coffin and I sat in front using my hands to hold it in place as we started on our long journey across the city. Seeing the look of surprise on the faces of the people as the police began stopping the traffic along the way to let us pass, we suddenly realised what a sight we presented. I began to wonder what my parents would say if they had been spectators.

In less than an hour we reached the hospital with our precious load, and what a joy to see the gratitude on Ibu Han's face.

Kathleen Sweeney (FMSA) is originally from Donegal. Her first experiences of Africa, recounted below, are from her time in Uganda. She has also worked in Kenya and, since 1998, in South Africa, where she now lives.

Uganda: the pearl of Africa

Nothing could really have prepared me for the impact that Uganda, a land of great contrasts, would have on me when I arrived there as a young Franciscan Sister in September 1967! Having been born and raised in wild, beautiful Donegal, I now found myself in a tropical and fertile land that was truly remarkable, vibrant, throbbing with life. I knew it as the source of the 'mystical' Nile and found that there is indeed a deeply spiritual quality to life there.

First of all there were the people of Uganda – smiling and friendly in spite of the troubled ethnic and political reality that they were living through. This had been a land of traditional monarchs and kingdoms whose power had been abolished and stripped away by the government. Yet, in a way, life seemed normal and settled for the people, who struck me as being forever on the move.

From the first day that I landed in Uganda, I noticed the women, always brightly dressed and with bundles on their heads, strolling along the roads and pathways. I learned that they are rarely in a hurry, chattering away as they go along. Children rolled about happily in the dust of the '*shambas*' or village compounds, or raced their homemade cars and hoops with great glee. And always the drums throbbed in the background. The fast and intricate rhythms add to the sense of vitality and intensity of life in Africa. No special occasion is complete without the throbbing drums and swirling dancers. The people are natural performers. During my first year in Uganda, Mount St Mary's High School produced a spectacular performance of *The Mikado*. Everybody loved it and we were well and truly transported to Titipu with the young ladies transforming themselves into a formidable Emperor, a handsome Nanki-Poo and an enchanting Yum Yum!

I believe that St Francis, who saw justice, peace and care of the earth as interrelated, would have felt at home in Africa. In Uganda, the many great lakes, snow-capped mountains, tropical forests and diverse wildlife seem to glorify the Creator as Francis did in *The Canticle of the Creatures*. The tropical climate, with seasonal rain twice a year, favours life in abundance. I can still remember the riot of colour in the compound of Mount St Mary's High School (where I taught during my first years in Africa). Opposite the school there were the rolling green hills of a tea plantation and, in the school compound, daring monkeys lived close to the shady trees, shrubs and multi-coloured bougainvillea. I remember so many exotic touches to life there!

Uganda is the final resting place of the foundress of my congregation, Mother Kevin Kearney from Arklow. In Uganda she is remembered as 'Mama Kevina'. With a small band of Sisters, she courageously faced the challenges of the times – they went there in 1903 – and tried to improve the quality of life for the people. In today's world there are many modern facilities and material resources but plenty of human deprivation in the midst of what at first seems abundance. What still remains, however, is the generosity of heart, resilience and sense of joy that has always marked the Ugandan people.

I think their flag says a great deal. The colours are black, red and gold, representing the people, the sunshine and the blood of their kinship and struggles. In the centre of the flag, there is a small white disc with a crowned or crested crane – a gentle and noble bird – symbolic of the people of that land.

CHAPTER TWO

A Funny Thing Happened

Paul O'Callaghan, born in Co. Dublin in 1980, spent three years living and working with VMM (Volunteer Missionary Movement) in four countries in East Africa: Kenya, Tanzania, Rwanda, and the Democratic Republic of Congo. In 2008, he wrote an unpublished book, *Travel tales from the Continent of Golden Joys – musings from the missions.* He is currently studying for a doctorate in child psychology at Queen's University Belfast, as part of which he has worked with former child soldiers in Uganda.

Exotic fare in Tanzania

When in Rome, they say, do as the Romans do. In my experience of eating abroad, though, I've discovered that there is no food that everyone always likes. Knowing cultural sensitivities and the pride people have in their local cuisine, I secretly vowed one day that I would try never to refuse anything I was offered in Tanzania unless I knew with absolute certainly it would make me ill.

So, when the parish chairman decided to offer around a mid-morning snack, I politely accepted. It was only after crunching the hard shell through to the succulent, sweet liquid inside, that I timidly asked what exactly it was I had eaten. Flying ants, I was told. The parish priest then took an ant and threw it to the dog – which refused to eat it!! A bad omen, indeed. Yet, if one forgets the fact that you are eating a large insect (minus the wings), I believe almost anyone could easily chomp their way through a small packet of them. Ever on the lookout for income-generating projects here, I did briefly entertain the idea of contacting the Omniplex chain of cinemas back home in the hope they might consider a new line of 'organic' snacks to be chewed while slurping a monstrous-sized coke and a computer-sized box of popcorn!

Perhaps the most bizarre-sounding fare I've ever eaten is what is commonly referred to here as *masikio ya tembo* (elephant ears). The parish cooks have a real gift in the culinary department and fry elephant ears with such perfection that they are mouth-wateringly delicious! But lest you think that the wild herds of Tanzania are being decimated by this local delicacy – elephants in Tanzania are a protected species – I should inform you that 'elephant ears' is the local name for 'tortillas' – thin, flat pancakes made from flour, water and butter and fried slowly in the pan. I suppose their large oval shape and firm yet doughy base is why the name was coined.

The Pallottine priest who runs the 1,000-acre grange is a crack shot. One night he shot two guinea fowl and a three-year-old male gazelle. That night, after skinning the gazelle and chopping the bones, we ate the meat for dinner, and again the following day. Gazelle meat is very tender and once you can put out of your mind the fact that you have killed and eaten Bambi, or at least Bambi's first cousin, it is a very tasty dish indeed.

Tricking the trickster

While game-meat may occasionally be delivered to the house by rangers or shot during a hunting trip, providing fruit and vegetables for the table involves nothing more than a visit to the local market. Yet a trip to Arusha's main market is nevertheless an assault of every single sense you possess. First, there are the smells: a pleasant, earthy smell of freshly picked and plucked farm produce mingling with the stink of half-rotten fruit and vegetable peelings discarded in the main gully that runs through the market place. Salted sardines add their pungent smell to the mix, while spices like ginger, cinnamon and paprika mingle with the farmyard smell of live chickens, creating a nasal adventure that must be experienced to be believed.

Then there is the sight of rows and rows of red tomatoes, green cucumbers and beans, purple aubergines and yellow bananas: a fantastic riot of primary and secondary colours blended together. And the delights of taste: fruit can be sampled before eating and sellers will slice open a mango or chop off a segment of watermelon and offer you a piece. People are friendly, and when you've got a bit of the language and know your numbers well enough to haggle over prices, the whole experience can be great fun.

The market is usually busy and trade is brisk. When you are foreign, all the sellers try to catch your attention, believing that the *mzungu* (European) will pay more than the standard price for everything. Young bag-boys descend on you like a flock of pigeons, each trying to touch your hand and offering to help carry your groceries for a few coins. But one thing I've learned since coming here is to always be wary of the person that is extra friendly. Such a case was Butcher Shop 60 where they sold beef, cutting strips from a huge hunk of meat hanging in the window.

The last time I had bought meat there, our cook had casually mentioned that the 3kg of meat I had bought the week before seemed strangely lighter than normal. I guessed what was happening and set to work to devise a trap for our butcher boy. He was all smiles as he measured out the meat. I deliberately turned away so he wouldn't suspect anything but watched out of the corner of my eye as he slyly changed the weights used to measure the meat. Before I left and paid for my 3kg of meat, I asked him to confirm there were 3kg in the bag. He nodded in agreement. In a surprising break from our usual routine, I then introduced myself and made sure to get his name too. The trap had been sprung!

I hurried off to a greengrocer in the market, a fellow parishioner and friend, to ask him to weigh the meat. It was 2½ kgs. I knew then I had my proof that the butcher boy had tried to swindle us. So, I returned to the shop and told them that I'd forgotten to get another kilogram of meat. He cut me off another hunk, weighed it and handed it over. I then thanked him for the 'free meat'. When he looked at me quizzically, I explained that I had been cheated through the use of wrong weights and that I was going to call the police. By this stage a crowd had gathered around, ever eager to witness a good verbal spat or a physical bust-up to relieve their boredom. The manager of the shop then addressed me in English, telling me that the butcher boy was an uneducated fool (his words) and had made an 'honest' mistake! He then asked me not to pursue the matter. I made sure to emphasise the point that honesty does not require an education, but left with everyone's dignity intact. However, I did leave the option of notifying the police hanging in the air and took a wicked pleasure in allowing them to sweat over the real danger that the police could come and shut them down for good or fine them heavily for theft.

It's worth remembering in any business transactions in the market that *caveat emptor* is definitely the rule of thumb.

Crowd-surfing priests

'Haraka, haraka, haina baraka' – There is no blessing in hurrying. This one maxim has come to epitomise for me the gift Africa has to offer the frenetic, tail-chasing world of the West. The continent that holds the cradle of humanity continues to teach us the art of stillness, through the beauty of its surrounding natural world and the emphasis its people place on spending time with others. The gentle pace of life in Tanzania was thus a perfect location for a spiritual year of prayer, reflection and contemplation: a sacred space to discern the onward path of the beginning of the rest of my life.

Despite the panoply of religious options on offer and despite the natural competition that must exist between pastors, priests and sheikhs to hold onto their respective flocks, Tanzania is one of the most religiously tolerant and harmonious countries in the world. Indeed, I believe that few countries would be able to emulate the level of respect for different religions that is so evident in this country. In this domain, I believe that Tanzania is a world leader and a shining example of how an officially secular state can also foster respect for all religions and the rights of people to freely gather, worship and choose for themselves what religion they would like to hold. Long may this tolerance and respect continue.

The music here is rhythmically repetitive, choruses tend to be repeated many times over with different verses, but the singing is never tiresome or tedious. Instead, it is uplifting, even hypnotic and certainly inspirational. Faith is celebrated as an integral part of life, and the churches have achieved a seamless blend, mixing prayer with simply having a good time.

Take for example the New Year's Eve midnight Mass, which began at the earlier time of 10.30pm so that Mass would finish at midnight. With the Mass finished an hour and a half later, the parish priest began the New Year countdown (in Swahili) from the altar: *kumi, tisa, nane, saba, sita, tano, nne, tatu, mbili na MOJA*. Then, suddenly, the whole congregation erupted with spontaneous hugging, whooping, shouting, ululations and dancing. Aisles became impromptu dance floors as the blend of cultures and tribes got down to the serious business of dancing and having a good time.

Some of the young Masai men present removed their *shukas* (black and red shawls) and swung them in the air like revolving electric-fan blades, dancing with backs and shoulders perfectly straight, up and down, jumping higher and higher to the beat of the music. Suddenly, amid the melee and general merrymaking, I looked down from the altar to see the parish priest crowd-surfing over the pews, supported on the hands of twenty people holding him completely horizontally and passing him down through the church!

It was a sight begging for a camera so I ran from the altar back to the parish house. By the time I returned, the crowd-surfing was over, but I discovered that my journey to the parish house had denied the fun-loving parishioners from carrying me around too, since the concelebrating priest and other novices also flew through the air, on wings of prayer and eager hands.

It was some party! The church was a perfect venue for dancing and singing and to cap it off, a trumpet player completed the festivities with the national anthem sung whole-heartedly and vigorously by the 500-strong congregation. It would bring a tear to a glass eye just to see the pride and pleasure with which children as young as ten years of age sing their national hymn with such enthusiasm and enjoyment.

Sr Louise Shields is from Co. Antrim. She worked in Kenya for ten years, and is now living in Middlesex, England. She is a member of the Congregation of Our Lady of the Missions.

Misadventures on the road to Dar es Salaam

Have you ever seen any of the 'Herbie' movies? Well, we had a magical blue Volkswagen too that landed its owners in all kinds of adventures! It was old and affectionately known as KME400 (its registration number).

One year, four of us decided it was about time we saw more of the African continent – so we opted for Tanzania instead of going to the Indian Ocean at Mombasa as we did every year. Excitedly, we crammed in everything but the kitchen sink, knowing there would be no easy access to shops, and if there was, probably nothing in them to buy! Our spirits were high. Sr Paul, our overall planner, set great store by 'playing things by ear'. As we sped towards the border, one of us innocently asked: 'So where are we spending the night?' 'Oh', answered the undaunted planner, 'I haven't actually booked anywhere. We'll just find a place.' KME400 shuddered, I'm convinced, as we all looked at each other in dismay.

Helen Keller once said 'Life is either a daring adventure or it is nothing'. We arrived in Arusha, a town that reminded me of the old western cowboy sets from the films. We eventually found a YWCA hostel. The landlady might have had a problem with the 'Y' part of the title when she saw us, but we got a gracious welcome.

With no food allowed inside, we went out onto the streets, but there were only dingy kiosks selling smoky goat sandwiches, questionable water and the local lethal beer. So Sr Paul had a bright idea and decided to fetch our gas stove from KME400; she smuggled it and some light food past the landlady. As we prepared, a sudden odour of gas wafted through the air. Something was very wrong. Gas was escaping at an alarming rate. It was an explosive situation!

As we opened windows and coughed and spluttered, there was a knock on the door. It was our landlady. I was pushed up by the others and told to distract her. With a cacophony of noise in the background, I tried to have a 'normal' conversation with her about the weather, keeping my back firmly against the door in case she attempted an entrance. I assured her that everything was *'sowa sowa'* (OK). She left, somewhat bemused. With that, we sat down in silence and ate our humble meal of bread and cheese, and vowed never to take on board again any of you-know-who's bright ideas!

So, with a protesting KME400 packed to capacity, we turned our sights on Moshi, a town at the base of Mt Kilimanjaro. After only twenty miles there was a sudden crack and KME400 went from chugging to crawling. We were in the middle of the bush. Sr Paul spied a lorry and flagged it down to get help. The driver shook his head and said he would bring one of us into Moshi to get a mechanic. Sr Paul volunteered and hopped in the cab. When the lorry was lost over the horizon we realised the risk we had let Sr Paul take. We decided to follow them, ever so slowly.

As we cruised along at ten miles per hour we passed through some small villages. Seeing *wazungu* (white people) caused a lot of excitement as young and old stood on the dirt roads and cheered us on. They were perplexed by our slow pace. Some small boys even came to meet us on their homemade wooden bicycles, shouting with glee as they overtook us in what should have been our 'fast' car. Sr Theresa didn't think this was funny and urged us to pretend that we were enjoying the scenery as we crawled along. She pointed at this and that, but all that could be seen for miles was featureless grassland. Not even a wild animal could be seen – only a few scrawny cattle who meandered along beside us in apparent sympathy.

In the late afternoon, we found a mechanic in Moshi. But where was Sr Paul? We were becoming more anxious. After a while, a beaming Sr Paul arrived with another mechanic. The lorry she was in had also broken down! She had spent the last few hours with this mechanic trying to find us. We paid him anyway for his trouble. As for our other terrible trouble, we seriously considered finding a ball and chain to keep her in one spot!

We spent a few happy days in Moshi, and climbed the lower parts of Kilimanjaro. Sr Paul suggested that we visit a friend of hers in Dar es Salaam. Our journey took us over dirt-tracks through the bush. The winding track climbed over the brow of a hill and as we sped merrily down the other side we failed to notice a rather large area of cotton soil (very sticky black mud). Our wee Beetle became embedded in the black mucky mess. 'Lighten the load', we all cried in unison and climbed out. The intrepid Sr Paul took the wheel and ordered us to push – by now we were up to our knees in the mud. All we got for our monumental efforts was mud, mud, and more mud – in our hair, in our faces, on our clothes, in our shoes. Still KME400 was stuck fast!

We went into the bush to gather sticks to make a platform to launch us out of the mud. But in the process we disturbed a colony of safari ants. Modesty was thrown out as we tried to pull these vicious pinching insects off one another. Then panic and fear set in as we noticed some large cat-like paw prints in the soil around us. We redoubled our efforts and at long last KME400 was free!

Just at that moment, coming towards us was a Masai warrior clad in traditional red cloth, his shoulder length hair dressed in red mud. In one hand he carried a spear, and in the other – an open umbrella! I don't know who looked more ridiculous: our culturally clashing warrior or us nuns caked in black mud. We didn't even merit a second look as our warrior strode majestically past us, even though we tried to greet him with the only Masai word we knew: 'Soba'. He probably thought better than to get involved with those crazy *wazungu* women.

We were welcomed at a lonely mission house by a solitary Irish priest. We washed our clothes and shoes at the nearby river. The priest enjoyed the company, for he had few visitors. Food in Tanzania was scarce at the time, so we restocked his shelves to thank him.

Dar es Salaam itself was a bit disappointing in the end. Soon it was time to go home, via the border at Tanga. As we neared Tanga, we saw a sign at the side of the 'road' that read *Slow Men at Work*. This could be taken very literally in East Africa! Just ahead there was a group of road workers having a heated discussion. No one told us otherwise, so we overtook their truck. Sr Johanne, who was driving, looked in the mirror and announced that those men in the truck were waving angrily at us. But why? We had just driven over a newly-laid patch of tarmac! The driver ahead of us had just done the same thing.

'We better keep moving', said Sr Johanne, 'the damage is done and we don't want a riot!' So on we drove. Then came a surprise. Over the next hill, who should we meet but another worker with a walkie-talkie – hard to imagine, so remote in the bush. He was waving us frantically to stop. We sensed we were in trouble.

'Well', quipped Sr Johanne, 'at least we won't have to worry about where we will stay tonight. We'll all be in the clink!' To his tirade in Swahili, we all played dumb. Exasperated, and realising he was getting nowhere, he finally gave up. He dismissed the witless *wazungu* with a wave of his hand.

Fr Tom Hogan is a Spiritan Father. From Tramore, Co. Waterford, he served in Kenya for thirty-one years. He now lives in Dublin.

Celebrating Christmas – in stereo
Soon after I arrived in Kenya it was time to start learning Kiswahili, so I went to Mgange Nyika at the top of the Taita Hills. The parish house had the most wonderful view – it faced Mt Kilimanjaro in Tanzania. At certain times of the year Kilimanjaro was covered in cloud, then suddenly it would reveal itself in all its glory.

It was my first Christmas in Kenya and I was still making my first efforts at learning Kiswahili. I was with Fr Vinny Browne and we were to celebrate midnight Mass in the church at Mgange Dabida. Vinny by that time had succeeded in getting a reasonable command of the language. So we agreed that Vinny would be principal celebrant and head preacher, while I would concelebrate, and be master of ceremonies. We were all set for the midnight celebration.

The Mass was going well enough, the choir was in fine voice, the traditional drums were throbbing and kiyambas were being shaken to accompany the Christmas carols. Vinny was making a big effort to speak in his best Kiswahili. However, his language skills were not good enough for one of the faithful at the back of the church. This man had already begun celebrating Christmas and was quite drunk. He had his radio with him. So he announced to one and all: 'This European can't speak our language, so I'll see the Mass here in Taita but listen to it from Dar es Salaam.'

He tuned the radio to Radio Tanzania, which at that very time was broadcasting midnight Mass from Zanzibar Cathedral. The man turned up the volume to full so we could hear clearly. The preacher from Zanzibar was really fired up and was certainly doing better than Vinny. The disturbance continued at the back of the church for a short while until the parish elders intervened and confiscated the offending radio. Later on, a church court was instituted by the elders and they fined the man one goat for the disturbance caused and for embarrassing Fr Browne. I seem to remember that the goat got eaten by an enlarged court!

The man who rose from the dead in Mwatate parish, Taita Hills, Kenya

One day, the Christian leaders came to inform me that a body had been found just beside the Catholic Church in the sisal plantation. This was serious business and I suggested to the elders that we go and tell the local chief and the police, who then accompanied us to see the body. We were unable to identify the body as the hyenas and other wild animals had been feasting on it for some days. The police asked us to bury the body and so we went to prepare a deep grave in the ground near the church.

Curious spectators turned up to see what all the excitement was about. Suddenly, one of the many onlookers shrieked, screaming this was the body of her missing husband! She recognised the decorated beaded Masai belt around the waist. That halted the funeral proceedings for the time being. The woman was a member of the Luo tribe and the man would have to be buried according to their customs: relatives would have to be called, a wake would have to be held and animals slaughtered and eaten. We sympathised with her, and the Church helped her financially with her husband's mourning ceremonies.

However, just three months later, a man got off the bus from Taveta. There was consternation and many people were frightened – for they were looking at a dead man walking. They had been present when he was buried and his grave was visible for all to see! He was glad to be back home in the village, but on alighting from the bus he was surprised when even his friend frowned at him and kept his distance. 'What have I done so wrong? I have paid most of my sister's school fee', he said, surprisingly. Eventually, someone came forward and told him that they had attended his burial!

Explaining that he was not a ghost, he began to tell his story. He had been given money to pay for his younger sister's school fees in Taveta High School, which was situated near the Tanzanian border. He set off in good time for the journey but, as luck would have it, the bus broke down on the way – fortunately, near a village where the weary travellers could get some food and drink. The day had been hot and he felt thirsty. He fell into bad company and went on a drinking and gambling spree.

When all his money had been drunk, or lost in a card game, he was dealt a great hand in the final game. He had nothing to bet but his watch and his wonderful beaded leather belt. He simply knew he could not lose. He played his last card and to his amazement … lost. Realising that the school fees were gone he was too ashamed to return home. However, he still had the bus ticket to Taveta and the bus had been repaired, so on he travelled, and he found himself a labouring job on the sisal plantation. When he had saved sufficient money, he paid some of the school fees and returned home to Mwatate, suitably repentant.

Everyone was astonished at the turn of events. He went home to his shack and his wife was overjoyed to see him. Being the good woman that she was, she came and thanked us for helping her bury her husband even though he was now back in the land of the living! She wanted to return the money we had given her. 'Not at all, mother,' we replied, 'the son who has been lost has been found. It's time for a celebration of life.' To this day he is known as '*Ufukuko*', meaning 'risen from the dead'.

But just *who* had we buried in the plot beside the church? Probably we will never know.

The washing of the feet in Mwatate parish

I had by now made some progress in learning Kiswahili and it was Easter time – my first in Africa. Sisal is grown in huge plantations in the area around

Mwatate. Sisal is used in making ropes and seating. We planned to hold the Holy Thursday ceremonies in the church situated on the sisal estate. It would be difficult, but I would be able to manage with the help of catechist Feliciano Mwendenao.

Feliciano was a refugee from Mozambique. Together with his wife and children he had fled the Frelimo conflict. He was to be my first close contact with refugees. So we prepared for the ceremony to be held at the church on the estate and all was arranged. There would be twelve people to have their feet washed and they were to sit on a bench. I was to start washing the feet of the people at one end of the bench and then continue up the line. It was all very straight forward. Since work was over for the day, people came from all around the estate for the ceremony which was held in the late afternoon.

The church was packed and the ceremony began. It was going well enough and I had finished my homily. It was time to do the washing of the feet. I got the water, towel and basin from the altar boys who were helping in the ceremony. I started from the left, knelt down and began washing and then drying the feet of the chosen people. I was nearly finished my duties when I noticed that I seemed to have forgotten one or two who were still sitting at the other end of the bench; I returned and washed and dried the feet of the forgotten.

Suddenly, the bench was full again! Maybe I had misunderstood? Perhaps it was twenty-four people had been chosen. Perhaps it was twelve men and twelve women; anyway I continued. Nevertheless, there were more and more people coming forward. I knew I was in for a long evening when I heard Feliciano announce: 'Father is washing everyone's feet ... this is a very big blessing, come forward row by row and be sure to bring all the children'.

So row-by-row they came, adults and children. By this time the water was nicely coloured with the red dust of the area. The towel too became a bright red colour. Maybe using a snow-white towel wasn't such a good idea after all! So every one had their feet washed – except myself – and all were blessed. It was a long process, but the people felt that they had made a good start to the Easter ceremonies.

Rachel Harte grew up in Belfast. Before leaving for China in July 2003, she worked as a high school teacher in Strabane for three years. Rachel's time in China has included trying to learn Mandarin at first, then teaching English in a local university. The following incidents are from her first years there.

Chinese takeaway

Language study meant a tough time for me. Throughout those first two years it was a continuous struggle to learn Chinese. Even getting the word for Hello was hard going. In Chinese that's *Ni Hao* – can you say it? Good! Our teacher had told us to practise saying *Ni Hao* to anyone we saw on the street – or elsewhere. I dutifully obeyed. However, on seeing a lady in my stairwell, I got quite excited as I was especially keen to get acquainted with what was presumably one of my apartment block neighbours. I smiled broadly and said, *Ni* Hi! She looked a little confused, gave a courteous smile, and moved on. Aahh! I'd managed to make a new word using components from both English and Chinese!

However, there were occasional glimmers of hope in that often-depressing time. Once, I was shopping in the city centre with a friend. It is usual to see street beggars there, including children. It's often so hard to know whether they are genuinely in need of attention or not, and they do tend to quickly focus on the white foreigner. The general feeling is that the kids are often being used by adults for profit.

That particular day a little boy came up to me and started kissing my arm, naturally asking for money at the same time. I usually carry some biscuits to give to them. He accepted my offering gladly. I asked him a few questions in Chinese which he answered simply, so I was well able to understand. He then stopped and looked at me and asked, *Ni shi waiguoren haishi zhonguoren?* – which means: Are you a Chinese person or a foreigner? I was so pleased that my language ability could fool the locals. Even a five-year-old beggar child can be a source of much-needed encouragement!

Newly confident, I decided it was time to go to a restaurant on my own. We new recruits had been given a helpful piece of paper with the names of various dishes. I carefully practised saying '*da pan ji*', which was translated as chicken and potatoes. On arrival I went straight over to the waitress and carefully said: '*Da pan ji*'. Amazingly, she seemed to know what I meant.

However, she also started to say many things that of course I had no clue about. Thinking perhaps she was asking if I wanted chillis added I pointed to my tongue and waved my hand around negatively to indicate chilli was not required. She seemed to get the gist. I also pointed to the polystyrene take-away boxes behind her and to the exit door to show I would be taking the food home and not sitting down to eat. Nevertheless, she motioned to the chairs to get me to sit down and poured out the usual complimentary cup of green tea.

Half an hour later, I began to wonder what was happening. At that point I was a little surprised to see a huge casserole dish coming out of the kitchen, and then to realise it was all for me. Perhaps I could have coped with this, but more embarrassment was to come. The waitress told me the cost and, after clarification, I realised I didn't have enough money to pay for it! I tried to get this across with more hand actions and she replied with a Chinese phrase which I knew meant 'no problem!'

I wondered, *Are they gonna give it to me for free?* Instead, one of the waitresses lifted the huge bowl and started to leave the restaurant, indicating I should come with her. As she gestured towards the surrounding apartments, I quickly realised she wanted me to take her to my home. We walked the five-minute journey mostly in silence, apart from when she stopped to speak to local people. They looked at me and laughed. I could only smile meekly.

On arrival at my apartment, I gave her the money and emptied the chicken and potatoes into various dishes so she could take the pot back. I rang a colleague to tell her what had happened. Through the giggles she managed to tell me that the dish I had ordered usually serves six people! The translation on the 'helpful' piece of paper has now been written more accurately so that future 'newbies' can be saved from my ordeal!

Fr James Good, born in 1924 in Cork, worked as a professor in several departments of University College Cork from 1955 for twenty years. In 1975, he moved to Kenya to serve as a missionary in the Turkana Desert, where he remained until 1999. He now lives in Cork.

Lost in translation

In middle age I decided to abandon university teaching and head for the Turkana Desert of Kenya. I did not worry too much about the language – in Maynooth (in addition to our Irish and English) we had Latin, Hebrew, and French. I had also studied in Austria, so German was added to the list.

On arrival in Turkana I found two more languages to learn: Swahili, a common language all over East Africa and relatively easy; and Turkana, a most difficult tribal language. I decided that this was too much, so at first I adopted the method used by some missionaries – preach in English, and then pause for the catechist to translate. One was told that the catechists were quite smart at this.

Alas! My first sermon was a disaster. In a loud, clear voice, I announced, 'Today is the feast of the Sacred Heart.' In an equally loud clear voice, the catechist announced, 'Today is the feast of the Holy Spirit.' Fortunately, I understood that much Turkana, but my sermon was left in tatters. When you think of it, can you blame the catechist? After all, the word 'holy' is the same as 'sacred' and 'spirit' can normally pass as a translation of 'heart'. So, learning the local language became imperative.

Meantime, my Swahili was coming along – at least I thought it was. Preaching one day in Lodwar prison, with a mixture of men, women and children prisoners for my congregation, I thought I was doing quite well until a heavily pregnant female prisoner confronted me. 'Father', she said – almost aggressively – 'Don't you realise that we Turkana women don't understand Swahili very well? Will you let me preach for you?' Taken aback, I did not know what to do, but I took a chance, not knowing what I was letting myself in for.

The best way I can describe the lady's sermon is to say that it was reminiscent of the hell-fire Redemptorist sermons of long ago. Inevitably, much of her ire was directed towards the men. She let them know in very clear terms that the crimes that brought them into Lodwar prison would land them in hellfire unless they changed their ways. She let the ladies off lightly: most of them would have been in prison because they could not afford to pay a bribe to a policeman.

I think the best *faux pas* that I heard in Kenya was the story of the priest who was preaching with great earnestness about the Blessed Virgin Mary. Very soon he found his congregation laughing uncontrollably, so he cut his sermon short. After Mass he asked the catechist what was wrong. 'Ah! Father,' the catechist said sadly, 'that was a beautiful sermon about the Blessed Kettle Mary!'

In Swahili, the words 'virgin' and 'kettle' are not unlike: kettle is an ordinary Swahili word, *birika*, pronounced like the vast majority of Bantu words, with the accent on the second last syllable, while virgin is an Arabic word, pronounced *birika*, an exception to the general rule.

So, no easy way for the poor foreign missionary. Roll on the happy day when local priests will take over the running of their own local church. Incidentally, I often wondered whether St Patrick ever learned Irish – his Latin wasn't particularly good, and he describes himself as a 'sinner, the most unlearned of men'. Ancient Irish would not have come easily to him.

Br Liam McCarthy is a Dubliner, and a member of the Franciscan Order. He has lived and worked in Zimbabwe since 2001.

Brush with the law

I live at the Franciscan Formation House, Tafara, just outside Harare in Zimbabwe. The young Franciscans studying theology travel each day to Holy Trinity College in the city. One day as they travelled back after their classes – the five of them fitting nicely into the Mazda 323 – they were stopped at a police road-block.

The officer told them to pull in off the road, park the car and get out. As they stood on the roadside the officer checked the tax disc, the insurance and then the wheels.

'This car is not road-worthy', he snapped. 'Look at those tyres! Who are you?'

'We are Franciscan students', they replied. 'We're studying theology.'

'What's that?', he asked. They tried to explain, and added, 'You see, we are going to be priests', hoping this would help their case.

'How do I know that?', he scoffed.

'We study Latin', they replied. He didn't seem convinced. Other police and some passers-by began to listen in to this unusual interrogation. 'Yes, we are going to be priests; you see we study Latin', said the senior man. 'Brothers! Line up, relax and join me in singing…'

So the Brothers intoned the *Salve Regina*, singing right through to the end. All were amazed and amused and smiled at this rendition of the antiphon to Our Lady – in Latin – by a roadside in Zimbabwe. The officer couldn't help smiling; he regained his authoritative voice and said: 'Go on! And get those tyres changed!' The Brothers got back in the car and travelled on home, pleased with their initiative. The next day they got four new tyres.

John and Marion Rowe volunteered to work in Sudan as lay missionaries with VSO (Voluntary Service Overseas) in the 1980s, after rearing their eight children. They were eventually pulled out due to the civil war, and now live on a farm in Co. Wexford. The following piece comes from John.

A Christmas crib

Christmas was coming and the school council of En Nahud, way out in the west of Sudan, was in session, planning for the big event. Marion and I were still in shock after finding ourselves sent into the remote Nuba Mountains to help the farmers there recover from a very bad famine. The shock increased when we found we had to learn Arabic in order to be understood by the people. That is why we had come for a crash course to the school in En Nahud. It was also where the bishop was sending his new missionaries.

The young missionaries had welcomed us with open arms – especially when Marion very rashly promised a Christmas pudding for these home-sick young men (but making and defending that pudding is a story in itself). We were with a very mixed lot from a great variety of countries and languages, and we often resorted to very basic Arabic to get by.

Anyway, Christmas plans. The parishioners were mainly farm workers from the south who would enjoy a celebration, and midnight Mass would be central. Jobs were allotted, and it fell to me and a very pious young Mexican priest, Fr Miguel, to do the crib. Slight problem: no crib, and no figures for the crib.

Crib? No problem – a little straw hut with a red light bulb shining down on a straw cot. Figures? Well, African clay modelling skills are world-renowned; asses and oxen, as well as men, women and babies, are familiar creatures everywhere, and a camel could be introduced for local colour. The Dinka people could handle that, no worries. But we did worry, slightly, when the clay models of the animals were produced with only days to go, and these looked very bizarre indeed – more like creatures from the dinosaur period. You would think these cattle herders had never seen a cow in their lives.

We held our breath waiting for the Holy Family who were promised for Christmas Eve. When they came at the last moment, in all their nakedness, poor Fr Miguel nearly had a fit. The infant was very plump and obviously far from newborn, and Mary resembled those Neolithic mother-goddess figures, very well developed top and bottom (especially bottom). The sculptor had excelled himself with Joseph, who was a very masculine figure indeed.

The good Fathers fell about laughing, and in fact thought it a very apt re-creation of the innocence of Eden – all but Fr Miguel, who very carefully placed the camel strategically across Joseph's masculinity. It was the only animal big enough to hide it, and with a hump in just the right place.

Christmas in En Nahud in 1986 was great fun!

Fr Pádraig Ó Máille is a native of Louisburgh, Co. Mayo. He went to Calabar, Nigeria after his ordination as a Kiltegan Father in 1957. Displaced by the Nigerian civil war in 1968, he worked in Galway until 1970, at which time he was among the first group of St Patrick's Missionaries to go to Malawi. In Malawi, he became heavily involved with the pro-democracy movement, and was eventually deported by the government for 'political agitation' in 1992. He is now retired in Dublin. Fr Ó Máille is the Honorary Consul for Malawi in Ireland.

What's the Efik for tone deaf?

One of my regrets on leaving Nigeria was that I had not mastered Efik, the language of the people among whom I worked. I had my excuses. As a teacher, I was constantly told I had no need of the local language. This was the theory. I was to discover later in practice that knowledge of the mother tongue of my pupils was, in fact, a distinct advantage in teaching English!

In 1957, when I arrived in Nigeria, language courses lasted for two to three weeks. Certain formulas necessary for hearing confessions were memorised, and there was a pretence that passing an exam guaranteed competence. An early bout of malaria meant I missed the first week of our language course and this left me particularly deprived.

I did make an effort. I joined the course the following year, and once in a while during school holidays I made an extra effort. After one such attempt I felt a growing competence. I decided that the time had come for me to attempt Mass in the local language. All seemed to go well until the first 'The Lord be with you'. I looked confidently over the congregation and intoned what I knew to be the formula. Instead of the staid reply that I expected, there was an outbreak of uncontrolled laughter, especially among the small children. Mothers sat about managing the situation with slaps and pinches, and the laughter was soon drowned out in shouts and wailing. I filed away the distraction for after Mass. I would find out the cause of the laughter.

It was simple. Instead of 'The Lord be with you', I had solemnly prayed for my congregation: 'The mosquito be with you'. It was a question of tones, I was told later. I had gone either high-low instead of low-high, or vice versa. I never mastered the difference and I doubt whether I would ever have fully mastered Efik. As well as being colour blind, it seems I am also tone deaf.

After several years I did make one final big effort, and after spending three weeks in what I considered total immersion in the language I felt a growing confidence. After Mass one morning, I found the local village head-man waiting to discuss something when I returned to my house for morning tea. I proceeded to greet him at some length, anxious to show the progress I had made.

I was encouraged by his beaming smile, but I had to ask him to repeat himself so that I might understand his reply.

Imagine my dismay to discover that what he was telling me, in response to my best Efik, was 'Please, Father, I do not understand your English!'

Br John Matthew Feheney is the author of *Caribbean recollections: Presentation Brothers remembered* (2009). Originally from Co. Limerick, he worked as a secondary school principal in Trinidad and Tobago. He now lives in Cork. Here he recalls a memorable incident involving a teaching colleague.

Just not cricket!
'B**st you, Matthew, you and your snakes!'

The speaker was my friend and colleague, Br Cyril. The intemperate language on this occasion might give the impression that Cyril was unrefined or foul-mouthed. But this would be completely wrong. No! He was as near a gentleman as you would meet. Nevertheless, this outburst was not unusual when he thought you were responsible for a calamity (especially if it involved his beloved college cricket team). The background to this incident was as follows.

Cyril was passionate about our college cricket team. But he also had some phobias. Two of these were *ophidiophobia* (fear of snakes) and *entophobia* (fear of insects). He was also curious, and this, when combined with either of the above phobias, can be dangerous. One evening, Cyril was watching an important Colleges League cricket game, keeping an eye on every move. Our senior team was playing and Cyril's special protégé, Ram, was batting for us. I was next door at my desk, marking student assignments. Like Cyril, however, I could also keep an eye on the cricket game if I wished, since my window was in front of my desk. While moving along the veranda, Cyril spotted a cigar case sticking out of a jam jar in which I usually kept pens and pencils. I had forgotten all about the cigar case. It was intended for a large thick cigar; I had received it (complete with cigar) as a gift some weeks earlier. By now the cigar had been smoked, but I had something else in the case. This was a small snake.

To explain why I had a snake in a cigar case: one of the attractive features of our house was the southern wall, constructed entirely from perforated bricks. The obvious benefit of the perforated outer wall was that it ensured a breeze through the house, thereby giving respite from the heat. The hazard was that it also permitted free entry to snakes, centipedes, mosquitoes and scorpions.

Now I had made something of a study of small snakes, since they regularly invaded the house. The snake is a peculiar creature in that it alternately craves two things that are diametrically opposite – wet and dry conditions. As it crawls through the grass, its skin is wet and it seeks a dry spot where it can curl up, dry out and sleep in comfort. As a cold-blooded creature, it also seeks warmth when it wishes to relax. During the wet season, on many a morning, when we came downstairs, we encountered small snakes curled up along the southern corridor. Obviously, one never came down without shoes! In general, these snakes were harmless grass snakes and you just used a stick to throw them out into the grass.

Occasionally, however, one encountered a coral snake (*micrurus nigrocinctus*), which is poisonous. This snake, however, has very distinctive markings of concentric red, yellow and black rings, so, once you can see it, you can avoid it. There is also a 'false' coral snake that is not poisonous, the markings of which are slightly different. An old rhyme provides a clue as to which is which: 'Red on yellow, kill a fellow; red on black, venom lack'.

Sometimes the snakes which crawled through the wall perforations during the night were not content to curl up on the plastic tiles of the floor. They went exploring the ground floor and their favourite hiding place was under the wooden pallet on which the refrigerator rested. Now the fridge of that period was an ideal neighbour for a snake because it combined the two climates which it craved. At the back of the fridge, hot air was noisily expelled, while, in the front, the door (which frequently failed to close properly) allowed cold air to escape from within. So, the snake could move around in the pallet frame under the fridge from back to front depending on whether it wanted warm air or cold air.

While the permanent residents in the house, being aware of these hazards, were rarely surprised by a snake, it was a different matter entirely when a visiting Brother approached the fridge without appropriate initiation. I remember one evening, as we prepared to retire to bed, the silence was broken by screams from a dour and taciturn visiting superior. He had gone to the fridge for a drink and had been 'confronted' by a snake. It took some minutes to reassure our visitor that the snake was harmless. But I fear that the incident may have gained us some low marks.

I had also discovered that it was quite easy to get a snake into a bottle. I just put an empty cola bottle in front of the little snake, gave its tail a prod with a stick and it promptly crawled into the bottle, thinking (I suspect) that it could crawl out the other side of this tunnel. All I had to do then was put on the cover and I had the snake in a bottle. I then got the idea of bringing one of these small snakes home with me when I went on vacation. Now snakes can manage to survive without food not only for days but even weeks and months. They just slow down their metabolism. So I began a further experiment. I held the open cigar case to the mouth of the bottle, tilted the bottle upward and the cigar case down, and the snake, without hesitation, migrated into the cigar case. I added a little water and then screwed on the cap, made a small hole, to allow entry for air, and decided to test the theory of snakes deliberately slowing down their metabolism by leaving the snake in the cigar case for a few weeks. Meantime, pressure of schoolwork forced the matter out of my mind and I forgot all about the snake in the cigar case.

On the day in question, despite the action on the field of play, Cyril could not resist examining the cigar case further. 'Oh, Matthew', he said, taking it in his hand and unscrewing the top, 'I am impressed with your taste in cigars!' As soon as the top was off the cigar case, the little snake stuck its head out and shot out its tongue to test the atmosphere. Cyril screamed and dropped the cigar case. The little snake immediately disappeared. But this was not the most serious development!

Ram, our top batsman, was at the crease at the time. He was at ninety-six not out and was about to take strike. Four runs would give him a century, which would be a record in our central division of the Colleges Cricket League. Our jubilant supporters around the grounds were chanting, '*Four runs! Four runs!*', to let Ram know that they were expecting a boundary. A spin bowler from the opposing team was running up to the crease just as Cyril screamed. Distracted, Ram momentarily took his eye off the ball and the result was disastrous for our record books. He was caught LBW. The umpire raised his finger, Ram was out, and Cyril, with a stamp of his foot, uttered the exclamation with which I started this story.

Though, as I remarked above, that language was not characteristic of the style and content of Cyril's normal discourse, it did, nevertheless, capture something that was part of Cyril's character and personality. This was a total dedication to his work, especially his role as games master. He did not merely observe a game of cricket, he lived it. It was typical of Cyril's open and candid nature, that, if you made a mistake, he told you so, straight to your face. This was one of the qualities that endeared him to his students. To them, what you saw was what you got. I knew Cyril for almost fifty years and lived and worked with him for twenty of these and got to know him well.

Fr P.J. McCamphill is originally from Dunloy, Co. Antrim. He was ordained in 1969 and appointed to Kitui, Kenya. He has been in Kenya since then, aside from a spell on vocations promotion in Ireland in the 1980s. He is now director of promotion and mission awareness in East Africa for the St Patrick's Missionary Society. He lives in Nakuru, Kenya.

Scrambled eggs on Christmas Day in Kenya

Life, as we all know, is like the curate's egg: good here, bad there. So too are parishes. Most outstations are fine. The people are lovely and eager. Back at the mission house, as you stroll contentedly under the quiet stars of night, you are happy. There are, however, some outstations that are not conducive to happiness. Both types existed on one of my regular Sunday safaris.

One outstation had a tidy little church under the protective shade of a huge rock that commanded a great view of the surrounding countryside. The people there were well-trained by the catechist. The second outstation, on the other hand, lay in flat, dry bush. And when entrepreneurial skills were being given out the catechist here must have been missing. His best talent was his ability to avoid scrutiny by me.

Thoughts like these entertained my mind on Christmas Day as I zigzagged between the potholes on my way from an uplifting Mass to the second outstation. So much so I failed to see a sudden sandy patch on the road in front of me. Before I knew it, I had parted company with my motorbike and was lying spread-eagled across the road. So was my Mass-box. A quick straightening of the handlebars and I was on my way again, my temper more than slightly frayed.

The village was a sight to behold when I rode in. Sitting under the hot sun in what had been the church, were a few hardy souls. There was no roof. A recent storm had blown it away, and nobody told me. So what could I do, but say Christmas Mass in a roofless church as the merciless sun walloped us.

Murphy of Murphy's law fame celebrated Christmas with me that day too. On my way home I stopped in the shade of my usual tree for a cup of coffee from the flask I always carry. The people had given me a few eggs and I had put them in my trouser pocket because my other bag was full and I didn't want them to break. And, of course, as Murphy had planned, I brushed against the motorbike and the eggs burst in my right-hand trouser pocket. An accommodating hole in the pocket made sure the yoke ran all down my leg.

I looked at my watch. My mother would be home preparing for Christmas dinner in Ireland. I could only manage a rueful laugh at the day I had just had in Kenya.

Martin Keveny is a native of Easkey, Co. Sligo. He was ordained in 1966 for the diocese of Killala. His pastoral experience has also included working in New York, and since 1994 he has been serving in the diocese of Miracema do Tocantins in Brazil. His brother, Fr Valentine Keveny, is a priest in Washington DC, and his sister, Sr Fionnuala Keveny, lives in Mayo.

A dog's dinner in the Amazon Basin

I arrived in the archdiocese of Southwark to begin my ministry as a 'rookie' missionary priest in 1966. Like many of my predecessors in the diocese of Killala, I cut my teeth in the south-west of England. This was a wonderful time to be a priest, in the aftermath of Vatican II. It was even a better time to be based in England, during the euphoria of their first and only World Cup victory. Every second Saturday, it was my delight to cross the Thames to Upton Park to 'blow bubbles' with three of the World Cup stars who played with West Ham: Geoff Hurst, Martin Peters and Bobby Moore.

As it happened, my arrival here in the Amazon Basin of Brazil in 1994 also coincided with the delight of Brazil's World Cup victory in the USA. Plenty of the paraphernalia that is associated with the World Cup greeted us on arrival. Bishop Thomas Finnegan had appointed me to the new diocese of Miracema do Tocantins in the Amazon Basin. So, at the age of fifty-four, I began a new mission, coping with a new climate, a new culture and a new language.

I remember that one of my most unusual experiences was on one February 11th. I was invited to a rural community, 115kms from base, to celebrate Mass on that day. After a two-and-a-half hour journey, mostly on a dirt-track, I eventually arrived at the house. I began Mass, stating that, 'Today is the feast of Our Lady of Lourdes'. The response of the congregation was one of disapproval, informing me that it was the feast of St Lazarus. Somewhat perplexed, I concluded the celebrations and, as is customary in the rural communities, lunch was prepared with plenty of chicken, rice, beans and a salad. I then noticed something strange happening – the women took a table-cloth and spread it on the ground outside the house.

The women then took twelve plates and heaped them with the rice, beans, chicken and salad and placed them on the table-cloth outside, each with a knife, fork and spoon. We all sat there in expectation, ravenous with the hunger. After fifteen minutes waiting, nothing happened. I thought that the people were waiting for the 'Padre' to begin. I duly stood up, took one of the plates of food and sat down to enjoy my lunch. However, I noticed that the people began to smile and nudge each other. All of a sudden, twelve people emerged from a byre with twelve dogs on leashes, leading them to the plates of food. Here was I, very embarrassed, eating a dog's dinner!

Then, I remembered the response from the beginning of the Mass: 'Today is the feast of St Lazarus.' In Brazil, people have great devotion to the fictional saint in the parable of the rich man and the poor beggar who lay outside the mansion expecting the crumbs from the table but who received none. As the Gospel puts it, the only comfort he got was from the dogs that licked his wounds. As well as this, many houses have holy pictures of St Lazarus, walking with a cane, dishevelled, covered in sores, surrounded with dogs. The people can identify very closely with St Lazarus as they, too, have been ignored by everyone – church and state. They have, in the past, suffered neglect, exploitation, discrimination and a lack of resources in health and education.

I must state now that when I am invited to celebrate Mass in the rural areas on February 11th, I always claim a prior engagement. The reason for this is that when the dogs had finished licking the plates on that February 11th, the women heaped the plates again with more food without washing them, believing that on that day no disease will be passed from dogs to humans. I do believe in miracles, but I must admit that my faith is not so strong as to accept this type of miracle! The story of what happened to me on that day has passed around the diocese, from parish to parish, and is now part of the folklore in our region in Brazil.

CHAPTER THREE

They Do Things Differently Here

Fr Michael Scott is a member of the Salesian Congregation. After his ordination in 1964, he spent some time teaching in England, and then spent thirty-four years working with local populations in the Amazon rainforest of Brazil. He returned to Ireland from Brazil in 2009, and is currently in Dublin.

Life in the Amazon Basin

This is the story, or part of it, of an Irish Rover, whose 'rovings' over the past couple of decades have been confined to the north-western regions of the Amazon Basin (the upper Rio Negro area), where the three countries of Brazil, Venezuela, and Columbia are in close proximity. Here all is forest – dense equatorial forests cut through by the countless rivers that form the great water basin of the Amazon, a basin that contains the largest proportion of fresh water in the world. Water, water everywhere and lots of it to drink.

Jauarete, where I live, is situated about forty-five miles north of the equator. From where I stand, stargazing, I can see the Southern Cross to the south of the line and the Plough to the north. The Pole Star is very low on the horizon and can only be seen occasionally, on a particularly clear night or morning.

The full title of the Salesian mission here is *Jauarete Cahoeira*, which means 'The Rapids of the Leap of the Jaguar' – the jaguar being fairly common in the jungle and the most feared of predatory beasts. The mission area is in the north-west of Brazil where two rivers join in an equatorial variation of the 'Meeting of the Waters' – the Jaupes, which is a tributary of the Rio Negro, and the Papuri. In between the rivers is a neck of land that belongs to Columbia. This means that on whichever river you travel, one side belongs to Brazil and the other to Columbia. In fact, of course, it is all Indian land and the international frontiers make little sense in this area of limitless jungle. Our mission is on the Brazilian side.

The climate is very hot here. Average temperatures are in the eighties. During the last few weeks the thermometer was registering 36°C (that's 96°F) and the humidity was equally high. In the rainy (or 'rainier') season, the river rises 2m after only a week or so of rain. There can be a difference of 8m or more (that is, 25ft or more) between the level of the river in the dry season and the wet season. However, I must confess I like the rain. It reminds me of our 'Irish mist'.

Jauarete comprises the mission centre and the parish. The parish extends over an area of 30,000 km², definitely not 'walk-aroundable' in a day. Everything in Brazil is on a grand scale (including corruption). There are ten tribes scattered through this vast area, some with only a few dozen members and some with hundreds, and each with its own culture, customs and language. However, the dominant language is Tucano and most tribes speak it in addition to their own.

With the exception of the Peonas, they are all 'River Indians', in that they live by or close to the rivers which provide a means of communication, an opportunity for commerce, and of course, fish. In this connection it might interest people to know that, although the Peonas do not wear clothes, the River Indians love to be dressed à la mode. Encouraged by the missionaries, they engage in shifting agriculture. This consists of clearing an area of jungle by the method known as 'slash and burn'. It's hard labour at the best of times. There are no bulldozers, Massey-Fergusons or JCBs around here!

In between the charred trees, wherever they can find a space, planting takes place: *mandioca*, rice, banana, pineapple and maize are the principal crops. *Mandioca* (manioc in English) is an extraordinary crop and the flour from its tubular-like roots provides the staple food for the whole region. One of the unusual things about *mandioca* is that you can cut off any part of its six-foot-high stem, stick it in the ground and off it grows again, as long as it has two 'eyes' – one below the ground which produces the roots and one above which provides the leaves.

Another, even more extraordinary thing is that *mandioca* is deadly poisonous and makes a liquid called *maniquiera* when grated for flour. The poison disappears when boiled and, so they tell me, the liquid makes a good drink. However, if someone is careless and leaves a basin of pre-boiled *maniquiera* outside the door and a cow passes that way, it's goodbye cow! The only advantage to this kind of mistake is that there is a juicy steak in the offing.

Incidentally, after boiling the *maniquiera* a white sediment remains. This is the famous tapioca (our every-other-day dessert in the romantic boyhood days of Pallaskenry). From this the Indians also make a kind of bread, *beiju*. The Indian cannot live without his *mandioca* flour – mixed with water it is often the only thing to eat.

So much for the River Indians. The Peonas, though, are quite different. They live deep in the jungle and are hunters by profession. They are also semi-nomadic. They are experts with the bow and arrow and the blow pipe (the darts are tipped with poison). They spend days or weeks on a hunt before returning to the village. At night they take with them a burning piece of wood that makes a natural torch that never goes out – the wood contains oil which keeps it slow burning. Contact with the Peonas is difficult, for obvious reasons.

Parish matters

As for parish statistics, the population is approximately 4,500. There are seventy-five villages: some of these are only *sitios* with one or two families; others contain from forty to one hundred people. There are forty-six small chapels and twenty-two schools. At the last count a few years ago the number of those completely illiterate was 460.

Each village has a catechist and a chief, the two being sometimes combined in the same person. The catechist is responsible for the sick, and is given a course in first aid and entrusted with a medicine chest. The chiefs are responsible for decision-making and organising community work. An annual course in all that pertains to agriculture – planting, the types of crop, raising of cattle, pigs and fowl – is held for the chiefs at the mission.

With two priests busy 'on the waters' there is only one left to look after the centre – and you can guess which one! The centre comprises the school (300 students – about 100 boarders in the boys section and about sixty in the girls), the hospital, and four local villages. In addition to the six Salesians, we have a community of seven nuns. The school provides the usual educational subjects, as well as carpentry, tailoring, some mechanics, the rudiments of agriculture, hygiene and first aid.

The mission hospital is practically the only means of medical assistance for the people of the area. The government has a post here and a nurse works in conjunction with the mission. Fortunately, we have a Sister in charge of the hospital who is also a doctor: she qualified in Poland before entering and coming to Brazil. Medically speaking, I am amazed that the government has done so little for the people in all these years. There seems to be a complete lack of interest in the native Brazilians, who are also the forgotten Brazilians.

The scourges of the region are TB, worms and a type of measles. There are numerous eye-diseases (yet you never see an Indian wearing glasses), there is too much tooth decay (there are no false teeth around either), and there's the ever-present malaria or the threat of it. I never realised how important it was to have teeth until I came out here! What does one do when one gets the devil of a toothache in the jungle? Grin and bear it! When it is a question of necessary operations out here, one simply suffers and maybe even dies. When you think of the money wasted on such things as armaments, cosmetics, dog foods and so on, it makes one wonder whether there's any real justice in the world.

Other allied problems in the medical field are malnutrition and the lack of hygiene. The houses out here are mud-floored and right from birth the children revel in the mud. There are no toilets, other than the river and the jungle, and water is taken straight from the river for drinking purposes. Doctors who come here – usually visitors, since none of them show any great desire to stay once they've seen the situation – are always talking of the need to build toilets away from the houses, but nothing is ever done. It would certainly be a worthwhile project to build good toilets in each village, but here again the means are lacking. If hygiene and sanitation were improved the health situation would also improve.

Some native remedies can be very effective. Vincente, a local *tuchaua* (chief), cured me of an eye infection on one of my river journeys. Vincente is a dapper little man who has a fancy straw hat (when dressed) and a limp – an unusual combination in these parts. Noticing that my eye had closed up and was eking pus, Vincente headed into the forest and returned with a long piece of *cipo* (a fat, thorny root). Holding it over my eye, he squeezed out drops of sap as from a tap. Taking these unusual 'eye drops' from time to time, my eye gradually got better. It is with this type of *cipo* that people in the forest sate their thirst when no stream is available. The sap is sweet and tastes like coconut milk.

While on the subject, another cure for this eye trouble caused by an insect called a *belida* (it can cause blindness if not checked) is to drop into the eye and onto the invading insect the small seed of the *alfavaca* plant. I underwent this 'operation' too, on another visit, when my eye – closed, swollen and oozing green pus – didn't respond to conventional treatment. A young Indian woman prised open my eye, saw the insect – 'big and white' – and dropped in the seed which apparently kills the insect. Whatever it does, my eye was improving by the following morning.

Trading and travelling

The only people who receive money on a regular basis here are the teachers in the village schools, and what they receive isn't much. People barter here rather than pay cash, which they do not have. Trading is on the exchange system, either with other villages, with traders on the river (there are few traders this far up, though, because of the fierce rapids), or with the mission *dispensa* (a kind of glorified shop).

Because of its geographical position, Jauarete is very much cut off from the outside world. Consequently, communication is one of the great problems. The only effective means over distance is by air. Each mission has its own airstrip, carved from the jungle with double-hard labour and copious amounts of sweat. Twice a month a small Brazilian Air Force plane leaves Belem, on the east coast, for Manaus and the Rio Negro, visiting each of the missions in turn and transporting mail, some cargo and passengers. The planes are old and not built for comfort, but the service is free so you are tempted to take your chances. Some of our Salesians have had hair-raising adventures but, thank God, there have been relatively few fatal accidents.

Rumour has it that the service is to be cut to once a month because of the high price of fuel. If it is, it will isolate us even more. Imagine being able to post a letter (like this one) only once a month. At other times a transport plane (a Buffalo) arrives, bringing bulk cargo and food for the various centres. This plane will also take passengers if space is available. It is newer, swifter and safer to travel in. Actually, the arrival of a plane is a day of high excitement for the mission population, for it reminds us that there really is a world beyond the jungle.

The missions have some marvellous friends in the Brazilian Air Force who really appreciate the work the missionaries are doing. One of these friends is the Brigadier himself, who cannot do enough for the good nuns and padres. He loves to visit us and, in fact, each year he spends his vacation in Uaupes. Last year he had films made of all the missions, presumably to show the 'big shots' what they are not doing for the Indians, and what is being achieved is not their work even though they sometimes like to imagine that it is.

Shooting the rapids on a mission upstream
The time is Easter and the year is 1998. On the Tuesday after the feast day our little boat, *Réalt na Mara* (Star of the Sea), moved out from the sandbanks of the mission port and headed up the River Icana in a north-westerly direction. Its occupants were two: the *'Padre'* and the *motorista* – a Baniva Indian. For the next two weeks we would navigate all the Rio Aiari and large sections of the Icana, both rivers part of the vast mission parish of Assuncao do Icana and inhabited by the Baniva tribe.

There would be many rapids to navigate – some difficult, some impossible, all dangerous. The first of these, one of the 'impossibles', was Tunui; all cargo had to be carried bodily over the sharp rocks and the boat guided carefully by means of a rope and local help through the churning waters at the river's edge. It was here that I consoled the village chief, Gentil, whose daughter – a girl of about fifteen – just a few days previously had been killed and partly eaten by a jaguar. She and a companion had crossed the river and entered the forest some fifty yards when she was attacked from behind. Her frightened companion fled to break the news in the village. By the time anybody got to the scene of the tragedy it was too late. The body of the girl was removed for burial. Later, some men hunted down and killed the jaguar. In the course of the journey we came across many people who were afraid to go to their plantations in the forest because of the presence of jaguars. This meant that they had to go hungry as without their manioc flour they have little else to fall back on.

Further up the river, the Aiari, a tributary of the Icana, we discovered that a young lad of thirteen had died after having been bitten by a *jararaca*, a very poisonous snake. The forest medicine proved ineffective in his case and the nearest hospital (the small mission medical tent, or the hospital in Sao Gabriel) might just as well have been on the moon – by fast boat it would have taken days, by canoe weeks! In these areas, many die for lack of accessible medical assistance and the necessary means of transport to avail of the same.

Travelling along Amazonian rivers in torrential equatorial rain is not at all a pleasant experience. Sometimes one has to stop and seek a place of safety due to lack of visibility and the agitated state of the waters. Our first stop on the Icana was at Pupunha, a village divided between Catholics and Protestants – but not on a war footing! There we passed the night – the first time I slept in the new chapel built with the help of the mission.

Some way up the river, with the pangs of hunger asserting themselves, we pulled into the side under the shade of some overhanging branches and had our morning coffee, with chocolate-spread toast. The toast wasn't exactly fresh, having been toasted some months before. Toast has a good survival record compared with other perishables in this climate.

From Jandu we went on to Maua, a village high above the river with the rapids rushing noisily below. Here too it was just possible to pass, though again the passage was a bumpy one. It was on then to Aracu Cachoeira (*cachoeira* meaning rapids). This was a very different kettle of fish. There was no way of getting past without help to bodily lift the boat up the steep falls, the approach to which was dangerous because of the forceful movement of the waters. Here it was impossible not to get one's feet wet and a lot of other parts besides – you just had to plunge in.

Travelling in our little boat, one had the impression that the forest was closing in on us like a giant octopus ready to engulf us in its tentacles. It often inspired fear. Finally, we glimpsed our destination, Eamandua, perched high on the river bank. At first sight all we could see was a steep muddy bank up which one had to climb almost perpendicularly on no particularly defined path – a false step and you were in danger of tumbling back into the river. Thank God it wasn't raining, and ... oh! ... the pains in the legs and the knees! At the top things levelled out into a little village of five houses built around an open space. The set-up, as is usual in Indian villages, is that of the extended family – the patriarch, or chief, surrounded by his sons and their families, in this case a total of twenty-one people.

Returning from our visitation we stopped with the Columbian Sisters of Teresi where I said Mass in my best Castelhano, leaving them with the Eucharist in their beautiful chapel. Afterwards, they treated us to dinner (a word I hadn't heard in a long time), at which we actually ate real potatoes and very good homemade cheese – the nuns keep cows. God bless 'em both – nuns and cows! It was the first square meal I'd had in days.

Continuing our journey on a full stomach (oh what a wonderful feeling), we called at the few villages we missed on the upstream journey. Finally, we reached Pari-Ponta as it was getting dark and decided to stay the night. We were already nearing Jauarete. The following day, at the stroke of noon, we disembarked on home ground: tired, sunburnt, a few pounds less in weight, but happy after an eventful trip lasting fourteen days, thanks be to God.

As a footnote, but nonetheless important for all that: I would like to add here for the benefit of all those generous people in Ireland, Salesians included, who provided me with money on my visit home last (to be with my father before he died), that the money has been used to build twenty-six good houses for the Macu Indians in a settlement about a day's journey from here. We also hope to sink a well there to give a better and safer water supply. The people are very pleased with their new situation. Grateful thanks to all who so generously helped and may God's blessing be with you through the coming year.

Sr Teresa Byrne lived as a Good Shepherd Sister in Egypt and Sudan from 1955 to 2005. She worked as a school principal, as well as engaging in parish work and other human development projects. She currently lives in Limerick.

Hospitality in Muslim Sudan

I have worked in Egypt for twenty-three years, and in Sudan for twenty-seven, from 1955 to 2005. In Egypt I was principal of a school, covering the whole range from kindergarten to secondary level. In Sudan I had varied apostolates – teaching, parish work, human promotion, et cetera, as the need arose. First I worked in El Obeid, Western Sudan for twelve years, and then on the edge of the capital, Khartoum. There, I was mostly engaged with displaced people who came to settle in a large desert area because of the war in the south of the country.

Sudan was and is a wonderful country to work in. Situated in the north-east, it is the largest country in Africa and in the Arab world. Sudan is home to one of the world's oldest continuous major civilisations, with urban settlements dating back to 3000BC. There are 599 tribes and over 400 languages and dialects are spoken.

People there knew little about Ireland, and the only way of helping them understand where I came from was by saying that Ireland was bordering England. The English were well known to them, having colonised their country. For many years I was the only Irish person in the parish where I worked. Later, others came, as did aid agencies like Trócaire, Concern, GOAL, and Ireland was finally on the map.

When I think of my years in Sudan, west and north, what comes to mind most vividly was the extraordinary sense of sharing and hospitality of these people whatever their state or religion. You always felt accepted. I was only a few days in El Obeid when I was invited by a young girl to her wedding which was, as was the custom, to be held in her home. The house where we were staying was near that of the bride and my companion and I set out walking. We were not sure of the house, but as we walked along the road we heard singing and dancing and presumed we had arrived.

We knocked at the door and were greeted warmly by those present, but to our dismay we knew no one and looked around in vain for the bride. We timidly asked if this was the house of the new bride. The young girls who were dancing told us the house we wanted was next door but that they too were preparing for a wedding the following week and that we would be more than welcome. As was the custom, the bride to be was being taught the bridal dances. We went on to the right house this time, but we were in admiration at our reception and how no questions had been asked as to our provenance or why we had come! We were strangers and we were fully accepted.

Another wonderful custom that I found uniquely in Sudan was the sharing of the meal during the holy season of Ramadan. Devout Muslims do not eat all day and after sunset neighbours in many areas come together, each family bringing a dish which is consumed communally. As we went around the parish during this time we noticed circles drawn in the sand with small pebbles. In the centre of the circle a cloth was spread, and the various dishes placed on it. It is wonderful to see neighbours assemble in this manner to share a meal in common after having prayed together.

When a visitor arrives at a Sudanese house a fruit drink called *tabrihana* – a refreshing non-alcoholic drink – is served (or in poorer families, water). Water is precious as it is often carried long distances in remote areas. Before partaking of the meal, water is poured over the hands of the visitor and a towel is presented to each one to dry them. A large tray is brought to the table with several dishes, all resting on beaded doilies made by the women. No knives or forks are used, but with the help of a piece of *kisra* (flat bread) the food is picked up. There is something significant about this eating together out of a common dish, a custom that unites family and friends.

Again, water is brought for washing the hands and the dessert served – this usually consists of sweets, like crème caramel. After dinner, guests may enjoy tea flavoured with cloves and cinnamon, or refreshing coffee. It is interesting to stand by and see the coffee being made. The women fry the coffee beans over a charcoal fire and then grind them with cloves and certain spices. They steep it all in hot water and serve it from the coffee pot, called a *gebena*, into tiny cups, after straining it through a special grass sieve. You are presented with cup after cup of this delicious coffee while the aroma of the roasted coffee beans fills the house.

This sharing goes deep into the culture of the Sudanese. Southerners fleeing the war zone came to Khartoum to the parish where we worked or other parishes situated outside the capital. Often it was the women and children who came, the men staying in the south. They arrived with literally nothing, but soon found refuge with friends, other members of their tribes. They were welcomed and nourished until such time as they could manage for themselves. Visitors too would come to spend time with family members and stay several days. They were never asked to leave, no matter what strain this laid on the family.

Many Sudanese sent their children to Khartoum for education, and again they were lodged and fed by the head of the family. I have seen over twenty children and adolescents settle into families and was amazed that all had something to eat. How, I cannot guess, unless it was a repetition of the miracle of the loaves and fishes!

On the occasions of weddings or funerals, which always lasted several days, one would see the women arrive with their pots and pans, helping for long hours with the cooking. Everyone attending had a meal, even in the poorest of families.

Kindness and care for others seem to be deeply embedded in Sudanese life. It would often happen that while out driving, my car would break down or get a puncture – all our cars were old and were not helped by driving in the desert, especially during the rainy season. But I was never afraid; other drivers stopped their cars and quickly came to my assistance. Repairs were completed and some kind words and jokes were exchanged and we were all soon on our way again.

There are so many other stories I could tell. The media are never kind to Sudan and daily I read of horrors and atrocities being committed in the south, or in Darfur. Very few positive events are reported – a pity, I think.

Sr Redempta Connolly is a native of Rosslea, Co. Fermanagh. She is a member of the Missionary Sisters of the Holy Rosary (formerly known as the Killeshandra nuns). She worked as a teacher in Sierra Leone, and now lives in Dublin.

Muslims and Christians

Sierra Leone is a Muslim country. Though Christians are small in number, the Church has a higher profile than its numbers warrant because most of the government officials have passed through our schools. Primary education is not free so the boys get preference, and about eighty per cent of the women are illiterate. I saw education as a way to a better future for the women. The Muslim boys learn the Koran in Arabic in the village.

In Sierra Leone, Muslims and Christians exist peacefully, and have great respect for religion. I met a few of my student teachers in Bo, the second largest town in the country, one day. They asked me for help to buy some books. I said, 'Gentlemen, I have nothing to give you, only my blessing.' At that, they knelt down in the middle of the street and waited until I blessed them. I was taught a lesson that day – you don't joke with blessings!

Sadly, the infant mortality rate here is very high and malaria is still the biggest killer. The mosquito breeds in stagnant water so simple hygiene can help save lives. I found that teaching the Sierra Leoneans how to make oral rehydration solutions for dysentery was as important as my religious work. They are inclined to ask the wrong question regarding disease. They ask *who* caused the disease instead of *what* caused it, so they consult the *moray man* (witchdoctor) rather than a health worker.

They have their own superstitions, but sometimes things that we don't understand we may mistakenly take as superstition, as I found out at the funeral of a local priest's mother. After the service in the village the burial took place across a stream, in the surrounding bush. Beside the stream was a bucket of water and a pile of small stones. I noticed each person placed a stone in the bucket of water before stepping onto the plank that served as a bridge over the river. The older Sister who was with me said, 'Don't you go putting a stone in that bucket because you don't know what that superstition means.' I let her cross the stream ahead of me, and put my own stone into the bucket before following. When we had buried the woman, I met one of my students and I asked him the purpose of putting the stones in the bucket of water. His reply was that it was to count how many mourners were at the funeral – so I was counted!

Paul O'Callaghan, born in Co. Dublin in 1980, spent three years living and working with VMM (Volunteer Missionary Movement) in four countries in East Africa: Kenya, Tanzania, Rwanda, and the Democratic Republic of Congo. In 2008, he wrote an unpublished book, *Travel tales from the Continent of Golden Joys – musings from the missions.* He is currently studying for a doctorate in child psychology at Queen's University Belfast, as part of which he has worked with former child soldiers in Uganda.

Monkeys: the tune they love so well

Although mangoes are available here in Tanzania all year around, the season peaks in March when one can buy massive, succulent, green or reddish-golden skinned mangoes in the market for less than ten cent. For the parish here in Arusha, the mango season heralds the start of the monkey season, as the primates love nothing better than to sink their sharp teeth into these mouth-puckering wonders. Close to the church, three or four very tall mango trees have been planted and when the wind blows they become a real hazard as the shaking branches can dislodge a one-pound whopper that plunges to the ground, completely flooring an unsuspecting Mass attender below! A troop of monkeys now include the parish land in their extensive territory and these cheeky tree climbers have selected our parish as the venue for their mid-morning constitutional, sprinting backwards and forwards noisily on the tin church roof during morning Mass.

One afternoon, I went to the parish office to play a few tunes on the parish keyboard. In the middle of Phil Coulter's *The Town I Loved So Well*, I suddenly became aware of a 'presence' beside me. This was no religious experience though, for as I peered through the net curtain, I became aware of a curious monkey, craning his neck and peering into the interior of the office, fascinated by the strange noise. As the window was open, he must have been less than a foot away from me. Flattered by the attention, I gave the song my all, turned up the volume and watched with interest to see what would happen.

Sadly, I couldn't maintain the little monkey's attention for long and soon he rambled off. But he was back in a few minutes and vaulted on top of an outside pew and listened intently for some more minutes. I almost thought he was swaying to the music, but that might be pushing it a bit far as these monkeys are constantly twitching, always on the lookout for the local children who like nothing better than to lob a big stone at an unsuspecting simian. I'm not sure exactly why they want to do this – it's not as if we eat monkeys here in Tanzania – but I suspect that many fear the monkey for bringing disease and some even blame the poor primate for originating the scourge of AIDS that has claimed the lives of so many here.

Teaching children in the nick of timelessness

An Irish judge, James Mathew, once commented that justice is open to all – like the Ritz Hotel. Like the Ritz Hotel, prison is also open to all, but frequently populated by only one social class. I found this to be as true in Tanzania as it is back home in Ireland. Prisons have always intrigued me and when I was given the opportunity to teach English to some young offenders in the main children's Remand Centre in Arusha City, I was thrilled at the opportunity to meet and work with these incarcerated kids. Those I met there challenged every view I had held about the penal system.

Teaching in prison here is indeed a challenging experience for any foreign teacher. For a start, nearly all the children speak little or no English, so one needs Swahili to communicate. In addition, many of them are illiterate, having missed an uncountable number of schooldays. Yet despite these obstacles the children are knowledge-starved and education-hungry. The Remand Centre is the only educational establishment I've ever taught in where the students requested that they continue studying maths instead of taking a ten-minute break as I had suggested!

But as eager as the children were to learn, they were even more eager for praise or any words of encouragement. I remember one day teaching the names of the animals of Tanzania in English class. Each child then carefully copied down these words from the cracked and pot-holed chalkboard. Each one then insisted on getting a tick once their work was done. One boy even worked during recess time to earn his blob of red ink.

With the aid of some Irish volunteers we bought a set of children's readers, each book for a different level of English. So, it happened that on Christmas Day, between morning Mass and roast turkey and Christmas pudding, a group of us from the parish were treated to a reading of the riveting exploits of Peter, Jane and Pat the dog! Spending time with the kids on Christmas Day and throwing a party they would remember for the next year was one of my happiest memories of Arusha, and the smiles on their faces made all the effort seem so worthwhile.

The solvent-for-chicken exchange programme

One of the most bizarre encounters I ever had was meeting a group of ten- to twelve-year-old beggars at the Kenyan-Ugandan border at 11 o'clock at night. Our bus had got a puncture so we all piled out and mingled with the sellers and locals there. Far from being caught up in their own youthful pursuits, as one might have expected, the kids descended on the stranded guests like beady-eyed hawks to beg for money. They appeared to be drunk, laughing uproariously one minute, then whining and shivering the next. I soon realised why.

The children were solvent sniffers. Each child had his own bottle or rag with which they got their daily, possibly hourly, fix. One child told me in slurred speech that they sniffed in order to sleep out in the open at night, in the cold. Seeing a man roasting meat over a fire, I approached him and negotiated with the ragamuffins to buy their bottles of solvent in exchange for half a chicken each. All four kids agreed, offering me their bottles in what could possibly be the world's first ever solvent-for-chicken exchange programme!

However, I was immediately faced with a dilemma for I couldn't dispose of the children's bottles in any of the bins nearby, for fear that the children would simply find them and reuse them. So, I stuffed them in my pocket and with bulging pockets bursting with highly flammable contents, I re-boarded our bus. To relieve the pressure in my pockets, I then immediately placed the bottles in my hand luggage in the rack above my head.

You can imagine then how I started to sweat when a police officer boarded the bus and walked up and down the aisle, scrutinising the passengers. If he'd asked me to open my bag, I would have been caught red-handed with what I'm sure must have been illegal substances. Thankfully though, he only gave me a cursory glance before moving on to the next person. I was mightily relieved to dispose of the rinsed-out bottles when I got to Nairobi. I just hope that none of our priests decided to recycle the bottles as drinking vessels. They may reach the conclusion that they've got a hard-core solvent addict in their community!

Nairobi: the cataclysmic clash of two worlds

Nairobi is both heaven and hell: attractive and appalling, friendly and frightening. Nairobi is not so much a tale of two cities as a city of two tales: stories of the haves and the have-nots. Seamlessly, less than a stone's throw from each other live the prosperous and the penniless, the lettered and the illiterate. On the one hand, Nairobi is a thriving, bustling borough boasting a rapidly growing economy. English is the lingua franca of business and social life in this cosmopolitan city, while cafes and restaurants sell every type of food for every type of palate. One can sample anything from pasta to sweet and sour chicken curries, from cream buns and chocolate éclairs to pancakes and maple syrup waffles.

As well as being a business centre, Nairobi is an intellectual hub for East Africa. Nairobians buy books, newspapers and magazines by the bagful as is evidenced by the number of printing presses in the capital, churning out high quality yet reasonably priced English and Kiswahili textbooks and novels. The city must also have one of the highest densities of third level colleges in Africa, while the National University of Nairobi has at least three campuses located in separate parts of the sprawling metropolis. For those who want to pursue a life of service to God in the church there is a panoply of biblical colleges and Bible institutes to choose from, while trainee priests and nuns are spoilt for choice with no less than three universities offering bachelor of arts degrees in divinity and pastoral studies.

Yet, Nairobi is also a city of contrasts. For a city that holds such promise, it is shocking to learn that about one third of its population live in slums. These deprived areas are about as densely populated as rush hour downtown Calcutta. Incessant petty theft and extortion are constant trials, while alcohol abuse and the violence that accompanies it must make life there one of the toughest on earth. It is a simply mind-numbing sight to witness the wooden and earthen huts and shacks roofed with iron sheeting, stretching as far as the eye can see. While visiting one family home, I discovered to my dismay that a whole family live in a two-roomed mud house, without any running water or toilet. During the damp and miserable rainy season the warrens of dusty alleyways turn to mud and become an ankle-deep quagmire in places.

The fault lines between the rich and the poor communities are not so much marked by geographical distances as by opportunity differences, pent-up forces sometimes colliding with cataclysmic fury. In the adrenaline-charged days of post-election violence that rocked Kenya, the Jesuit university seminary of Hekima College, where many orders – including the Pallottines – study, was to be the flash point for one such confrontation. Hekima College plays host to some of the brightest and best of the Catholic Church in Africa. These in turn bring their extensive philosophical arsenal to bear on discussions on the role of knowledge, freedom, intention and will in moral decision-making.

But this day's lecture will be different. For today, two worlds are about to collide. Outside the gates of the college an angry mob has gathered. A shrill alarm from a lecturer's private car is confused for a police siren and the group of stick-and-stone-wielding youths from the local slum, angry with the government and the heavy-handed police, are looking for a target to vent their pent-up rage. Angered to the point of violent action by the mistaken belief that someone in the college has called the police, the gang threaten to rampage through the campus, potentially destroying everything that lies in their path. Panic spreads among the students. Some turn to prayer, others head towards a side entrance to escape, while a small band of hotheaded young males want to fight the invasion and defend their college.

But today wisdom, the Swahili translation of the name of the college, wins out. The president of the college brushes the chalk dust from his clothes and heads over to the young people outside. As luck would have it, he is of the same tribe as the group of angry young men and his reassurances in their own mother tongue eases the tension. The gang turns away from the college; life and property are saved. On the way down the road they attack a landline telecommunications centre in Nairobi, smashing the windows with stones, bricks and sticks before running down the street and disappearing among the warren of back-streets and alleys that is the slum of Kibera.

Catherine O'Sullivan is a member of the Institute of the Sisters of the Infant Jesus. She has worked for fifty years in Malaysia, Peru, Northern Ireland and Bolivia. She is currently living in Ireland.

Peru: temporary escape from desert places

The bus bounced and jolted along the foothills of the Andes on its way to Canto Grande, a little town nestling in one of the valleys that intersects the west coast of Peru. It was the annual outing of the *Hatun Runas* (Important People), as our senior citizens were called in the village of Collique. The excitement in the bus grew as we left the desert behind and a carpet of green with trees and flowering bushes came into view. It struck me very forcibly that here were people not only on a picnic but also on a journey to get in touch with their roots. Everyone, without exception, had been brought up close to the soil, and as the bus rattled and rolled we were getting closer to the sap from which we would draw sustenance during our dry and thirsty days in the desert.

As we poured out of the bus, it was obvious that the 'ohs' and 'ahs' and other exclamations came from deep within, as we breathed in the unpolluted air of the countryside. The overspreading trees and new-mown grass in the church compound where we gathered smelt sweet and welcoming. From the height on which we stood, we had a panoramic view. The nearby river flowed past hamlets and farmland and then broke into a lazy meander. On the other side, barren hills hugged the horizon and were littered with boulders lying where they had tumbled aeons ago.

The gurgling river seemed to be calling us to descend the winding path that led to its banks. We made our way down, picking our steps between rocks washed white by the winter floods. Like children brimming over with happiness, we all wanted to wash our faces and bathe our feet in the crystal water and smell the freshness of the luxuriant vegetation. The first contact with the cool spring water brought shrieks and chuckles that resounded in the neighbourhood. After some time, we chose our favourite rock and we sat there in the warm sunshine refreshed by an easterly breeze.

As one o'clock approached, we gathered on the green bank to enjoy our lunch, amid chatter and laughter. The wonderful spirit of the exchange and sharing of food touched me deeply, symbolic of a much deeper sharing in daily life. Lunch over, groups dispersed to enjoy the countryside, while some of us, unable to walk too far, paddled in the shallow water or sat on the rocks reminiscing about life and sharing the stories of our hopes, pains and fears. There was a sense of timelessness in this area, a timelessness that is unique to quiet places.

From my vantage point on the rock, I saw one of the women, who suffered from dementia, lovingly touch the bark of a century-old tree while mumbling to herself. With the same gesture as if warming her hands to a fire, I saw her draw energy from the spirit of the tree, a common belief in these areas. As I drew near, discreetly, to join with her in this sacred ritual, I heard her mumble '*Tarapoto … Tarapoto*' – the name of the place where she was born. I was deeply moved by this woman, normally silent and confused, who was now drawn back to reality through the presence and touch of a magnificent tree.

As I stood rapt by this experience, our companions returned loaded down with plants and herbs, cures for every ailment under heaven. The joy and exuberance that they felt here in the open space and their sense of harmony with the surroundings filled me with mixed feelings. While sharing in their great joy, I also felt a stab of pain at the deprived life they were leading in a sunbaked desert village, a stark contrast to these lush green pastures. But these resilient people had had the capacity to uproot themselves and possessed an inner strength to break through the harshness of the desert soil and set down new roots so that their children would be able to reach full potential. Just as roots, interconnected and interdependent, bind together and draw support and sustenance from each other and from the earth, likewise these stalwart people supported and sustained one another.

As we made our way back to the village, we felt our communion with nature had a healing influence. Life had been purged of some of its sordidness and our hearts began to beat with renewed joy and hope. And as our bus moved closer to home, churning dust clouds in all directions, our *Hatun Runas* continued to sing enthusiastically amid clapping and cheering.

Bolivia: life in the mountains

Bolivia is a beautiful country stretching from the awe-inspiring snow-topped Andes to the lush jungle areas of the Amazon rainforests. The mountains offer spectacular scenery, perpendicular slopes, and a maze of sharp peaks. The mountain roads sweep up and up, making the ravines all the more menacing as one dangles between life and death. It is a land full of surprises, ranging from the remnants of ancient civilisations to colourful indigenous cultures and colonial treasures.

But the greatest riches are the people of Bolivia whose resilience and exuberance challenge the harsh reality of everyday life. The majority are of indigenous descent, and for that reason the Andean culture is more evident here than in other places in South America. Spanish is the official language but more than thirty indigenous dialects are spoken throughout the country, the more important being Aymara and Quechua.

When I first arrived in Potosi, the highest city in the world, the fact came home to me very quickly that I was more than 4000m above sea level. Owing to the rarefied air at altitude, I puffed and panted my way up some of the steeper streets. Our house was situated in the mining area of San Cristobal, in the shadow of Cerro Rico (Rich Mountain), a conical-shaped mountain pock-marked with the many entrances to the mines. I shared community life with four young women who were studying in nearby colleges.

The visa was a big preoccupation during those first months. After consultation with the immigration authorities on arrival, I was told I had to apply for a new visa. This meant clearance from the police, letters of recommendation, medical examinations, thumb prints and all the other requirements necessary for the issuing of a visa. Several trips had to be made to Potosi. When I was on my final trip, many visits later, the young lady in the immigration office said to me. 'Now that your visa is almost ready, when are you going to start working on your identity card?' You can imagine my face!

The great benefit was that I came to know every avenue and street in Potosi. The city, though neglected, is a living museum and boasts of some of the best collections of colonial and Bolivian paintings and architecture. There were thirty-three churches within walking distance of our house, each one a museum in itself. In the city plaza, smartly dressed people mingled with *campesinos* in their traditional costumes. The women wore brightly coloured *polleros* (skirts), hand woven blouses and shawls. Bowler hats of different design rested precariously on their heads, revealing the province of their origin. The majority of them carried a baby in a colourful wrap on their shoulders. They would sit for hours on the sunny side of the street selling their wares or knitting or working on a spindle making thread from raw material. They did everything and anything to supplement the meagre income of their husbands, the majority of whom were miners. I often sat with them and gleaned lots of knowledge on their way of life and customs.

The wonder of the city soon vanishes as you approach the nearby mines, source of the city's riches. It was in this region that enormous quantities of silver and gold were extracted in colonial days. More than 5000 miners, many of them very young, are still at work here, dynamiting and digging with picks and crowbars for minerals of inferior quality. The average life span of miners is about forty-four years because of silicosis and other lung ailments resulting from the dusty and claustrophobic work conditions. Small wonder too, that they have to rely on stimulants like coca leaves and a swig of alcohol to endure the heat and the back-breaking work.

Other Bolivians live in forgotten villages in very isolated mountain areas. The young have little access to secondary education because of lack of funds and the great distances from schools. Some of the more fortunate students live in very modest hostels attached to country schools. Since their villages of origin often operate outside the currency system they have no way of paying for their accommodation other than in kind. Donations received from generous people in different parts of the world help to cover additional costs. Like many others, they have to migrate to neighbouring countries at an early age to look for work, where, very often, they 'got lost'.

Shortly after my arrival I had the opportunity to visit one of these schools. It was a real adventure. We travelled up unpaved mountainous roads overlooking sheer precipices and razor-edged ravines, round a series of hairpin bends, each revealing a view of mountain ranges higher than the last. At one stage, we all had to get out of the truck to push it up a steep incline! I experienced my worst moments when we had to stop on the edge of precipitous falls to make way for on-coming jeeps. Any false move on the part of the driver could have landed us in the abyss.

It was difficult to imagine the distance people had to walk to get to any kind of a centre or village. This was home for so many resilient people. Children watched over their flocks of goats, sheep and llamas, a familiar scene in these areas. There were signs of hardship everywhere. The school was situated deep in the mountains, with conditions very basic. Yet they provided a much-needed education for the young people.

The Sisters lived in the small village of Azangaro, and taught in rural schools, as well as reaching out to the families of the surrounding districts. They had managed to bring more than 600 rural women together in different groups to learn new skills and produce beautiful intricate tapestries and items of clothing which they later sold. Workshops were organised and young village women studied reading, writing, maths, health education, cookery and organisational skills. These young women shared what they learned with other women who were unable to attend the sessions.

In San Cristobal, Potosi, scholarships were given to the most marginalised to discourage them from working in the mines and to enable them to concentrate on their studies. These students in turn did voluntary service, often teaching the children of miners, who were offered an alternative education outside of school hours. Basic Christian communities were initiated as a way of decentralising church activities and creating a network of communities where people could share and pray in a family atmosphere. This experience also motivated us to search for creative responses to the harsh realities of life, based on solidarity, sharing and celebration, qualities that are so much part of the Bolivian culture. These community gatherings filled us with hope and enthusiasm, giving us the courage to travel together with a song in our heart.

The festive spirit is very much part of the Bolivian way of life, generating extraordinary creativity. Through song, dance and folklore their cultural and religious traditions are handed down from one generation to the next in an integrated and life-giving way. Anyone who has been privileged to live for a time with marginalised people can never be the same again.

As we re-enter the world where wealth, power and prestige are seen as the way to happiness we are wary of these trappings, having travelled by another route – sharing, friendship and celebration.

Sr Pauline Leahy of the St Joseph of Cluny Order has been working for many years in adult education programmes in The Gambia.

When the rains came
It was June – hot, humid and oppressive. Looking around at a dry, weary land without water, we longed for the refreshing rains – not only for ourselves, but also for our thirsty land, our animals, our farms, and to keep our wells supplied too.

On our way to St Joseph's Adult Education and Skill Centre in Banjul, we noticed the clouds were coming together, as if to gain the strength needed to burst open the skies. It grew darker, and the definite smell of rain was in the air. Yes, we felt sure we would soon welcome a torrential downpour. Inside, the classrooms grew dark. As so often happens, there was no electricity.

Suddenly, thunder rolled around the skies. Lightning flashed, and the dark became even darker. Dust whirled around the streets; they looked almost resentful, as if they did not want to be disturbed from their sleep of several dry months. At first, drop followed welcome drop. Then, rain and thunder beat together. Streets were emptied of people as everyone rushed for shelter, caught by the suddenness of the deluge.

Students were flooding into the classroom downstairs, wet, cold and laughing. A change of clothes was a must, and in minutes, there was a sort of fancy dress parade. Don't ask where things came from – necessity is the mother of invention, and what a mother she was that morning. As the girls huddled together to warm themselves, Sister was seen crossing the road to the Naar shop. She came back with the makings of a surprise breakfast. And how the students showed their initiative! Water was soon bubbling in cans on a fire, and in no time plastic cups and spoons came out of hiding. Steaming cups of sweet Ovaltine were being passed around. Candles were lit and placed on the tables where they created haloes of light that pushed away the gloom and framed the scene. Everyone was happy, chatting and laughing, celebrating the first of the rains – and just wishing this could happen more often.

Helena Cusack is a Good Shepherd Sister from Co. Waterford. She has served in the Philippines, Indonesia, Singapore, Malaysia, Australia, New Zealand, the UK, and on the South Pacific island of Guam. She now lives in Ireland, in her home county.

Life on Guam, an island in the Pacific Ocean

When I learned that I was destined for Guam, my first desire was to find out where in the world this unknown place was situated. Having spent some time with the map, I found it between Hawaii and the Philippines, the largest island of the Mariana group. I soon learned a little geography, and found that it was only about thirty miles long and eight-to-twelve miles wide. It actually originated as a volcano that erupted from the Pacific Ocean.

The original inhabitants of the island were called *Chamorros* and came from Malaysia. Approximately 100,000 of them lived entirely self-sufficiently in villages organised into districts under local chiefs. Today, there is a mayor in charge of each village and he is recognised as a person of some authority. The Spanish brought colonialism to Guam. In 1898, immediately following the Spanish-American war, Guam was ceded to the United States, who use it as an important military base. Guam elected its first civilian governor in 1970. This is how things stand at present.

I had previously spent some time in the Philippines and shorter periods in Indonesia, Singapore, Malaysia, Australia, New Zealand and Great Britain. Before I arrived in Guam, I wondered if I would feel isolated on such a small island. But on the contrary, as time went on I met people from other nationalities whose ancestors had come here as a result of the various conquests of the island; I began to learn about these cultures and soon had many friends. As there were people here from many different countries, I felt more like being at the centre of the world, it was so cosmopolitan.

Guam has many attractions. The water has a turquoise sheen and is always warm. I once went to the seabed in a submarine: a great variety of fish accompanied us as we travelled along! However, the sea is not always so pleasant. Typhoons hit about four times a year and were very frightening. At such times we were without electricity and water, sometimes for months at a time. The well became very important – not only as a water source, but also as a meeting place where we got to know our neighbours.

The usual way of transport between the islands was by boat, but recently an aeroplane has been purchased. It is known as the 'missionary plane' because it takes people on business through various islands, as far as Fiji. One difficulty was that on the island of Naru there was no airport, so the plane had to land on the public road! Consequently, all other traffic was at a standstill until it took off again, about an hour later.

The native people have mixed feelings about the presence of the American forces on the island. The number of military personnel on the island has been reduced in recent years but this has also meant a reduction in employment opportunities, leaving many of the work force out of work. There has been a campaign going on to return the land vacated by the military to the descendants of the original *Chamorros*.

The island has definitely gained a lot over the years by way of funding for education, health and welfare from the United States, but unfortunately it is losing its own culture and carefree way of life. Like the rest of the world many young people are involved in drugs, contributing to violence and social and family breakdown. The ministry of the Good Shepherd Sisters consists of two shelters: one for women and children who have to leave home because of family violence, and a second shelter for children, aged 0–18 years, who are on their own. Both shelters are called *Alee* – from the lee, or sheltered, side of a ship in a storm.

Fr Enda Watters is a Spiritan Father who studied in UCD, Jerusalem, and Chicago. He has travelled to over thirty countries, on every continent, in roles as varied as magazine editor and secretary of the Irish Missionary Union, as well as being a pioneering missionary in Brazil. He wrote about some of his experiences in his book, *Missionary memoirs*, published in 2009. Fr Watters currently lives in his hometown, Dublin.

Meeting the *Ju-Ju* man in Nigeria

Before long I was introduced to traditional religion – or 'paganism' as it was then called. Side-by-side with Catholic households in Nigeria one found traditional believers. *Ju-Ju* shrines were in evidence everywhere. At one such shrine in a place called Iwollo there was a large, very well-carved statue of a man and woman in an explicitly sexual pose. Converts to Catholicism had to formally renounce all such traditional practices, but nevertheless some kept *Ju-Ju* objects in their homes through superstition. When a parish mission, of the type we knew in Ireland so well, was held in a parish, one of the big moments was when *Ju-Ju* objects were taken from the houses and burned publicly at the end of the mission.

It was in a mission called Amaigbo that I visited a *Ju-Ju* shrine and met the '*Ju-Ju* man'. He had a fine house and five wives, one of whom was named Eileen! He was obviously doing good business, as there were plenty of signs of fowl having been offered in his sacred grove. There were feathers everywhere. He was dressed with tusks and bones and carved black figures. In his little *Ju-Ju* hut there were various bones and skulls and he himself sat on his haunches behind a curtain beating a drum. There was white paint on his eyelids and under his eyes. He was quite agreeable to speak to and seemed pleased when I asked if he could be photographed.

On one occasion I decided to take a photograph at a *Ju-Ju* stall in the market where there were birds and feathers on sale. The man there asked me to show my authority, so I showed him my Fides Journalist card and he agreed. He said that he had been to the United Kingdom and had seen photos of African people there that he did not like. Hence his reluctance.

Catherine Veale, from Dunhill, Co. Waterford, joined the Good Shepherd Congregation in 1950. Her first mission was to Sri Lanka in 1951, where she taught in a collegiate school in Colombo for twelve years before engaging in social work with the Good Shepherd ministries. In 1979, she pioneered a new foundation in Madagascar. She served there until 2000, when the young Malagasy Sisters took over the work. She went to work in Ethiopia, but returned to Madagascar for a further year. She is now retired in her native county.

A revelation in a hovel in Madagascar

Our first Good Shepherd foundation in Madagascar opened in 1979. The four Sisters chosen were from four different countries: France, Belgium, India and Ireland. Our internationality was a symbol to the people of the universality of the Church. The bishop of Fianarantsoa who invited us wanted us to start our mission in a rural area and to get to know the language, culture and mentality of the people first-hand.

The day I arrived – 21 February 1979 – I went to the Benedictine convent in Ambositra, where others had already begun the language course. A building became available to us in Sandrandahy, so after a few months we were ready to take up the parish challenge. Two of us could speak the language fairly fluently by then.

Sandrandahy, our parish, had Mass on big feast days, but otherwise our parish priest celebrated Mass in one of his twenty parishes, where we also attended. My attention in Sandrandahy was drawn to a special collection towards the end of Mass. A small sickly woman with a large goitre came to the front of the church with a little basket and people came forward and put in a coin. After the ceremony I questioned the catechist about this.

Here is the story: this woman was Maria and she had a sister called Madeleine. They lived alone out in the hills. Madeleine had been a cripple for eighteen years and could not move; she was also blind. This collection was their only source of income. When I heard the sad tale, I wanted to visit her and the catechist agreed to take me there at once. We had to cross paddy fields and rocky hills before we arrived at the little house.

The doorway had been sealed up to keep out trespassers and roaming animals, so we climbed in through a window. Inside I could scarcely distinguish anything, but gradually saw a litter in the corner with an emaciated figure lying there. It was Madeleine. The dirt, neglect and destitution of the whole scene was unbelievable, something I could never have imagined, but when we greeted the patient, she was no ordinary self-pitying soul – she showed such a lively spirit and an intense interest in life.

She knew we had just come from Mass, so she questioned us about everything in the parish, showing an amazing vitality of spirit. After our conversations we began to pray, and it was she who led the prayers. Looking at her, I thought of Jesus on the cross. She had been there more than eighteen years, nailed to the bed, suffering not only neglect, but pain and hunger and discomfort of every kind. Her next prayer astounded me: *'A prayer before the crucifix'* – I was transfixed at the words! At that moment I was looking at Madeleine but seeing Jesus!

It was a moment of revelation and truth for me. He is alive in each baptised person, and I saw Him stretched on the bed that day. What followed moved me even more. She continued to pray, this time croaking a hymn, the *Magnificat* in Malagasy, which in very simple words says: *'I am happy – faly aho!'* Madeleine meant it; it was evident in her tone.

Who could ever imagine a poor, forgotten human being, bedridden for eighteen years, still capable of saying: *'I am happy, so happy'*? I must say I came away that day a changed person. I had seen things I had never seen before. There was a bonding between us – she talked so freely with me. I continued to visit her whenever I could, bringing her necessary food and clothes. I also paid one of the local women to clean the house and wash Madeleine.

Sadly, she was near the end of her days of suffering, and some weeks later as I approached the house, I was told she had just died. I was happy to help with the last rites, to give her the winding sheets and necessary things for burial. In this area of Madagascar the dead are shrouded in a *lamba* (a sheet usually made from the wild silk worm) before being laid in the tomb. Madeleine is still singing her *Magnificat* in heaven. Of that I am sure.

Fr Ted Smyth is a native of Moynalty, Kells, Co. Meath. He was ordained in 1953 and appointed to Kenya, where he worked in the diocese of Eldoret from 1953 to 1966. He taught in Ireland from 1968 to 1979, after which he returned to Kenya. He remained in Kenya until 2008. He now lives in retirement in St Patrick's, Kiltegan, Co. Wicklow.

The amazing *matatu* – what a way to travel!

When the social history of Kenya comes to be written, many subjects will have to be covered. But one subject without which that history would be incomplete has to be the part played by the humble *matatu* in the coming to life of the young nation. Kenyans are inveterate travellers and at the birth of the new nation there was no transport system in the country. A small group of pick-up owners got an audience with the new president, Jomo Kenyatta, and were given the franchise to find a way to solve the problem.

At the time the chief coin in the currency was the penny. The minimum charge for a ride in a converted pick-up was three pennies. '*Matatu*', derived from *tatu*, the Swahili word for three, became not merely the amount of the fare but also the name of the vehicle. Within a short period, the name *matatu* would become synonymous with a terror machine barrelling along every highway and byway in the country. The *matatu* was the way to travel. No matter what the circumstances, the *matatu* never passed you by, and nobody disputed the truth of the saying that 'the *matatu* is never full'.

The capacity of the *matatu* was open to interpretation. The normal bench arrangement could accommodate four persons on each side of the vehicle provided you 'sat square'! But often three times that number were hamburgered together and the flag raised for take-off. At this stage, there was neither male nor female, young or old, among the passengers. And if a few more passengers were spotted along the roadside, to leave them stranded would be unthinkable. And if there were seven or eight passengers hanging loose in space at the rear door, the trip was all the more profitable.

Despite the numerous shocks to your bone structure, the *matatu* was often a very merry machine. It was democracy come to town and, despite discomfort, it was a great leveller. There was great fun and endless dialogue. Instead of floating along in a plush coach absorbed in your own ipod or newspaper, you were one of a bunch of good companions. You had joined a community and the conversation flowed freely. It is regrettable that in recent times the *matatu* has come to be seen as Kenya's worst murder machine. It was seen as somewhat cool for a driver to speed along with his vehicle loaded to the gunnels and the front wheels barely in contact with the road. A little more acceleration and the *matatu* could become airborne. Rules of the road were for the weak and feeble-minded.

Wherever people met, the *matatu* menace was discussed. Over the years, tales of tragedies multiplied and horrendous crashes were reported daily. Often, the local hospital was unable to cope with the victims, and the ordinary patients would be discharged to make room for the injured. Only the numbers of dead were spoken about. The maimed, the lame and limbless were never mentioned. As to what caused the accident, nobody ever knew because the driver and his assistant, if they survived, vanished from the police radar and, some time later, when the dust had settled, casually reappeared safe and sound, looking the picture of holy innocence.

Now at last the transport minister has cried 'Stop'. The annual death toll has convinced the authorities that the system needs to be reviewed, and that the travelling public has to be protected. Draconian measures have been put in place. Every public service vehicle must be fitted with seat belts and a speed governor. The whole resources of the nation are mobilised to enforce the new regulations.

But there are consequences. No one quite realised that this cheap form of transport was so essential to the life of the nation – an essential component of social and community life. In Kenya, people travel to town for no particular reason at all; just to see their neighbours and chat and stay for as long as they wish. They want to feel free to wander around, in and out of the kiosks and shops. Who knows what bargains can be found? When you were ready and all your business done, the people's car would take you home and at a low cost. Since the new regulations have come into effect the cost of travel has more than quadrupled and as a consequence prices across the whole spectrum of living have soared.

Did the *matatu* lose sight of its original charter? Whatever the answer, one thing is certain – the name of that amazing vehicle, as well as that of its founding father, Mzee Jomo Kenyatta, will have its place in the history books of Kenya.

Sr Margaret Mary Ryan (RSM) is a member of the Sisters of Mercy. She worked as a teacher, firstly in the Philippines from the 1950s, and later in Africa.

The extraordinary women of Kenya
Now that I am back in Ireland and involved with a Commission for Women, I have begun to make comparisons between the experiences of women here and women in Africa and in the Philippines. I worked in the Philippines for nine years from 1959 to 1969, and in Africa for ten years. In between those journeys I taught in a girls' secondary school here in Cork, so comparisons can be made very easily. What a difference between the two experiences! Indeed, women in Ireland have much to be grateful for compared to their African or Asian counterparts.

Right now I will confine myself to the African scene. When I went to Africa first, I was teaching in a boys' school in Njoro, Kenya. The pupils were upper class and intelligent; their aim was to achieve high points so that they could progress to further education. The school was only a ten-minute walk from where we lived, but my early insight into the life of African women took place within those ten minutes.

I used to call every Friday 'Good Friday'. Why? Every Friday during that ten-minute walk, I would meet countless women – and even little girls – carrying loads of wood on their backs. These cut-offs were available at the local sawmills on Fridays. You could take what could be carried on your back for one shilling, so the bigger the load the better, money-wise. The expenditure of energy or the discomfort experienced didn't seem to matter. Men and boys would sometimes be seen carrying wood in hand-drawn carts or across bicycles but *never* on their backs. For them that would not be 'cool'!

I went eventually to teach in our Mercy School for girls. This was a primary school and the pupils who attended were those who were not accepted into the native schools because they were not expected to stay in education. It was here, meeting the mothers of the pupils, that I discovered the resourcefulness and ingenuity that best describes the African woman. The Kikuyu women in particular are noted for their unfailing loyalty and dedication to the family, to the tribe and to the Church. Missionary priests will tell you of their gratitude to these women who do so much work within the parish. Their contribution is enormous – acting as catechists, washing church linen, washing church floors, cooking for festivals as well as arranging and monitoring church ceremonies. Having worked hard doesn't deter them later from donning their *kangas* – multi-coloured Kenyan wraps – and dancing and singing to their hearts' content.

The famous 'Kikuyu cry', which they can produce ad lib, marks the zenith of their enjoyment – real euphoria! It always reminded me of those 'Kitty the Hare' stories we were told as children where the cry of the banshee was always included. It could be described as a high-pitched wail that initially sent a shiver up and down your spine. However, like so many other aspects of foreign culture, it gradually grows on the expatriate! At ordinations, confirmations, episcopal visits and other such occasions, it became a familiar and ever-welcome sound.

Women in Kenya do most of the *shamba,* or garden work. No flower garden though! Maize and beans are staples, and their production for family needs is the responsibility of the women and mothers. In the planting and harvesting seasons they head off in groups equipped with their *jembes,* what we call spades. They usually have the *watotus* (babies) on their backs and, on arrival, leave their precious bundle on the headland, while they themselves dig, plant and reap. Dealing directly with Mother Earth poses no problem for African women.

On Saturdays, they clean the churches, and, during the rainy season, the caked mud has to be removed in preparation for the next day's worshippers. It is quite common to see many bare-footed adults at Mass on rainy Sundays – feet being easier and cheaper to clean, as well as being more durable!

Despite their heavy workload and amazing energy – and their vast potential – Kenyan women have very little involvement in politics or in the public
sector of life. However, they have won themselves a very special place in the
hearts of all missionaries. *Mná Kenya – bua agus beannacht!*

Emily Byrne is a Good Shepherd Sister from Co. Wicklow. Her sisters, Kathleen
and Teresa, also entered the Good Shepherd Congregation. She lived and worked
in Sri Lanka and Singapore from 1948 to 1992. She now resides in Waterford.

Passing on the flame: the Singapore experience
The fifth of seven children, I was born in Killabeg, Co. Wicklow and went to
school with the Brigidine Sisters in Tullow, Co. Carlow. I was professed as a
Good Shepherd Sister in August 1948 at the age of twenty-three, and given the
religious name Gabriel. In December 1949, after serving for a year in Sri
Lanka, I was transferred to Singapore. I remained there for the next forty-three
years. This was a very different mission from Sri Lanka and a challenging one.
Singapore is a small country, densely populated, where different races from different cultural backgrounds, speaking different languages, and eating different
foods lived harmoniously together. That was my first surprise.

Few of them were Christian but they had their own strict sense of morals
and their own values. I learned this very soon after arrival. I was teaching a
class of five-year-old children of different nationalities. Asian parents gave their
children pocket money to spend in a tuck shop attached to the school while
English parents usually did not believe in giving their children money. Every
day I observed a Chinese boy call a few English children together to ask them
what they wanted. He then went to the shop and returned with sweets and ice
cream and passed them around.

I mentioned it to his father. The young man explained: 'We Chinese
believe in teaching our children when they are small to share with others. So,
every morning as I give him his pocket money I remind him that it is not just
for himself, that it is to be shared with those who don't have money.' I learned
a lesson that day. I saw that boy grow up, get a well-paid job and become an
extremely generous man. I asked myself, who is teaching whom?

Singapore at the time was a British colony. Most people lived in bamboo
huts, and only the 'elite' went to school. But this changed very quickly when
they got their independence in the 1950s. Schools were quickly built and everyone could be educated. High-rise apartments were put up so that every family
could have a decent home. Teaching was very rewarding since children were

anxious to learn: parents encouraged their children to make the most of the opportunities which they had never had themselves.

It was a privilege to work with these people. In the early days we engaged a young Chinese man to help around the garden and to drive a small car we had acquired. He came to work the first day in his bare feet. He was very happy when a Sister gave him a pair of shoes. Having worked for some time with us, he said he wanted to better himself and so he was leaving to drive a taxi; a few years later he had invested in some buses to drive children to school. This is only one example, and it was a pleasure to be part of a success story.

In the mid 1950s, we opened a novitiate to train local Sisters. As vocations increased, we Irish missionaries learned to live in international communities and to work alongside our Singaporean Sisters. As time passed, these Sisters were able to assume positions of authority and we were happy to work under them. In due course, Singaporean Sisters were going abroad as missionaries. They went to Thailand, to the Sudan, to Kenya and to China. The wheel had turned full circle.

I had seen Singapore grow from a colonial state to a gigantic metropolis. In 1991, the Singapore Good Shepherd Sisters had their third locally-born Provincial. I felt that the work of Irish missionary Good Shepherd Sisters was done, and so I decided to return to Ireland, proud and grateful at having been part of the Singapore story. In 2009, a Singaporean Good Shepherd Sister was chosen to be part of the Order's General Leadership Team.

Last month, I received a CD from a Singaporean Sister. I was struck by the words. I quote just the refrain:

> *I am standing on the shoulders of the ones who came before me.*
> *I am stronger for their courage; I am wiser for their words.*
> *I am lifted by their longing for a fair and brighter future.*
> *I am grateful for their vision, for their toiling on this earth.*
>
> *I am standing on the shoulders of the ones who came before me.*
> *I am honoured by their passion for our liberty.*
> *I will stand a little taller; I will work a little longer.*
> *And my shoulders will be there to hold the ones who follow me.*

Michael O'Donovan, from Union Hall in west Cork, grew up on a farm with his five siblings. Born in 1947, he was ordained a Divine Word Missionary in 1980. The following year he went to Papua New Guinea, and he has been there since. He spent the first twenty-four years in the Sepik River region, living and working with the local people. He has also taught in a seminary, and now works at a retreat house. The following are extracts from Michael's letters home from Papua New Guinea.

January

It rained most nights during the Christmas period. One night it rained so heavily that I complimented the owner of the house I was staying in for making his thatched roof waterproof. More than once, elsewhere, I had woken up to find a waterfall coming straight down on the mosquito net.

After Christmas a group of us went upriver to purchase a large canoe. If you take out the world map and follow the Sepik River right up the Indonesian border you could put your finger on the spot where we bought the dugout canoe. I have plans to power it with an inboard diesel engine. It would cut the travelling time and expenses by half.

On 4 January, a Timbunke man, Theo Jue, was grabbed by a crocodile – his body has not yet been recovered. Theo and his wife Monica were out fishing in their canoe when Theo decided to take a bath. It seems that the crocodile was resting in that very spot and took Theo under. It is the first time in living memory that a Timbunke man has met such a fate.

The elders in the village blame the youth for the incident, because they misbehaved themselves at a dance in Aibom by getting involved in a fight with the people of Shortmari. When the fight got out of hand the Timbunke youth took off with an outboard motor belonging to Shortmari. The Timbunke people have returned to Shortmari since with the price of the motor and a bunch of betel nut to settle their differences in the customary Sepik fashion. Timbunke people hope this will get rid of the crocodile spell, which has the village living in fear.

Next month the crocodiles will start nesting. This is a concern for the locals who depend on the young crocodiles for a living. If the crocodiles move to a new territory to lay their eggs, the owner of the land is the rightful owner of the newborn crocodiles.

The tributaries of the Upper Sepik are also drying up to a trickle. One village, Yaragai, just across the mountain from here, has a large canoe. They call it the 'Blue Bus'. It's now in dry dock waiting for the rain to return. Once, when the canoe arrived here in Ambunti, full of people, I started counting the passengers as they disembarked. One of the passengers saw what I was doing and told me that they once had eighty-four people in the canoe. That day I counted sixty-eight people and I thought surely it was the limit. Luckily, none of the passengers was overweight!

April

The village of Apan prepared the liturgy for Holy Thursday, and Malu led the Way of the Cross on Good Friday. Masanbuk and the teachers of St Joseph's School were responsible for the liturgy for Holy Saturday night. A horse-load of firewood was stacked neatly at the school ground and fourteen bamboos were laid along the route of the candlelit procession to the church. The bamboos were cut into six-foot lengths and stuck upright into the ground about twenty feet apart. The cavity of the bamboo was filled with sawdust, soaked in diesel and set alight to give off a bright red flame.

The lighting of the fire was organised by Masanbuk. Over a dozen human figures came down the mountain dressed in traditional style, each waving a brand up and down to increase its burning power as they approached the pile of timber. They danced around the wood several times, before suddenly turning towards their target and setting it ablaze. As the fire grew bigger and brighter, we stood about thirty feet away from it and sang hymns. The Easter candle was lit and so were a hundred smaller candles. The fourteen bamboo flares were already in full glow as we headed up the mountain towards the church as part of our Easter Vigil, the service of light.

One of my old friends, Ambrose Lisan from Yindkum village, died last month. Ambrose went on a few foot-patrols with me when I was looking after six villages in Tringe parish. On my visit to Yindkum last January, Ambrose recalled the day I nearly pulled him into a flooded river near Buckenbowi. Across the twenty-foot river was a fallen tree trunk acting as a bridge. When crossing Ambrose held my hand, but the log started to sway when we reached the middle. I lost balance and we both went see-saw on top of the log. Only Ambrose's life-long experience at pole walking kept both of us on the bridge. Whenever we met in his house afterwards, the day we did a river dance at Buckenbowi was sure to be retold. May Ambrose dance in Heaven today.

June

On 25 June, I blessed a new bush church at Bangus village. It was a marvellous occasion with great support coming from the main centre here in Ambunti. Their church leader, Ambunigi Aboran, gave us a short history of Bangus. He told us he was a young man when he organised the building of the first church in 1948. Fr Kowalski came to open it and he brought along five rolls of cloth.

He cut the cloth and gave each person a piece to wear like a bath towel around them. That was the first time the people of Bangus had ever worn clothes, a bit of a turning point in their history.

Ambunigi went on to tell us he joined the army in 1950 and after that the Catholic Church ceased to function in Bangus. He is sixty-nine years old now and he wants to start again where he left off forty-nine years ago. In the intervening years the Seventh Day Adventists and the South Sea Evangelical Churches have contributed enormously towards the development of this village, which has over 600 inhabitants.

After Mass the people gathered in front of the home-made grandstand to hear the nine guest speakers. I was the last to speak and there was little left to be said so I changed the subject. I told them to dress well, look smart and feel good about themselves; to educate their children, not to lose their culture; and to look after their bush (ground). I don't know if they understood what the Irishman was trying to tell them, and I was wondering too: which was the better world, theirs or mine?

That night we held a prayer meeting next to the church with the stars and the moon shining down on us. Before we left, the leaders gave me a coconut to plant on the church grounds. It's their custom, a bit like signing the visitors' book, only the coconut has a much deeper symbolism.

July

Life keeps moving on at this end. I recently made a trip to Walfain and I had to climb over a steep mountain. When I found the going tough, the local people told me I was getting a bit old now for mountain climbing. I think they will soon be right! Though, I always feel good after such trips when I return home.

Once we reached the mountaintop, Simon, the church leader, produced a fresh coconut for me to drink. It is always part of the trip to rest for half an hour once we reach the top. Our conversation is often focused on the people who live in the distant hills. Today we spoke about Yembiyembi – but it was all very positive. A Yembiyembi girl has married into Walfain, and is taking a leading role in church activities. For some years I was looking after Yembiyembi when I was stationed in Timbunke, and now we were able to talk about the people we knew there. With the passing of the year, I was told, a few of those are now resting in peace somewhere in the distant hills.

When we arrived at Walfain we congregated outside their bush church on top of the mountain ridge for a prayer meeting which went on for two hours. After that, some people sat and talked all night while the women prepared and cooked the meal for the following day. The six-day old moon gave us light until midnight, and two Tilley lamps kept the hilltop aglow until morning. When the dawn broke the village rang out with bird song and other forest creatures were also making themselves heard, all welcoming the new day. After the Mass and baptisms, the meal, which mainly consisted of fish and sago, was brought to the church grounds and shared out among the different communities. There was perfect contentment. I thought we were the happiest people on the planet, as there was no stress or strain on anybody and the people were enjoying being together.

Could you guess what I received one Sunday for an offering? We have a collection every Sunday, and as you know, people also contribute vegetables, fish and sometimes a live rooster. On this particular Sunday there was a roll of toilet paper in the basket. You see, my parishioners think of all my needs!

November
During the month of October, Damien, Anton and myself were on a pastoral visit to Walfain village, and well out of sight of the Sepik River when word came to us one night that the river had gone down and the lake, which we had crossed by boat, was drying up. The people told us we should get back to Ambunti as soon as possible or we would have to wait until the next rains arrive. We left next morning and four carriers helped us to take our belongings over the mountain and down into Yaragai village where our boat, with its fifteen-horsepower motor, was waiting for us.

The lake had indeed turned into a mud plain, but the channel had still enough water for myself and Damien to use two oars. The problem was to know where exactly the water was as the channel zigzagged from side to side. Hundreds of white egrets gave us some indication as they stood knee-deep in the water watching us pulling and shoving our boat for two hours.

At the mouth of the lake the water was rushing out carrying hundreds of dead and living fish along with it. Several women from the nearby villages were out in their canoes collecting the live ones. One woman pulled her canoe close to our boat and threw live fish with both hands into our boat. Another woman came from the other side and did the same. Luckily the water was about two feet deep at this point and we could use our engine again to bring our extra cargo of fish out to the main river and back home to Ambunti.

One thing which hasn't changed here is the barter system. The women walk three hours out to the Sepik with their garden crops and exchange them for fish from the river people. I brought along some Catholic newspapers to sell. I had to leave them behind in exchange for fruit from their gardens.

This year, the pastoral workers made a nice light canoe for the parish. It is specially designed to get through narrow and shallow waterways and it can easily be lifted over the logs that block up the creeks from time to time.

One Sunday morning, as I was heading upstream in my speedboat, I met a family coming to church in their canoe. The father was standing up in front and the mother was sitting down behind with a child sitting on her lap. In between were four small children. As I passed by, all the children waved to me with great enthusiasm. I thought to myself they were as happy in that canoe as if it had been a Mercedes-Benz.

Remembering New Year's Eve, 1999

Here in Ambunti parish, we celebrated the new millennium our way. Young and old in their hundreds came together on New Year's Eve to share a meal; it had been prepared by the women the night before. The menu consisted of one ton of sweet potatoes and taro, five meal bags of cooking bananas, five containers of fresh fish, five crates of chickens and a young heifer weighing 500kg from Timbunke farm. When the meal was cooked, it was all brought together, still in the pots and saucepans, and laid out on canvas at St Joseph's Community School. Each person brought along his or her own plate and spoon and we sat down on the grass to enjoy the last meal of the millennium. It was a real community experience.

As the New Year approached, all knelt down in silent prayer, to give praise and thanks to God for the moment it was. Then the church leader, Sailas Jrajumb, beat the wooden drum and we knew Papua New Guinea had entered the new millennium. With that, we all stood up to recite our slogan, 'Immanuel 2000', and the usual handshakes and good wishes were exchanged and the celebration went on throughout the night.

Midnight Mass lasted until two o'clock and at that stage most of the children and babies were out flat on the canvas, fast asleep. Several mothers who had devoted the night before to the cooking were unable to make it through the second night and they too were on the canvas sound asleep. As I said, it was a real community experience and if you felt like sleeping – well, it was the most normal thing to do at two o'clock in the morning.

A few coffee pots were heated up and more coffee and sugar were needed to get through the last four hours before dawn. Before the sun rose everyone was on their feet again, dancing in the charismatic style, and at the break of day we turned towards the rising sun to recite once again the slogan 'Immanuel 2000'. This was it, a new day had dawned, a new millennium had begun and it was back to our humble homes to continue life as usual.

The Apans crossed the river in their canoes and went upstream. The Malu people walked down to their homes along the riverbank of the Sepik. The Massambucks went up-mountain to their living quarters on the hill and the rest walked back to their settlements in the town. Most parents were still carrying sleeping children in their arms and over their shoulders. When the young children awake from their sleep and when the babies grow up, the parents can tell them how they celebrated the new millennium with song, dance, and prayer, and with a community of 800 people.

CHAPTER FOUR

Living Dangerously

Fr Brian Treacy is a Kiltegan Father from Co. Limerick who has been living in Kenya since the 1960s.

Friday, 11 December 2009

What a day! Paddy Hyland phoned me from Kericho at my mission in Tenges around 8.30am, and as always I asked immediately how he was. Usually he says: 'Great, never better', but this time he said: 'Dreadful! Gerry Roche was murdered by robbers last night!' As the terrible details became known, we were shocked and extremely distressed. It sounded as if the scene was truly awful. One thing that helped distract from the shock and numbness, I suppose, was the number of phone calls and messages that I was receiving – I must have got about sixty calls from Kenya and, later, from around the world.

Saturday, 12 December 2009

This morning, Saturday, I felt I had to go to Kericho to see the lads there. I picked up three Irish nuns from Baraka, Molo, on the way. They had just been wondering if someone would drive them. I think we all have a sense of the Lord's presence among us at this time, and there is a remarkable feeling of peace in all of us now, once we got over the initial horror. It's not that we are in denial; in fact we have talked at length about the whole thing, which I think is very helpful, and the support we are getting from everyone is quite remarkable.

Gerry has a very large family in Ireland – I think there are eleven siblings – and they have requested that his body be brought home to be buried in Athea. He is the baby in the family. They are the ones suffering the most right now. There will be a Mass in Kericho on Thursday, and the body will then be taken to Nairobi for transportation home. Paddy Hyland and a nephew of Gerry's will accompany the body home.

It's not our first experience of murder – one of our own, Martin Boyle, was killed about twelve years ago, as was a good friend, Br Larry Timmons from Baraka, shortly afterwards. This year two or three other priests have been murdered in Kenya, so it seems it has become one of the hazards of life as a missionary. Last week a gang of robbers who broke into his house attacked our own Sean Weldon at night, but, thank God, they didn't harm him. So that's the story for now, and life goes on.

On top of that I've just got word that there was a very bad accident between Nakuru and Nairobi. After a big family get-together, sixteen people were travelling in one vehicle trying to get to the main road, when it went out of control and overturned. Eight of them were killed, and the other eight are all in hospital with serious injuries. Some of them are from Londiani, and I know them very well, including two lovely little girls. One, Monica, is eleven, and Mary is only three. What a tragedy for the extended family.

Thursday, 17 December 2009

We had Mass today for Gerry in Kericho, and it was a very emotional day for everyone. In one sense it was very sad, but in another way it was a wonderful occasion. There were many tears, but it was great to see the thousands of laity who turned up, plus five bishops, maybe 120 priests and hundreds of nuns. Our own Bishop Mossie Crowley led the Mass, and Martin Barry gave the homily. He was a classmate of Gerry and a close friend.

Two of the African bishops broke down in tears as they spoke at the end of Mass. There was a great sense of togetherness as a Church, and you could feel that it didn't matter a hoot what was the colour of your skin. We were all in it together. The Mass was in the open air of course, and, thank God, the ferocious rain of Kericho kept off until after we had left.

I'm back now in Baraka with my novices on retreat, and I feel kind of drained after the day, but I know that we are on the road to recovery. Somehow, attending and participating in a funeral has a real healing effect on people. You begin to accept what has happened.

Fr Des Hartford was a Columban Father, originally from Lusk, Co. Dublin. He was assigned to the Philippines in the 1960s, charged with helping to forge better relations between Muslims and the minority Christian population. After the episode recounted below, Fr Hartford's health deteriorated and he returned to Ireland, where he passed away in 2004. This piece, written by Fr Hartford, was sent by Fr Cyril Lovett, a colleague in the Columban Society.

Hostage!

On 27 October 1997, I had come to a local beach after being invited there to meet representatives of Muslim rebels who had been fighting to establish an independent Islamic state in the south of the country. Some years previously, the rebels had signed a peace agreement with the government of the Philippines. They insisted that some of the promises made then had never been fulfilled. When I arrived at the designated meeting place I was put into a jeep and driven for about thirty minutes into the mountains, where I was told the leaders were waiting for me in a school.

But instead, I was abducted! They hoped that by capturing me they would apply pressure on the government to fulfil the promises made when the agreement was signed. By the time of my capture, I had worked for nearly thirty years in the promotion of peace in this conflict zone.

My eight captors, who ranged in age from thirteen to early twenties, were heavily armed. They made me walk a further two hours into the mountains. I felt relatively calm at this point. They told me they were demanding thirteen million pesos from the government. Though the radio said nothing about my capture, I soon learnt that the Philippine army had been mobilised. My greatest apprehension was that the army would try to rescue me by force.

In the days that followed I was frequently moved from one location to another through swamps and forests and occasionally had to sleep in the open under the stars. My usual shelter was made from a few bits of wood covered by leaves of nipa palm. As time passed I was growing a bit more apprehensive. There were petty annoyances too. When it started to rain, the mosquitoes became a constant nuisance. On occasions I, along with my guards, had to flee at short notice from other armed gangs, who wanted to take me prisoner for their own purposes. A quick wash and shave in the river and we were on the move again further up into the mountains.

In a village we passed through, many people came to look at me – but were warned not to tell anyone of my whereabouts or they would have their brains blown out. My guards were generally treating me kindly, though. They talked among themselves in the Maranaw dialect, which I also spoke, about the poverty in the mountains, about religion – and about sex, of course, and their fantasies of marrying beautiful white women.

I kept praying and reminding myself of the importance of being positive. On the fifth morning of my captivity the local sultan was waiting for me. He assured me that I was in safe hands! He also told me that my release was only a matter of time. It was so frustrating to think that many people were worried because of me. I spent that afternoon improving one of the hostage's English, at his request. He tried out his English on me.

'What is your favourite soup?'

'Mushroom', I replied, getting even hungrier at the thought.

'Huh?' he responded. He had meant 'soap'.

The following day, however, I experienced real fear. There was shooting all around; yet another armed gang had come to take me. We quickly packed and moved on into the forest. My guards promised they would die defending me. I became resigned to the possibility of dying at this point, and the fear gradually subsided.

My next makeshift hut had a beautiful view of the mountains but no protection from the wind. Security was light by now. Escape would have been possible except for the fact that everyone in the surrounding country is on the side of my rebels. At times I struggled with hatred of those who had betrayed me. I felt almost at breaking point, as much from mental and emotional as from physical fatigue. I cried that night for the first time in years.

Next day, I was moved through cornfields and ravines in the hot sun to a shelter of banana leaves in a camp with forty heavily armed men. Late into the night, a woman began chanting the eight volumes of the epic poem of the Maranaos. At 2am she decided to call it a day. I slept in fits until the Muslim call to prayer at 4.30am. I heard a few hours later that the army were approaching. One man from the village encouraged me to escape. One of the guards suggested he was open to a bribe. But by now I estimated there were over a hundred armed rebels in the area. At one point a rapid order was made to lie down on the ground. After darkness fell I heard a horse and rider galloping past in the night. It had become very tiring and distressing.

As we were moving continuously to avoid detection by the army (not to mention the other armed rebel gangs), I wrote a letter to the Governor asking that the army not become involved. By now, my energy was completely gone. A clatter of wild monkeys passed by, jumping from tree to tree. The anxiety of the guards was making me even more anxious. After dark, we were on the move again under a bright moon, at times running and slipping on the mountain path. I was in a strange mental condition at this stage: I seemed to have gone beyond fear. It was almost exciting, as if it was all just a dream. Then, I began to resent again this inhumane confinement.

Eleven days into my capture, my guards informed me that it was almost over. On our way to a village, I recall that we got some coconuts off a tree. People there told me that as many as 500 soldiers were searching for me. It is amazing how we had avoided them for so long! That afternoon, there was great commotion again. I was given a black veil worn by Muslim women and told to cover my head. I was also told the rebel leader was negotiating with the army, who were nearby.

Just after dark, the rebel leader told me that at last an agreement had been finalised. The guards asked me for forgiveness. By now I felt no animosity towards them – they had, after all, put their lives on the line to protect me from other gangs. I walked for a further two hours through the forests of Mindanao, still under armed guard. Apparently, they were afraid of snipers. Eventually, thank God, I was handed over to the Philippines army. Freedom!

After my ordeal I visited the President of the Philippines, Fidel Ramos, and thanked him for respecting the appeal of Church leaders not to attempt to release me by force. He went on to assure me that the promises made to the rebels would be respected when some other conditions had been fulfilled.

I remember afterwards a reporter asking if I had ever thought of making a run for it. Any temptation in that direction disappeared the first day when I saw one of my captors shoot a bird for dinner through the neck at about one hundred feet range!

Sr Louise Shields is from Co. Antrim. She worked in Kenya for ten years, and is now living in Middlesex, England. She is a member of the Congregation of Our Lady of the Missions.

Midnight robbery in Ruaraka

It was happening all over our part of Kenya. A band of thieves was systematically robbing the Catholic missions. We sensed that our turn would come. When it happened, however, we were totally unprepared.

It was 11pm on a Sunday night and we had all retired to our rooms. Except for the continuous racket of hyperactive crickets outside the windows, everything was quiet – the calm before the storm! Suddenly, the stillness was broken by the echoing of a car horn. Sr Theresa and myself came out of our rooms simultaneously, convinced that we had heard the horn of one of our own cars parked at the side of the house. Foolishly, we decided to go out and have a look. Robbery didn't even cross our minds.

Suddenly, five tall figures emerged from the shadows behind the cook's house. I froze. Theresa reacted quite differently. She yelled, 'They're here! They're here!' – she sounded as if she was welcoming long-awaited friends! Then she began to rebuke them, 'You people – we leave our homes and families and countries. Look at what you do to us!' The robbers paid not the slightest heed to her for their only thought was to get the car keys. One of them tore the watch off my arm and swept into the house. By now the other Sisters were awake.

Pandemonium followed. Everything began to happen at once! Sr Olivia had the presence of mind to lock her door. Guessing that her intention was to get help on the intercom, one of the robbers broke the door down. Sr Pauline found a whistle and began blowing for all she was worth. The robbers threw things at her, but to no avail. Sr Cecily was elderly and sick. A tall robber stood over her demanding her money. She just kept repeating, 'I am sick. I am sick.' I think he got sick of her response and left her alone. Sr Theresa managed to get back to her room and yelled out the window 'Help! Help!' to the priests in the neighbouring house. Unfortunately, they heard nothing.

Myself – I went looking for the car keys. We had always been told to give these sometimes ruthless and violent men what they demanded. I handed over the keys, they grabbed a few things and left as suddenly as they had arrived. Anyone watching the chaos unfold might be forgiven for thinking it was an episode of the Keystone Cops!

As they drove away, we just stood there in silence, numb with disbelief. With the tail-lights disappearing into the night, we suddenly became aware of sounds on the gravel outside. Fearing that one or two of the robbers had been left behind, we grabbed things to throw at them. It was a good thing we didn't, for it was the priests from the mission, in various states of undress and looking bleary-eyed, finally alerted by the commotion. They were armed with *pangas* (machetes), sticks, even a spear, and were ready for action. Typical! Some folk are never around when you need them.

Sleep was impossible that night. Dawn came very slowly. We were relieved when it did. Sr Pauline had sustained an injury and had to be driven to the hospital. I went with her. They made me stay for a few days as I was suffering from severe shock. Poor injured Sr Pauline had to drive herself home!

We had been lucky in spite of everything. Other missions did not escape so lightly – Sisters were tied up, held at gunpoint, beaten, and worse. In a similar attack a night-watchman was killed. Someone, somewhere, was praying for us that night.

Heather Martin (née Evans) comes from Greystones. The following stories are from her time working as a maternity nurse in Tanzania with the lay Anglican organisation BCMS (now Crosslinks). Heather and her husband David now live in the greater London area.

Wildlife encounters

The moon was bright and I was on call that night. I woke to hear footsteps coming to my window, and then listened for the word *'hodi'*, but it did not come. So I decided to look out but could not see anyone. Later, I fell asleep, and was not called to the hospital that night.

In the morning I asked Ernest, 'Who passed my window during the night? I had heard footsteps…' He went to look and came running back, wide-eyed. 'Did you go to the hospital last night?' I answered that I hadn't, telling him I had not heard the call for *hodi*. 'Sister,' he said, 'it was just as well you did not go as it was a *simba* (lion) who passed your window!' Ernest was our cook and he, like many of the men, knew the paw marks of the different animals. I thanked God for His protection yet again.

Another night, as I did my hospital round about 10pm, I was walking with the staff nurse between the children's ward and the male ward when I shone my torch towards the rubbish heap. Two eyes shone back, and I murmured to the staff nurse, 'There's a hyena.' She asked me to shine my torch again. When I did she told me it was a leopard – so we made our way along to the male ward rather quickly! After my round there we went out of the building and I shone my torch along the path that led to our house. There was the leopard again, about twenty-five metres away on 'my' path. A hungry leopard is a very dangerous animal indeed.

We returned quickly to the ward, pretending we had forgotten to check something or other. Needless to say, we spoke in English as we did not want to alarm the patients. About ten minutes later there was no sign of the leopard, so the staff nurse lit a pressure lamp and told me that leopards do not like the light.

Two student nurses went part of the way with me, then I ran the rest of the way home with my torch and a prayer for my safety. They in turn ran with the pressure lamp back to the hospital, possibly also praying as they ran! As there was no way of telling them I had arrived safely, I went to bed, grateful that I was in God's care. I prayed for the student nurses too.

Paul O'Callaghan, born in Co. Dublin in 1980, spent three years living and working with VMM (Volunteer Missionary Movement) in four countries in East Africa: Kenya, Tanzania, Rwanda, and the Democratic Republic of Congo. In 2008, he wrote an unpublished book, *Travel tales from the Continent of Golden Joys – musings from the missions*. He is currently studying for a doctorate in child psychology at Queen's University, Belfast, as part of which he has journeyed to Uganda to work with former child soldiers.

Tension in the air: Testee No. 95 to the waiting room
I've got to admit, I hate waiting rooms. There is something about the highly-controlled tension bubbling beneath the surface there that makes me want to

crack inappropriate jokes about death and illness, or else bolt out the door, magazine under arm and doctor's card in hand. But when the room is a partially constructed, unplastered and unpainted concrete casing, the desire to escape and put a thousand miles between me and the needle-wielding nurse is off the Richter scale. Allow me explain how I ever got myself into this situation.

You see, on one sunny Saturday morning, after a week's seminar on Behaviour Change, fifty young people from the parish accepted the invitation to discover their HIV status. A nurse and counsellor were duly contacted and, wandering into the room to see what was going on, I was directed by the young people there to an empty seat in their circle. Thus, I became patient number ninety-five, awaiting an AIDS test like millions of youths across Africa who are courageous enough to discover their HIV status.

Sitting in our cold, plastic chairs, in the semi-built parish centre, one could almost taste the smell of fear and anxiety in the air. One by one, we were summoned into an adjoining room where a nurse in starched flannels invited us to be seated. My greatest concern at that moment was not that I might have AIDS – I knew the chances of that were miniscule – but my big fear was that I might get AIDS from the needle used to test me!

However, seeing the nurse remove a sterile needle from a sealed packet quickly allayed my fears. After a small prick into a vein that had appeared like a birthday card pop-up greeting, the procedure was over, the torque removed and a cotton-wool swab placed on the injection site. It was at this stage that our fretful wait began. One of the boys beside me commented that although it only takes ten minutes to know the result, that ten minutes seemed more like a whole year.

Finally, the call came: 'Namba Tisini na Tano' (Number 95). I approached the unsmiling nurse and was asked to take a seat. She then studied me for what seemed like an eternity. The tension was killing me. 'Just tell me', I screamed inwardly, 'I can't take the suspense.' Slowly, she turned and uttered those immortal words, 'Congratulations, you are HIV-free.'

I thought to myself, *I'd known that already, even before I was tested,* but there was something about having to go through the test, share the nerves and tension of the other young people and wait for the result, that made me want to jump up, sweep the phlegmatic nurse off her feet and carry her on a lap of celebration around the room. However, dignity and decorum won the day. I thanked her and left with a burning desire to tell the next person I met that I was positively HIV-negative!

Not all of our group were so restrained though. Girls hugged each other, laughing and crying tears of joy. The boys beamed, whooping, shouting and charging around the parish grounds like condemned prisoners who'd just been given a presidential pardon. Sadly, no such pardon is available for any religious student found to be HIV-positive. Most religious orders in Africa now insist that all their students be both TB and HIV-free before joining, so during novitiate or postulancy year, the Brothers and junior Sisters troop down to their local HIV testing centre and join the queue of those who dare to know their status.

Of course, knowing your status is one thing. Accepting your status when the result is bad is something else completely. After the HIV testing in our own parish, I was surprised to hear from the young people themselves that not one of our group had HIV/AIDS. With infection rates as high as fourteen per cent in Arusha and with young people at particular risk, the odds of a clear round for all participants were slim. Indeed, knowledge may also lead to denial, a refusal to accept one's condition. If the denial is so strong that it doesn't affect a person's behaviour, the future is grim indeed, not just for them but also for those who love them and pay dearly for this love.

Nevertheless, the fact that so many young people were tested and the fact that so many good results were announced is cause for celebration and may yet make the dream of a 'HIV-free generation' a reality in a continent that could really do with some good news for a change. However, the scourge of the virus is never far from people's minds for we are reminded daily by the ever-present and inexorably repetitive advertisement on television that 'A dream of a HIV-free generation begins with you'.

Colin Nevin lived in Israel from 1991 to 2002, firstly as a catering manager with the Anglican organisation CMJ in Jaffa, and then as chef de partie at the Hilton Hotel in Tel-Aviv. He currently lives in his hometown, Bangor, Co. Down.

Tension and friendship in the Holy Land
Anyone who has embarked upon a missionary posting soon realises that there is a lot of practical work to do alongside the spiritual. Such was my role as a missionary for CMJ (Church's Ministry among Jewish People), a 200-year-old Anglican missionary society founded in 1809. I had to work in a hot and humid kitchen feeding people's earthly appetites as well as their spiritual ones. The Gulf War was raging at the end of 1990 when I was living and working as *sous-chef* in the Dolphin Hotel in Great Yarmouth, Norfolk, England. At the time the nightly news bulletins were relaying scenes of tension as Saddam Hussein lobbed Scud missiles on Tel-Aviv with impunity. I had no idea that I

would eventually end up in the Middle East working in a virtual war zone, and having to adapt to the language and culture of that troubled region.

A lot could be said about my time in Israel. I eventually stayed ten years. I learned to speak Hebrew, to sing and dance in Hebrew fashion, and I read the Bible in its original Hebrew. I spent four years working for CMJ in Jaffa, followed by six years as *chef de partie* in the Tel-Aviv Hilton. I learned about all the Jewish festivals and made friends who invited me into their family gatherings. I shared in the happy and sad times, and even in the difficult times when suicide bombers were making life unbearable in the inner cities.

I learned that being a 'missionary' in Jewish eyes was anathema, as it was viewed as a threat to the Jewish way of life. I also learned from experience that I could meet and come alongside people in a more meaningful and sincere way living among them than by being a technical 'missionary' in a church compound. I learned that the Jews were still reeling from memories of centuries of persecution, often at the hands of the Church and professing Christians.

I also had my own gas mask and underground bomb shelter like my Israeli neighbours. I stayed put during some of the most difficult years in Tel-Aviv – this touched my Jewish friends, who said: 'All the do-gooders go whenever there is trouble.' I witnessed the national outpouring of grief when Prime Minister Yitzhak Rabin was assassinated. I had also the experience of preparing food for Tony Blair (the then UK prime minister) and his Israeli counterpart, Binyamin Netanyahu, when they were having peace talks in the presidential suite of the Tel-Aviv Hilton.

After a decade I was denied a further work permit and prepared to return home to Bangor. I organised a little farewell on the banks of the Yarkon River near my apartment, as it was not considered safe to meet in crowded venues such as cafes and restaurants. Another suicide attack hit Tel-Aviv that weekend. One friend telephoned to apologise that, due to the mood in the city, she would not be able to attend; I fully understood and was not expecting many others to turn up as I prepared a barbecue in true Israeli style. To my utter amazement over one hundred people showed up from all walks of life: neighbours, shopkeepers, work colleagues, other foreign workers. It was a poignant night and I will always remember it. My favourite word is still *Shalom*.

Fr Brendan Carr is a Spiritan missionary who served in Angola from 1983 to 2000. He has a masters degree in mission theology from Graduate Theological Union in Berkeley, California. Since returning from Africa, he was parish priest at Kimmage Manor for six years. Fr Brendan, who is now based at SPIRASI (Spiritan Asylum Services Initiative), on whose board he sits, is responsible for the congregation's new office for volunteer lay missionaries.

Lesser-known martyrs in Angola

Sadly, the blood of Christians has been spilled in too many countries in Africa. In Angola, many priests, nuns, catechists and church workers lost their lives in the service of the church – mostly in ambushes on the perilous roads, or as victims of that horrendous and indiscriminate weapon, the land mine. Some of these were singled out for their outspoken criticism of either the government or the rebels in times of civil war. While perhaps not martyrs in the strict sense, they gave their lives in the service of God's people. There were those too who died, specifically, for their faith.

I wish to record the story of two people, both catechists, whose names will hardly appear in any forum other than here, but whose lives and deaths were a witness to what the Church often terms 'heroic virtue' when speaking of the saints. Francisco Chihutu and Doreteia Kamala, in different towns of north-eastern Angola, spent their lives in service as catechists without any remuneration for their work. Both, at different times, succumbed to brutal death by beatings from their own relatives and community, the price often paid for being accused of having cast a spell on someone who had died or was seriously ill.

Francisco and Doreteia consistently fought against the witchcraft mentality among their people with its devastating consequences for innocent individuals and families. Any death, but particularly that of a young person, inevitably forces a family to call in a 'diviner' to ascertain who bewitched the deceased, for the death of a child by natural causes is a concept difficult to accept in this culture. Christians commit themselves not to participate in the divining process or make accusations of witchcraft, yet it is sometimes very difficult to resist peer and family pressure. It was ironic that Doreteia and Francisco, having opposed such practices all their Christian lives, should in the end be accused of evil intent and bewitching another.

In Francisco's case, he was not initially accused of being the witch. Someone in his enlarged family died and he was being compelled to take part in the divining process, which he refused to do because of his faith. He was first ostracised from the community, a horrible punishment in itself, then eventually was accused of being a witch. When he continued to refuse to partake in the diviner's ritual, the diviner ordered his death by clubbing and stoning.

From a distance it is easy to view such deaths as callous and illogical. Up close, they are the result of tremendous fear of the spirit-world and often of a power struggle within family or clan. As in any human group, from the very sophisticated to the most simple, the universal social evils of greed, selfishness and corruption are also at work.

Doreteia was accused by members of her extended family to whom she had given refuge when they fled from a war zone. Out of envy of her position in the community, and the perceived access she had to material goods because of her friendship with the missionaries, when a crisis arose over a death in the family some targeted her as the witch. Friends related afterwards that she knew she would be accused, for she had sensed animosity towards her matriarchal position in the family for some time. She had the opportunity to flee, but decided to remain, encouraging the Christians of her family to face down the evil plot.

She was set upon in a melee of kicks and clubbing, and left for dead. Her grandson got her to the local hospital and informed the missionaries of what had happened. Still conscious, she asked for the last rites. In her last hours she often broke into prayer and song, including hymns that she had composed herself in her own beautiful Chokwe language.

I had shared ministry with Doreteia for many years; no Christian life has personally inspired me as much. She is still an inspiration to me and to many. Whenever reciting the short litany of the saints as we do at baptisms or in the prayers for the dying or in the great liturgies, her name, her face and her witness always find a place among the saints of my litany.

Fr Maurice McGill, from Ardara in Co. Donegal, is a Mill Hill priest who served in Cameroon. He currently lives in Dublin.

Times of fear

The life we choose can be a dangerous one. The news this morning, 11 October 2009, contained the snippet that it is one hundred days since Sharon Cummins from Clontarf and Hilda Kawuki from Uganda, GOAL volunteers in Darfur, Sudan, had been kidnapped by armed men. As I was beginning Mass for returned missionaries in All Hallows College this afternoon, I was handed a piece of paper with a request for prayers for Fr Michael Sinnott, a seventy-nine-year-old Columban missionary priest from Wexford, who had been abducted by a gang from his house in southern Philippines earlier in the day. I hope that by the time you read these words all three will be with their families and friends. Two other Columban priests have been victims of kidnappers in the southern Philippines in recent years – one was released unharmed, one was shot dead.

An American classmate of mine and an English priest were taken from their parish in Benitu, southern Sudan, in early 1983. They were marched over a wide area for more than forty days before being handed over to the Sudan Council of Churches. By the 1990s, the leader of the armed gang had become a junior minister in the Sudanese government. When the American met him by chance on the pavement in Khartoum, he complained that the ransom promised by the Churches for the release of the priests was never paid!

Thank God, I have no experience of the trauma of kidnapping for ransom, but I had a number of fear-filled hours during two armed robberies in Bamenda, Cameroon, in 2002. One incident was particularly frightening. With Sr Colette, a Holy Rosary Sister, I had completed a six-day retreat for seven nuns and five priests at a prayer house attached to a Dominican convent some ten miles from the town of Bamenda. At 1.30am, I was woken by footsteps directly outside the window of my room. Within seconds, there was a sound of glass smashing in the room across the corridor. The Sister who was staying there began to scream.

I went to the door of the Sister's room and shouted at the man doing the smashing that I was going to call the police. He demanded that the outside door be opened. Someone was smashing the window of another room towards the chapel end of the corridor. It was obvious that a gang, numbers unknown, was trying to break in. I tried to alert the Dominican convent by intercom but got no reply. Sr Colette, I learnt later, was trying to contact one of the priests in the major seminary that was only about a mile away, but the mobile phone reception was poor. Luckily, the priest answered. Unluckily, he was not in the seminary but ten miles away in one of the town parishes … and his phone was out of credit.

Amazingly, it took a few minutes to wake up one of the retreatants; he, a Capuchin priest from Eritrea, had gone through a war there and was used to loud bangs in the night! As the gang were forcing an entry, we gathered in the chapel, and in the dark began to pray. The Confiteor was said, absolution was given, and the rosary begun. It took the gang some fifteen minutes to smash through the steel protectors on the window of one of the rooms. One or two of them then entered the house and forced open the main door and the door at the end of the corridor. A gang of four or five arrived in the chapel. A torch was shone on our group, and then one of the gang, as if giving a well-rehearsed speech, announced: 'We have come on a mission to collect the money from you and from the big safe…' He paused, and addressing a local Capuchin priest said, 'Hello Brother.' (The Capuchins brought food to the local prison a few times a week.)

I informed them that we were a group who had come to pray, we knew nothing of a 'big safe' and we had no access to the convent. My mobile phone was taken from under my chair and we were ordered to lie on the floor. I could not find a space, so I was ordered to go with them and to show them my room. It was at the other end of the corridor beside the side door; and from the state the room was in, it was clear that it had already been visited by some of the gang. I was taken outside and ordered to lead the gang to the convent. The distance was about twenty yards across a lawn with flowerbeds. I was in my pyjamas and only had slippers on. The rain of the previous day had stopped, but there was a slight drizzle. There was a dim light over the entrance to the convent.

The next few minutes passed slowly. At the front door of the convent, I was surrounded by five or six men; two had handguns, one had a hatchet, and the others had various implements in their hands. I was several times ordered to open the door; my answer that I did not have the keys was met with threats, especially from the man with the hatchet. Next, I was asked to show them where the fuse box was. Again, I had to say that I did not know. The main speaker was a stocky middle-aged man who, presumably thinking I was lying, repeatedly said to me: 'Respect yourself, you are an ancient. Respect yourself.'

It struck me that from his accent and demeanour that he was an *'officier'* from the French-speaking part of the country. I told them that they would find little money in the convent as the Sisters tried to live on the produce of the farm. The last group who had attacked the convent got 1,500 francs – less than €3. After a discussion among themselves in a local language, one of the gang began to hammer at the door. Another was trying to loosen the protectors on the windows with a crowbar. A few swings of the sledge hammer damaged the bottom of the door, but there was a steel gate behind it.

At that moment the convent alarm sounded. It was not a loud alarm, and would not be heard at the nearest house about a quarter of a mile away, but it certainly frightened the thieves. I was forced to my room and told to sit on the bed. When I got up to put on my socks and shoes to cover the small cuts on my feet that I got from walking over the flowerbeds, I was shoved back down. Just then a car horn began to sound quite near to the gate of the convent. The man guarding me slipped out the back door.

Soon, I heard two gunshots quite close to each other. Finding a pair of trousers, I dressed quickly and went along to the chapel. I was greeted with some relief by our group. Everything went quiet until the intercom from the convent rang: the Sisters were anxious about our welfare. They explained that Fr William from the seminary and two night-watchmen from there had come and that the gang had fled. The priest phoned by Sr Colette had, by a roundabout way, managed to contact Fr William in the seminary. Fr William with the night-watchmen in the car had driven slowly towards the convent, sounding the horn repeatedly as the car neared the convent. When they reached the convent gate Fr William, who had brought his old hunting gun with him in the car, had fired into the air. He was answered by a gunshot from somewhere in the darkness of the bush.

A large number of people had gathered around the convent by 3.30am. One of the senior Sisters, the only survivor of the founders who had come from the Netherlands nearly fifty years previously, offered the retreatants Valium tablets. There were no takers. Most of the group in the prayer house had lost some valuables. As well as the phone, I lost some money, my car keys, a belt from my trousers ... and a bar of soap.

The local gendarme commander arrived and did some interviews; he asked us to write down what had happened. Two gendarmes were left to guard the convent for the rest of the night. When the people went away, the group of retreatants celebrated Mass and had a very early breakfast. There was no investigation by the gendarmes. I came home on leave a few days after the robbery, and on my return heard that the commander had been moved elsewhere before an investigation could begin.

During 2002, the Capuchin and Calasanzian houses and a number of private houses in the Bamenda area were also attacked by gangs. Some of the residents fared much worse than I did. Early in 2003, driving near to the lawless area of Bamenda, I saw a group of people around a body on the road. A thief had been caught and had been given the 'necklace' treatment (where a car tyre is thrown over the person and set alight). I had only a brief glance at the partly burned body, but it struck me that it could well have been the enforcer of the robbery at the Dominican prayer house.

A month or so later, a large gang attacked the office of the Baptist hospital, some twenty miles from Bamenda. The gendarmes came on the scene quickly and there was a brief shoot-out; one of the gendarmes was shot dead. A gang member, who was caught, spilled the beans on the other members of the gang. Their leader was a policeman. The whole gang, including the policemen whose gun killed the gendarme, were rounded up and imprisoned far away from Bamenda. I often wonder if the *'officier'* leader of the gang at the retreat house was the same policeman. There were fewer robberies around Bamenda in the following years.

The first reaction to a situation of violence is fear and a certain panic. Then, the realisation comes that you have to do your best to deal with what is happening, and with that a feeling of calmness surfaces. Advice received in the past comes to mind: do what you are told, do not look too closely at the thieves, speak clearly but only when spoken to, and above all do not try to answer violence with violence.

The first missionary, St Paul, wrote: 'I have been in prison more frequently, I have been flogged more severely, many times exposed to death. Five times I have been given the thirty-nine lashes by the Jews; three times I have been beaten with sticks; once I have been stoned; three times I have been shipwrecked, and once I have been in the open sea for a night and a day; continuing travelling, I have been in danger from rivers, in danger from brigands, in danger from my own people and in danger from Gentiles, in danger in the open country, in danger at sea and in danger from people masquerading as brothers…' (2 Corinthians 11:23–26).

In my time I have been in 'danger from bandits'; how would I have coped with Paul's many ordeals? He carried on with his work, as I shall carry on with mine.

CHAPTER FIVE

War and Peace

Fr Patrick Reilly, a Columban Father from Co. Meath, worked in China before the Communist Revolution. He was arrested and imprisoned for a year by the Maoists for alleged subversive activities, before eventually being expelled from China in 1953. He worked with Irish emigrants in Britain until 1963, at which time he was appointed to the Philippines. He returned to Ireland in 1982, working in Co. Meath until his retirement in 1992. He passed away in 1998. Fr Reilly's account of his ordeal in captivity in China is provided courtesy of a colleague in the Columban Fathers, Fr Cyril Lovett.

Fourteen months in solitary confinement

For fourteen months I had been in solitary confinement in Communist China. During those long months I had hardly spoken to anyone – apart from my guards and interrogators. I had no bed to lie on, nor extra clothes to cover myself from the cold. I was forced to sit in one position for sixteen hours every day. I was allowed nothing to read, not even a letter from home. Twice a day the cell door opened and a meagre ration of rice with a tiny bowl of vegetables was brought into my dark cell.

I saw my body withering away. One day they weighed me. I was astonished to discover that I had gone from twelve stone to only six stone in weight. I was all aches and pains and drained of energy. A few times I tried to stand upright, but collapsed. I was convinced I was going to die. My wish was to say just one more Mass before I died. But how could I, locked up in solitary confinement in a Chinese jail?

One day, in August 1953, something startling happened. When my cell door opened the guard gave me steamed bread instead of the usual rice. Bread! Now, all I needed was wine for the Mass. Momentarily full of confidence, I could only wait … and hope. As the days went by, however, my eyes deteriorated until I became completely blind in the left eye and almost blind in the right. I reported my condition to the guards. They brought a doctor to my cell. He examined my eyes and said the nerves were bleeding due to lack of vitamins, and suggested that I be given better food, and also fruit. I was convinced that I would get neither.

True enough, the food remained the same. But to my surprise a Communist official told me they still had the money that was in the drawer of my desk the day I was arrested, and that with it they would buy some fruit for me. 'We do not want as much as a thread from the Imperialists', the guard told me. No prisoner to my knowledge had ever got this privilege of being allowed fruit. To my amazement, he asked me what fruit I would like. I asked for grapes.

A bunch of grapes was handed into my cell that same evening. I still had the white shirt I was wearing when arrested. I tore the two cuffs from the sleeves and washed them in my ration of drinking water. When the cuffs had dried, I made a little bag of one cuff, put some grapes into it, and squeezed the juice from them, gathering it in my rice bowl. This juice I then poured into a little bottle that I had kept hidden in my cell. It had been given to me with some medicine a few days after I had been arrested to impress me into believing that the Communists treated their prisoners well. Having put the juice from all the grapes into the little bottle, I corked it and hid it. Some days later, the cork popped from the bottle. The juice had fermented. I now had wine. I could now say Mass!

However, not being allowed to move in the cell, and being constantly under guard, I had to be very careful. I wiped a small portion of the cell floor that would serve as the altar. Then I waited for my opportunity. Towards evening I heard the guard on duty scolding another prisoner. I knew by his tone that he was going to spend at least ten minutes questioning him. I got up and spread the cuff of the shirtsleeve on the section of the ground that I had cleaned. Dressed only in my shirt and pants, and barefooted, I knelt down. I hurried to the consecration. I could not delay. I could not savour the moment. All was over in a few minutes. The guard was still scolding the other prisoner.

Fr Brian Treacy is a Kiltegan Father from Co. Limerick who has been living in Kenya since the 1960s. He was living in the Rift Valley when tribal violence broke out following elections at the end of 2007.

LIVING THROUGH A CRISIS — MY DIARY FROM THE KENYAN ELECTION
IN 2007

Tuesday, 11 December 2007

On Saturday I presided over the profession of one of the Franciscan nuns at Baraka, and it was delightful. The Mass lasted a couple of hours; it was a lively affair, interspersed with spontaneous singing and dancing in the African fashion. You lose all track of time when there is that kind of spirit in the congregation.

The General Election is coming up on the 27th: the campaign has been violent at times; a number of people have been killed. Things are looking ominous, and there could easily be serious trouble in some parts. There is a kind of feeling around that if the opposition party does not win that they might cry foul, and cause mayhem. Thank God it's very quiet here so far in the Londiani area – a potentially dangerous tribal flash point. At least the nomination process here has been relatively open.

Friday, 28 December
It would seem that the voting yesterday went very much along tribal lines, voting *en bloc* for either the opposition leader, Raila Odinga, or for the incumbent, President Kibaki. That is a pity, as it brings us back to tribal politics, which can be a very explosive and divisive way of ruling any country. Sadly, there is a general tendency to go that route in post-colonial African politics. As of this hour, it seems that the result is too close to call. There is a mood of relief so far in the country that at least there was peace on election day.

3pm There's a biggish delay in announcing the results of the presidential election, and there are already demonstrations and some violence around the country as people suspect that there might be some vote-rigging going on. There is a rumour just now that tyres, and even cars, are being burnt on the main road 2km away. There are reports of cars being stoned in Kericho, our main town. People here are just trying to keep a low profile and praying that all will be well. Unofficially, it seems now that Raila Odinga will win, which is all to the good. At one stage last night it seemed that Kibaki might win the presidential race, and Odinga have a big majority in parliament. This would be a recipe for a disaster, I think.

Sunday, 30 December, afternoon
The security situation in Kenya is deteriorating by the hour. The final results of the presidential election have still not been announced. Each side is accusing the other of massive rigging, and it does seem that something very fishy is going on. Quite a number of results that have come in from constituencies give total figures higher than the registered number of voters. This time it seems that the Kikuyu, who support sitting President Kibaki, may be responsible, but they are also accusing the other side of the same thing. It is a recipe for absolute chaos in the country – and that is exactly what is happening.

There are reports of serious rioting and looting in almost every major town in the country.

As I write this (4pm), the situation is worsening again. It seems that there was serious violence some hours ago in a Kikuyu village near our junction with the main road. The village is home to thousands of people, mostly Kikuyu, many of them having fled there after the tribal clashes of 1992–3. It seems that they were able to repulse the attack, with help from armed police, who seem to have been quite good and on alert for the past day or two. People have been fleeing their homes, many of them seeking sanctuary next door in the police station where there is little room for them.

For the past couple of hours we have been getting a trickle of people coming into the mission, carrying small possessions. There are already about fifteen adults, and up to fifty kids, who are running around, totally oblivious as to why they are here. I can hear their delightful laughter as they play. For them it is a kind of adventure or holiday. Some people are bringing their valuables: one man has just arrived with his computers. He runs a computer shop in the town. It is a sad scene, which we had hoped we would never see again.

5pm Just now a young African nun came in, in a state of great fear. Her *matatu* (taxi) had been stopped on the road, and surrounded by a group of Kipsigis 'warriors', armed with spears and machetes. They wanted to know which tribe she belongs to. If she were a Kikuyu, a Kisii or a Luo, then she was in trouble. She hid her identity card, and told them that she was just on her way to Kericho, so they let her go. She then had to hide in a good Samaritan's house, who eventually brought her to another woman who is a Catholic. Eventually, with the help of a policeman, she made her way to the mission here. She broke down in tears of relief when she arrived. She will stay with us here until it is safe to travel; it may take a few days.

Later this evening a young Kisii priest came in for shelter as well; he too got stopped on the main road. It was around the same time that they announced on the media that President Kibaki had been re-elected. It sounds as if there has been a serious element of rigging in his favour – for example, the results of one constituency favouring him were inflated by something like fifty per cent. So this kind of news will do nothing whatsoever to cool an already very explosive situation. There will be more serious trouble in the next few days.

Monday, 31 December

Not a very auspicious end to the year. We had about 150 people, mostly women and kids, sleeping in our hall last night, and I woke a few times to the sound of gunshots. Sometimes it is just the police scaring off potential attackers and arsonists. I got a call late last night from David, our catechist, saying that they were expecting to be attacked at any moment and I should inform the police, who are next door to us. I went there, but most of them were out investigating other attacks, and their phones were not responding. Luckily, just before I went to bed, I got the officer in charge and he told me that they would try to do something. They did go, and people were very happy today that the attackers had been scared off just as they were on the point of setting a house on fire.

Tonight we are expecting many more refugees. They sleep here at night, and then move back to the town during the day. No shops opened today, everyone is too scared. There is no transport of any kind. I ventured out a few miles through Kipsigis country, and it was deceptively peaceful: people working in the fields, but also a lot of young lads gathering on the roads discussing the situation.

I got a call from David a while ago, asking me to go to his house and collect a Kisii man who had been attacked earlier and still had an arrow lodged in his arm. I started off with considerable apprehension, and had only gone about 100m when some women stopped me and told me not to go on as some youths ahead had blocked the road and were stoning cars. If I had to go, I would need a police escort. So back to the police station again, and sure enough they gave me two policemen, who sat very visibly in front with me. The youths scattered on seeing this show of force, and we had no problem getting through to the injured man.

8pm It looks like all hell has broken loose, and our parish is burning, possibly hundreds of houses burnt in the past few hours, and the police seem to be powerless to stop it. They seem to have orders to shoot over the heads of the 'warriors', who are not a bit scared of that; and not one of them has been arrested. People of Kikuyu and Kisii origin are now fleeing in terror, and right now we have up to 2,000 people in our compound, I would guess. They cannot all fit into our hall and church. I phoned the senior policeman who said there were not enough police to go around, and their vehicle had broken down. Hopeless! Why they don't call in the army I simply do not know. This seems to be the story all over the country.

My own reaction tonight – it is hard to know. You just feel hopelessly frustrated: there is so little you can do. You can't drive into these areas on your own, and even if you did you would simply be endangering your own life and maybe others as well. All day long people say, 'I hear my house has been burnt', 'I have lost everything!', 'This is the body of my father (or son, or brother) who was killed…', 'My old grandmother is out where there is violence, could you please help us?' Somebody just sent me a text message wishing me a happy New Year. Right now, it is hard to imagine it.

Eventually, you just have to develop a kind of shell for inner protection, and you simply say: *'Pole sana!'* (meaning 'very sorry to hear that'), and you pass on to try to comfort the next person. People understand that we cannot help everyone. Apart from the one police Land Rover, our two pickups are almost the only ones in the whole parish that are reaching out to the refugees, dead and injured. But we do have to arrange an armed escort each time with the police, and this takes time. When we reach some incident, we find that there are not only dead or injured but a crowd who all want to be carried to the mission for safety. The vast majority of the people in the compound here are not Catholics at all, but they are very appreciative of our efforts.

Tuesday, 1 January 2008

Things have got even worse: about 3,000–4,000 people are sleeping in the compound, but with the horrific news of the barbaric burning of people in a church in Eldoret we decided that tonight they must all sleep out in the open. Last night we had close to 2,000 sleeping in the church, plus others in our meeting hall, and others again in the dining hall of the pastoral centre, with many again in the open as they could not find even an inch of space inside any of the three buildings. They are scattered all over the grass and right up against my bedroom window. Despite the temperature dropping at night to near 0°C, I have not heard a complaint from anyone; they are just happy to feel secure. Right now (10pm) I can hear them, laughing and joking in their 'beds'. Extraordinary spirit! I've heard our own hospital here in Londiani has closed down after some of the 'warriors' entered and warned the staff against treating Kikuyu and Kisii people.

Today the police got some paramilitary reinforcements at last, so that should help a lot. However, this is only a drop in the ocean, and they are still shooting over the heads of these young guys, who are only laughing at them, as they continue to burn and shoot their arrows at innocent people.

Wednesday, 2 January – Sunday, 6 January

One thing we have all noticed here is that we hardly know what day of the week it is when we are asked. I've been so busy I am writing this on Sunday afternoon, and having a real job remembering what happened since Wednesday. It is actually difficult to keep track of things from day to day as we hear new tragedies every hour, and requests for help from so many people.

Con and Martin have been great at ferrying people, and they remain very calm and collected in very trying circumstances. One great advance in technology has been the mobile phone, which has enabled people to keep up with developments.

I like to go around just greeting the people on the compound to keep their spirits up, but there is always someone who asks you to rescue their mother or grandfather or whoever is out there somewhere. Or else people beg us to bring in their store of maize and beans. We try to do our best, but we are beginning to realise that our Toyota pick-ups are totally inadequate for the tasks.

Thank God I have had 'rest days' in between the hard ones, as it is emotionally very draining seeing the people's suffering and terror. Yet you can only admire them for their astonishing resilience: 'We will be back, peace will come, and we will once more live in harmony, God will help us!' This kind of thing from people who may have just had one or more of their family murdered, or had all their property burnt, their food stores, everything.

I think Thursday was the day the army finally arrived, four big lorries of them, to the delight of the refugees. These guys hopefully will calm things down and take more control of the situation. Up to now, the police and paramilitaries have been shooting over people's heads. We don't think the army will do that.

We have had many communications from international relief organisations, including the Red Cross, UNICEF, Concern, and Médecins Sans Frontières. We have had phone calls from around the world asking for interviews, helicopters hovering around us several times each day, but not a single iota of aid has arrived so far. We have requested lots of blankets, food, and polythene sheeting in case of rain. Thank God, the weather is very dry and warm during the day, but it is very cold at night. There is a minor outbreak of diarrhoea among the kids. Our toilet facilities are seriously over-stretched.

Yesterday (Saturday) was a rather 'quiet' day for me, mostly spent around the mission here. The Franciscan Brothers and the Sisters from the dispensary in Baraka came to visit us here, and they brought medicines, some food, etc. We have set up a small clinic with a volunteer nurse here, and have patients arriving all day long. But medicines are very scarce. Luckily, the Red Cross have been in a few times (mostly assessing the situation), and the one person who was very ill they were able to take to Molo Hospital, about fifteen miles away.

Martin has gone out for the funerals of three victims. He took the three bodies in his pick-up to their homes, and on the way was interviewed live on the Pat Kenny show! That was a really hard day for him, as he knew well two of the people who had been murdered.

It is hard to get statistics of what has happened in the parish, but our estimate is that about twenty-five people have been killed, and something like 1,000–3,000 houses burnt to the ground. You can imagine an average family of about six living in each house. It is very hard to understand how people can burn other people's houses and all their food stores. In Kipsigis tradition this is one of the worst sins a person can commit and it brings a curse on the person who does it. 'He doesn't deserve to live!' they would have said. Yet still in their hatred – of the Kikuyu, especially – they seem to be able to ignore this.

Everyone has heard of the appalling horror in Eldoret a week ago when the raiders locked the doors of a church that was sheltering many children, then set fire to it. We hear about fifty died, mostly children. One woman described how she managed to get through a window with one of her little children, and then one of the raiders caught the child and threw him back into the fire. Stories don't come much more horrific than that.

Today was much quieter. We are wondering if the largely tribal war is about to end – everyone's dearest hope. We had decided yesterday, Saturday, to try to follow our normal Sunday Mass programme for the out-stations, even though it involved crossing the 'war zones'. This time we would go to the churches without any security, and hoped that people would respect that. Which they did. I said Mass first in a Kikuyu church and then in a Kipsigis house (the people there were too scared to come to our main church). In both places, all I could think was that all these people on both sides are really good people, and it is as if something really evil gets into people to make them fight and kill each other.

Martin said Mass here in the main church with a goodish crowd, then set off for Kipsirichet church, in a Kipsigis area. On the way, he encountered a big barricade of telephone poles blocking the road. He was manoeuvring around the barrier by going up the side of the ditch when his engine conked out. Somehow he managed to get it going again, and continued on his way to say Mass. Very courageous I thought. Personally, I think I might have turned back. Afterwards, he was lucky to be able to limp back home safely.

This morning I conducted a funeral for one of the victims. We went to collect the body at the mortuary of the local hospital, where all the staff had deserted – the attackers had threatened them. Someone whispered to me that there were still a few patients at the hospital, and so we went. We found one poor young woman there who was obviously dying. We said a prayer with her and she died a few minutes later.

I phoned Paddy Hyland in Kericho a few days ago, and he has had similar problems to us: thousands displaced, houses burnt, etc. It is hard for him, as he is living alone at present, and that can be traumatic. In his own inimitable style, he gave me a colourful account of one day that he had bullets whizzing just past his ear. From past history, we do know that Paddy would make a very good fiction writer... Seriously, though, he was here in Londiani during the clashes of 1992–3, and he is still regarded as a hero in these parts for the way he helped people then without fear or favour.

Monday, 14 January
Huge numbers of international organisations have been coming to visit us: Concern, GOAL, Red Cross, Médecins Sans Frontières, etc., etc., plus a host of government officials. Most of them want to make an 'assessment' of the situation, they want statistics – how many women, children under five years, between five years and ten, and so on. It is a bit frustrating to say the least, as how the heck could we even think of statistics, surrounded as we are by a couple of thousand cold, hungry and scared people. I suppose that is how these organisations work; in Nairobi they are trying to coordinate their relief activities.

Hundreds of email and text messages have been pouring in – from around the parish, from elsewhere in Kenya, and from the world beyond. Many of them will have to wait for some time until we get the opportunity to reply.

Parliament opens tomorrow, and it is expected to be a rowdy occasion, to put it mildly. The opposition are planning demonstrations against the presidential poll, which they insist was rigged. Most of the people here who have been attacked and driven from their homes feel that if the opposition party had got into power, things might have been even worse than they have been. That opposition party, led by Raila Odinga, has been advocating something called *majimbo* – devolving power from central government in Nairobi to regional administrations. This idea is laudable in theory, but what has happened here in Rift Valley province, for example, is that the Kalenjin people, of whom the Kipsigis tribe are part, feel that this whole area historically belongs to them, and so they have attacked violently people from other tribes, and they make no secret that their aim is to drive them all out.

However, if all the Kikuyu people in Nairobi decided to retaliate and drive out all the Kalenjin, it would be a recipe for total disaster in the country. It is a very short-sighted policy, but some politicians love to incite this kind of barbaric activity.

Thursday, 17 January
So for the past few days, I have been trying to put together statistics from around the parish. We know of 25 who have been killed. 968 houses and stores

have been burnt, from a total population of 1,227 adults and 2,434 children. The list comes to twenty pages of type. The numbers who have been displaced in the wider area run to several thousand.

Help has continued to pour in for the past few days in the form of food, clothes, soap, blankets and even basic cooking kits for people who have lost everything to the arsonists. We have had a French team from Médecins Sans Frontières here, and I must say that they have been great. There are four French and two local nurses, and three drivers. They are young people with unlimited energy; so nice and cheerful, and highly organised. They leave early in the morning, have no lunch, and are still delightful company late in the day. They have been given the job of co-ordinating aid for the whole of Kericho – responsible for logistics, statistics, provisions, communications, food and medical supplies, reports, etc.

Sunday, 6 December 2009 (almost two years later)
No rain yet in Tenges, or just a few drops now and again, which is just as bad, as it produces no growth. Yet the rain is only about ten miles away as the crow flies, but just doesn't reach us. The situation is very serious. I spent a week at retreat in Baraka, and there was plenty of rain there, with crops growing very nicely. It was also cold there with the temperature one morning in the chapel at 12°C.

The political temperature has also cooled a lot in the past year. Kiltegan organised a reconciliation meeting at Baraka a few weeks ago between the warring factions in the 'troubles', or 'post-election violence' as they prefer to call it. We had about fifteen priests present from all sides, plus twenty or so lay people. Our chief facilitator was, unusually, a Muslim lady called Dekka from a very remote part of Kenya on the Somali border. She was an extraordinary lady – highly intelligent, with a very good grasp of how to handle the situation when things tended to get hot.

Two of our own priests assisted her in the facilitation: Gabriel Dolan, who has been very active and is well known in justice issues here in Kenya; and Nicky Hennity, who spent about sixteen years in Rwanda after the genocide. In general it was a good meeting; it was really the first time that people had got a chance to sit down together and try to talk things out, offering some hope for the future.

Born in 1921, Fr Kevin Longworth was a Westmeath man who played Gaelic football for Longford. In the 1940s, he set off for Nigeria, where he was to serve for most of his missionary life until he retired to Kiltegan, Co. Wicklow in 2002. He also lived in New Orleans, New York, and California, and became an American citizen. He published his memoirs, *Harvesting memories*, in 2003. Sadly, he passed away in September 2010.

The Nigerian civil war

'Cry havoc and let slip the dogs of war' – Julius Caesar, Act III.

I was in Adiabo when the coup occurred in January 1966. We heard of the killing of Prime Minister Tafawa Balewa. It was very significant that the new military commander was an Ibo man. We heard of the plans of the leaders of the coup to 'clean out the Augean stables', to rid the nation of corruption. New legislation ensured that members of the Ibo tribe held the majority of senior posts throughout the country. This was seen as a plan to ensure that Nigeria would be under Ibo control.

No wonder we had the ugly counter-coup in July, followed by the killing of about 30,000 Ibo in the north and the frantic exodus to their homelands in Onitsha and Owerri during September and October of that year. We in Calabar heard of the brave Kiltegan men in Minna, under Ned Fitzgibbon, who saved the lives of many Ibo.

I saw army uniforms for the first time in August when Col. Ojukwu came. I met him that night at a cocktail party. We had no idea then that he would soon be the head of the secessionist State of Biafra. Under Ojukwu's leadership, Biafra declared its independence in May 1967, citing the slaughter of Ibo in the north, among other reasons. War inevitably followed, and we in Biafra soon found ourselves under siege.

These were dangerous times. A dawn approach by Nigerian troops to the town of Ogoja coincided with the ringing of the bell in the Catholic Church. This was taken by the soldiers to be a deliberate warning of their approach. When the town was captured, John Mahon of the Kiltegans was held at gunpoint for questioning. The late Tom McCracken had some rough experiences too when the boys travelling with him were taken out of the car and shot before his eyes.

There was a lot of suspicion. I remember once I had a burial service to perform in Afa Oku, and, as was my custom, I left the graveside after I finished my prayers, leaving the filling of the grave to the family. I had just arrived home when a MiG fighter came over and dropped some bombs on the prison, and some shrapnel passed through the roof of the staff quarters at the education office. I heard later that some people at the funeral were convinced that I had some secret contact with the bombers. I picked up a piece of the jagged metal shrapnel at the education office and kept it on a bookshelf at my home. In due course my house came under a routine search by the army, now frequently engaged in 'combing' – looking for enemy infiltration. My cook, Michael, hid the piece of shrapnel before it could be seen. He had a better knowledge of his people than I had. It was hard to take these constant searches of my home, and also to be stopped and searched by your neighbours. I had a feeling that many were anxious to put on an exaggerated show of loyalty to the Biafra regime.

As the tide turned against the Biafrans and the Nigerians closed in, we were greatly concerned as the Church and its agencies were accused of supporting the secessionist regime. Some priests and nuns began to slip out to Cameroon via Oron, using the local 'engine boat' – a dug-out canoe with an outboard motor. The dangerous trip to Ikassa took four hours if all went well. One day, we met some priests from Onitsha (one of whom was Barney Kelly), who felt fairly sorry for themselves at having had to turn back that morning when they heard gunfire from the direction of Calabar. They had to wait several months before exiting via the makeshift airport at Uli.

During this time of emergency I was stopped for questioning by three men, one of whom wore the uniform of the local militia. I heard nothing more until the following Saturday morning when a jeep stopped in front of my office and a tall red-capped sergeant strode into my office. He announced that the Colonel would like to see me. I told him I would of course be happy to meet the Colonel. I had been thinking of meeting him in connection with Mass services for the growing number of militia in Uyo, so I told him I would follow him in my car. He agreed. We drove towards the administration area, but I became disconcerted when we swung into a square surrounded by mud-walled, mat-roofed houses. The sergeant led the way into a bare room with a table and one or two chairs and announced in a formal manner: 'You are now under arrest.' I kept my cool, and asked, 'And what is the charge?' 'The Colonel will tell you at his convenience. Now you must be searched.'

Some hours later I received a note from the local Provincial Secretary, whom I knew to be a zealous administrator of all wartime regulations and who also was the conductor of civil defence. I read the words: 'Contempt for the Government of Biafra'. This actually came as a relief: now I knew that I was not in detention for any specific indiscretion and, to tell the truth, I was a wee bit proud to be charged with contempt for the Government of Biafra at that time.

There was a new moon that night and I slept until a group of new prisoners were brought in sometime during the night. I overheard someone saying that these people were caught trying to contact the Nigerians who were infiltrating the creeks around Oti Oron. In reality they were just poor fisher folk who happened to be in the wrong place at the wrong time.

After my release, I watched as the Nigerian army continued to advance. One evening when I was in Uyo, two MiG fighters zoomed over the town at treetop level, sounding like angry wasps as they sped away. I saw a bomb drop near my house in the distance, so I reckoned I had better stay where I was. The house and the unfinished church were at the junction of five roads. It had indeed been a near miss! Thank God, they seemed unable to get direct hits on any of their targets.

As the noose tightened on Biafra, things got steadily worse. One night the whole valley seemed to erupt with gunfire; it seemed a massive battle was raging for the capture of Uyo. This was to continue for two very anxious days. At dawn we dared not go to the chapel for Mass. Soon, mortar fire began, and we started to make provisions for our own safety if a shell should bring down the roof. There were some empty beds, so we got wire netting and put it on top of the supports for the mosquito netting, and placed mattresses on top. It felt a bit safer, lying on our beds listening to the incessant noise outside. One very heavy blast sounded as if a shell had exploded just outside, so we stood beside the staircase for some time with wicker baskets as makeshift helmets.

That was the longest day. The hours passed so slowly and the shooting showed no signs of letting up. I imagined as I lay on my bed that there must be a sniper holed up behind a tree beside the house, and they were trying to take him out. In the early afternoon lull (even soldiers take a siesta), the rooster crowed once or twice. I could have wrung its neck. We feared that it would draw attention to us, and at any moment we would be confronted by frenzied fighting men. We later heard of two Methodist missionaries in Okigwi who were killed in similar circumstances.

We had draped our white cassocks on the veranda wall as a sign of 'surrender' in the event of the Nigerian soldiers coming to the house. Soon a jeep came up our driveway, filled with red-capped soldiers and one civilian; he had contacted the army to ensure our safe passage from Biafra to more secure 'Nigerian' territory. In a few minutes we were in the open jeep driving past the busy looters, who probably thought we were prisoners – which technically, I suppose, we were.

We had to learn how to live in a new situation when the Nigerians took control and a sort of peace returned. I got a lesson on the first Sunday I went out with my Mass-box in Uyo. I ran into a group of self-appointed vigilantes and one wisp of a lad insisted on inspecting the box. I stoutly refused. We

traded words and when he said that the 'Reverend Fathers' were Biafran sup-
porters, I caught him by the neck and threatened to take him before the
Commander for spreading rumours. I was galvanised and tensed up more than
I had realised, but I must have frightened him as we were allowed to pass on.
Spreading rumours was a serious affair in the Uyo world; the consequences
could be fatal.

Revd J. Leslie Crampton grew up in Crumlin, Co. Dublin. After serving in
Northern Ireland, he, his wife Janet, and their one-year-old daughter moved to
Rhodesia (now Zimbabwe) in 1973. There, they worked under the auspices of the
Anglican USPG – Leslie as a rector and Janet as a nurse. Two more children were
born in Rhodesia, before they moved to Co. Wexford in 1982.

Zimbabwe: I remember the first day of 'one man, one vote'

I remember the day in 1980 when the election results were announced, when
Zanu-PF under Robert Mugabe won with a great majority. Prior to this, Ian
Smith had been the white Prime Minister, and no black person had ever voted
in an election here. I think most Europeans thought that there would be a
communist-style government under Zanu-PF, as the ministers were known as
'Comrade'. Also, I think most of us expected Ian Smith and other leading
white politicians to be assassinated or jailed. In fact, Mugabe did not treat the
white politicians badly, but was quite severe in his treatment of those of his fellow black Africans who were not supportive of him.

Janet and I had the privilege of voting in that election. Everyone who
voted had to dip their right hand in dye or ink to prevent anyone voting more
than once, because there were no voting cards.

In Fort Victoria (now Masvingo), where I was rector and where our children went to a government-run school, we were party to the introduction of
integrated education for white and black children. I very much welcomed this
development. However, many parents of white children were concerned that
their children would be disadvantaged by this, because they thought black and
coloured children would struggle to keep pace academically.

Children entered primary school aged six – but many black children had
never been issued with a birth certificate. The school authorities were able to
carry out an interesting test to decide the child's age. If a child could put their
right arm over their head, and hold their left arm with their right hand, then
(s)he was old enough to enter primary school!

Times of change

Trade sanctions at that time meant that petrol was scarce, so getting around was difficult. Also, there were only simple items to buy in a shop – although we even had a Spar supermarket in Umtali (now Mutare)! This was not unlike today of course, where people literally need to be millionaires in Zimbabwe to buy basic commodities like bread or maize. So, we grew our own fruit, thanks to good water conservation by the Rhodesian government.

I personally did not experience any friction between the white and the black people, although this is not to say it did not exist. As we were living in a white-European area, we mostly spoke English. I did learn some of the local Shona language and could read the liturgy to the Africans in Shona. However, I needed an interpreter for the sermon or for announcements – I felt this was a weakness in my ministry.

I lived in times of great change there. Before we left Umtali, we had the privilege of attending the consecration of the very first black African bishop in Rhodesia, Peter Hatendi. I served under Bishop Hatendi for two years, and then under Bishop Jonathan Siyachitema in the new diocese of Lundi. Their consecrations were both significant and joyful occasions: people literally sang and danced in the aisles of the cathedral.

Sheilagh Jebb served as a nurse with the Anglican organisation CMS Ireland in Nigeria, from 1950 to 1976. After that, she also worked in Yemen, Sudan, Sierra Leone, and The Gambia. Her father, Revd Charles W. Jebb from Ardee, Co. Louth, was a pioneering missionary in Nigeria from 1907 to 1933. She declined an OBE for her work from Queen Elizabeth II, and published her memoirs, *Going for God*, in 2008. She has lived in Bangor, Co. Down since 1992.

Smuggling refugees during the Nigerian civil war (1967–70)

In 1967, I planned to take my leave and visit Yankiri Game Reserve. But this was not to be, as travelling soon became fraught with difficulty. There had been horrible tales of Ibo people – even children – being killed in the north by the Hausas among whom they had lived for many years, their own part of the country being overcrowded. As the Ibo were enterprising and clever and were literate in English, they tended to get the jobs in the railway and post offices, and some others became prosperous traders. But they were also quick-tempered and lacked the refined manners of the Hausa.

I saw lorry-loads of these refugees streaming south, some with no idea where to go, as many had never before been to their 'homeland'. At the mission station, the Ibo steward hardly dared leave our compound for fear of being identified. One day Bishop Kale phoned: 'Get your Ibo to some safe place.' We went to bed not knowing what to do. We could not drive them to their 'homeland', given the amount of army and police checkpoints. We had heard of passengers being taken off public transport vehicles and asked to say the word *toro*. Most Ibo pronounced it *tolo* instead, and were killed or harmed. However, a Yoruba tribeswoman told us she could find a safe place.

Our Ibo driver was dark-skinned and could pass as a Yoruba, and he could also speak the Yoruba language. The Ibo steward, on the other hand, looked like an Ibo, so at each checkpoint we had to try to hide him and divert attention away from him. What was supposedly the most dangerous checkpoint, we approached with much trepidation, only to find the barrier wide open. The driver hesitated to go through, as the soldiers often shot at the tyres if this was done, but nothing happened. We reached the safe house, where the two Ibo went into hiding.

On the way back, at the same checkpoint, the road was barred and dozens of soldiers swarmed around my car. They emptied everything out, and demanded to know what I was doing. I told them I had been visiting friends, and was eventually allowed to go home.

Bishop William Slattery is a Franciscan, originally from Killenaule, Co. Tipperary. After working in South Africa – in Johannesburg, Ladysmith, and Pretoria – he was appointed head of the diocese of Kokstad, his current location, in 1993. He has published writings in Zulu, Sesotho and Xhosa.

Pretoria seminary

The most difficult time was when there was a hanging at Pretoria's Maximum Correctional Centre prison nearby. It was in the years between 1984 and 1991, and some of those executed were condemned for opposing the apartheid state with force. I was Rector of the National Seminary in those years. The executed were heroes to the black seminarians, who held a prayer vigil on the night before each execution. The minority of white students felt such times as tense and confusing. They had had to do military service under the policy of national conscription.

These were the years after the Soweto uprising of youth, and the slogan was 'Liberation before Education'. This put further pressure on African students as their peers outside saw them as opting out of the struggle. As a body the seminarians were good, but they were young and easily disturbed.

Other African countries were more physically demanding than modern South Africa, but during apartheid the country was a social hell. Apartheid was built on centuries of vicious segregation. Unfortunately, it had been very successful in dividing people on racial grounds. Students from all racial groups met for the first time in the seminary, having previously known nothing about each other. The staff were Irish Franciscans.

We allowed the students to celebrate the martyrs of Africa, and to celebrate the heroes of the Africans' struggle. I used to smile at the songs sung by the seminarians in Zulu and Sotho; they were generally revolutionary, but thankfully the white students did not understand the words. In this situation of national chaos it was of prime importance to insist on spiritual direction. We were lucky in those years to have with us Fr Con Murphy (SMA) and Fr Kevin Egan (OFM) as spiritual directors, who understood the human yearnings of the seminarians.

Perhaps the most dramatic moment was in 1985, when the students decided to march on the Union Buildings in Pretoria, the seat of the government executive. This was the symbol of white power, and it was illegal to go within a mile of the place in a protest march. The students wanted to present a letter of demand for the release of Mandela and to have democratic elections. It was a difficult decision to allow them to go. The previous week, when university students had protested in Johannesburg, the police opened fire when students disrupted traffic. However, having agreed with the students that they should wear their cassocks and not disrupt traffic or be violent I allowed them to go. About thirty-seven of the ninety students set off.

On arrival at the Union Buildings, the students found the deputy minister of foreign affairs holding a press conference for foreign journalists. The international media had heard the old excuses for apartheid before and felt that the apparition of these clergy, praying rosaries and singing hymns, and marching on government offices, was much more newsworthy. Some of the students with relatives overseas received phone calls later from London and other parts of Europe. The protest had gone around the world.

Many of these students have now become excellent priests and bishops around South Africa. The apartheid era was a difficult time, but a time in which one saw the work of the Holy Spirit in human souls. Those seminary years allowed our students to mature in their humanity.

Once, a student explained to me what apartheid had done to the African's self-esteem. As a child he had gone with his grandfather to buy a cow from a white farmer. His grandfather was a respectable, elderly African gentleman. The item of clothing that the old man prized above all else was his hat – he would not allow any child even to touch the hat. His lovely hat defined him. His grandfather and the young white farmer began to haggle about the price of the cow, and the young boy saw something amazing. His grandfather had taken off this sacred hat in front of the young man and was crumpling it behind his back as if it were a paper bag. The student explained that for him this symbolised what apartheid had done to the African soul.

It was a great grace to have been with young African people at that time. They were very generous in mind and spirit. Their ability to tolerate and learn from overseas people like myself in the heart of their struggle was generosity itself.

Fr James Higgins (SMA) was born in Co. Sligo in 1924. He has been teaching and ministering in Nigeria since the 1960s. In 2004, he published his memoir, *The pilgrim soul in me*.

The soldiers turned their attention to us

The Nigerian civil war – when Biafra, in the south-east, tried to secede from the Federation – began in May 1967, my first year there. I recall two incidents very vividly.

The local commander in Auchi had permitted six girls, who were unable to return to their homes in northern Nigeria, to stay in the Sacred Heart College in Ubiaja. Unfortunately, one Sunday evening when returning to the college compound, they were spotted by some Biafran soldiers patrolling in a jeep. They were recognised as northerners and were taken to the local headquarters in Igueben for 'questioning'.

The parish priest, Bill Kennedy, was informed, and he went there immediately. The local officers weren't very happy to see him. They insisted that they must keep the girls overnight until they saw their boss in Auchi. But Bill was adamant. They were placed under his protection, and if they were to be kept by the guards he would stay with them. Eventually, the guards gave in to the wishes of the parish priest. Fr Bill took the girls back to Ubiaja where they remained unmolested until Liberation Day. No doubt he saved them from a frightening experience. One of their captors had reminded him: 'See what their brothers did to our sisters in northern Nigeria.'

The other incident that I remember most clearly occurred at 'liberation' time. The Federal troops had halted the Biafran advance, and the Biafrans were retreating rapidly. One morning, Bill Kennedy and I noticed a commotion near our front gate – some locals had brought in an Ibo man who was unlucky enough to remain behind. The soldiers approached him and made him kneel down. Bill and myself moved towards them, but tempers were high, and there was little we could do to save him. Bill gave him conditional absolution, and he was shot there in our presence. The soldiers turned their attention to us and shouted at us, accusing us of interfering and siding with the Biafrans.

We walked slowly back to the house amid this torrent of abuse with guns pointing at our backs. Cold sweat was pouring off me during that forty-yard walk. I think neither before nor since did I feel death so close. It was a Saturday afternoon. The commanding officer forbade us to leave the compound without his permission.

Sr Elizabeth McCarthy, from West Cork, spent twenty-six years in Uganda, living through the Idi Amin regime. She also lived in Cameroon, Burundi, and Kenya. Prior to working in Africa she worked in England as a teacher, studied for a Masters in Paris, and did part of her early formation as a nun in Belgium.

When Tanzania invaded in 1979

Our community house in Mbarara, Uganda, was situated on the hill of Nyamitanga, close to the cathedral. I remember one morning as I opened the door to go out to Mass at 7am, I saw what seemed like a convoy of soldiers heading straight for our house. One soldier approached as if to enter. Not quite sure what to do, I greeted him as if he was a civilian! 'Can I invite you for a cup of tea?'

He was having none of it. 'You move, I shoot,' he retorted, pushing past me, followed by several others. I stood rooted to the spot until they had passed and then made my way to Mass. We later discovered that the army had heard a rumour that a convoy of weapons had come to our mission so they came to search the house. On entering the room of Sr Katie, one of our older nuns, the soldier had told her to take her cases off the top of the cupboard. 'I think you are stronger than me. You do it', said she. And he agreed! Br Karl, a German Brother, was asked to lie down, which he did. In crisis moments one's actions or reactions are not at all premeditated. On that occasion our students, though frightened, were not molested in any way.

A slightly scarier episode happened in Fort Portal. We had evacuated from Mbarara and were being housed in a small staff house attached to the training college of Kinymasika, which was then directed by our Sisters. One night the besieging 'liberation army' from Tanzania invaded our compound. Their main aim was to take our car and any others around. As a precaution we had removed the battery, because a car, after all, was a life-line. They were furious and made their way to our small house and pounded on the fragile door. We just prayed that the knocking at the door would cease. It did, eventually. We were yet again saved through the power of prayer.

I was due for home leave a while later. En route to Kampala/Entebbe we called in on the Medical Missionary Sisters at Kitovu. A huge crater had been made by a bomb just beside the house. The town of Masaka was decimated. The relief of going home was mixed with sadness at leaving some others behind amid all the destruction caused by war.

Four of us set out for the airport early on a Sunday morning. Mona and I had collected a new Toyota car at Mombasa some time previously. We were about half way to Entebbe when a car drove up beside us and guns were pointed in our direction. Diane handed over the keys of the car. We scrambled out. There were four men, and I was confronted by one of them. I recall he was wearing a red shirt and actually looked more frightened than I was! 'I could shoot you', he said. Recalling a passage from scripture, I took off my jacket and handed it over. I suppose that was taken as a sign of surrender, and off he went. I remember the screeching of tyres as they made off, leaving us white as sheets and penniless on the roadside. Soon enough, a bus passing by noticed our predicament. They offered to drive us to Kampala and the police station.

Many friends helped us to rearrange tickets, which had been in my jacket pocket, and procure travel documents. I reached Brussels Airport in the middle of the night and was received with open arms by our community at Rue de Lindhout. A few days later they got me on a flight to Cork, and home.

Paul O'Callaghan, born in Co. Dublin in 1980, spent three years living and working with VMM (Volunteer Missionary Movement) in four countries in East Africa: Kenya, Tanzania, Rwanda, and the Democratic Republic of Congo. In 2008, he wrote an unpublished book, *Travel tales from the Continent of Golden Joys – musings from the missions.* He is currently studying for a doctorate in child psychology at Queen's University, Belfast, as part of which he has journeyed to Uganda to work with former child soldiers.

Rwanda: weeping for the children who are no more

Rwanda is infamous for the genocide that occurred there in 1994. Although a visit to Kigali's Genocide Memorial is an ordeal that is both distressing and disturbing, it is an obvious starting point for anyone who wants to understand the political events that set Rwanda ablaze at the beginning of the 1990s.

The lawns of Kigali's Genocide Memorial site are immaculately clipped, the borders are flower-lined, and the balcony of the old colonial house is dazzlingly white. It is hard then to come to terms with the fact that here, in this 'picture-postcard perfect' place, over a quarter of a million murder victims lie buried. In the space of one hundred days, close to one million people were savagely murdered, two million people were displaced and a staggering half-a-million women and children were violated, many by men who knew they were HIV positive. An attempted 'final solution' of a whole ethnic group was orchestrated and carried out under the eyes, ears and nose of the international community which, ignobly, failed to intervene.

For many who visit the memorial, the most poignant part of the presentation is the upper room, dedicated to child casualties of war and genocide. Here, the impersonal toll of the statistics is enfleshed as one reads the names, favourite food, favourite drink, and last recorded words of a minuscule sample of children who lost their lives. One example sticks in my mind. It is of a little girl of no more than seven who is fleeing with her mother from the blood-thirsty mob pursuing them with machetes and knives. She pleads with her mother to protect her as she pitiably informs her that she just can't run anymore. She is killed immediately after witnessing her own mother's bloody demise.

The question that I asked myself over and over again during my time in Rwanda was how a nation could possibly mend the fabric of a society that had been rent asunder by such unspeakable barbarity and inhumanity. Despite the new-found prosperity, caused in part by extensive investment by a conscience-pricked international community, one still gets the impression that Rwanda is a spring-loaded high-tension trap that could snap at any moment.

This feeling of underlying tension was confirmed when I heard that, last March, a guard was shot dead while on duty outside the site of the Genocide Memorial in Kigali. A sign perhaps of the simmering discontent that exists with the 'official history' of the genocide that tends to paint one side as the victims and the other side as the perpetrators.

Yet the government of Rwanda continues to ensure that no-one will forget what happened in 1994, by erecting memorials, preserving genocide scenes, holding a month-long recollection every year and making sure all Rwandan children study the genocide in school. Can we say the same thing as an international community? After all, it was European policy that first created these ethnic divisions and then refused to intervene when terror visited their streets and homes. May God and the Rwandan people forgive us all.

Sr Louis Marie O'Connor was born in Kanturk, Co. Cork. She worked for more than forty years in Sierra Leone, as a teacher and in organising projects and supports for local women. She has been in Ireland since the mid-1990s.

Man's inhumanity to man: from war to peace in Sierra Leone

Rumours of war became a reality for the people of the Kono district of Sierra Leone in October 1992. Rebels roamed the area, showing respect for neither life nor property. People fled in terror. Thousands of displaced men, women and children moved around in search of safety.

At this development, we Sisters of St Joseph of Cluny in Makeni, in the Northern Province, experienced a range of emotions – shock and disbelief at first, then deep compassion for those who knocked at our door looking for help. Our community in Makeni kept in constant contact with our Sisters in Magburaka, eighteen miles away. On our way there one day, towards the end of October 1992, we met people walking with bleeding, swollen feet, children tagging along crying with hunger, fear and fatigue. Men and women had small children tied to their backs; the older children carried their possessions in pitiful bundles on their heads. Where could these wretched refugees go?

Thank God, the people of Makeni opened their hearts and doors to complete strangers. Many a home had up to forty people sleeping in it at night. They slept on every available space on the floor. But where to get food for them? Where to get proper lodgings for them? The problems were enormous and it took a lot of pushing and pleading to move those in authority to assist these helpless people. Eventually, funds were provided and administered by Caritas. The local authorities gave the displaced people a large plot of land. They got together to clear the land, dug wells and latrines, and encouraged families to build mud huts. Everyone helped and soon the 'Camp for Displaced People' became a reality.

Many of the neediest came to our Loreto Clinic. As we Sisters sat down to lunch one Saturday, an emaciated man came to the door looking for food. He was sick, hungry, tired and alone. We gave him a hot meal, some clothing and food to take away and he set off to find his brother. Later in the evening, a mother with eight children came. They were in rags, their feet bleeding, they were hungry and had no shelter. Loreto Clinic was opened and each one was seen to. The eldest boy had sickle cell anaemia and needed care. Caritas had given food, clothing and a sum of money to the Sister in charge of the clinic to be used for such people. Our help was so much appreciated by the mother and her children that night.

The influx of people increased. Hundreds of them arrived sick. As far as possible nobody was turned away from the clinic. Those too ill to be treated by us were referred to the St John of God Brothers' Hospital in Lunsar, forty miles away. The Brothers were wonderful, always trying to help those referred by us. Here I must say a word of praise too for the local clinic staff. All were married women with families. Not once did we hear them complain of the long hours of hard work required to help these poor people. Some took displaced people into their homes. All have shown a great example of Christian leadership in a basic Christian community.

The stories told by the refugees were heart-rending. One day, in the midst of the orderly chaos, a mother and her five children arrived looking for help. All work and all talk ceased as we listened to this weeping mother's story. She had been running away with her children when they ran into an ambush. She was stopped at gunpoint, and watched as her oldest boy, fourteen years old, was told to lie on the ground to be decapitated. She cried and begged so forcefully that the rebels relented and told them to get going. That had happened two days previously. This little family had already lost their father. They had walked all those miles through the bush and were now turning to us for help. The staff all came forward and, in the total silence following her harrowing story, we and the patients prayed together for healing for the family and for peace in Sierra Leone. Fortunately, we were able to help them. The mother attached herself to the staff and did odd jobs around the place so they were assured of food each day.

A young man came for treatment for horrific wounds sustained while being tortured as a 'suspected rebel'. Man's inhumanity to man left us trembling again that day. Both arms were like raw meat where the ropes used to tie his arms, elbow to elbow, behind his back, had cut into his flesh. His hands were paralysed. Have you ever tried touching your right elbow with your left one behind your back? We all tried in the clinic that first day. We all failed. We dressed his wounds as best we could, and gave him medicine, food and clothing. The anger of that young man, his fear and hurt were so deep and his protestations so loud that I took him for a long drive to allow him to give vent to all his feelings. After a few days we brought him for physiotherapy and eventually for skin grafts at the Leprosy Hospital in Masanga, about thirty miles away. He recovered gradually.

People with infected sores were treated daily. Dozens of poor people were limping or had lost upper and/or lower limbs. Malnutrition was found in people of all ages. It is heart-rending to see an emaciated mother struggling to suckle her equally emaciated baby and to feed her other hungry children too.

We purchased, using funds kindly donated by families and friends of the nuns, high protein food to give to those malnourished people. Only God can reward the donors. We continue to pray for them daily.

During the early part of 1993, we saw hundreds of children with measles. Many were so weak that they did not survive. The director of UNICEF visited our clinic and learned that we were receiving no help with medicines. When he saw the numbers and the help being given, he immediately ordered several cartons of medicines and made the order a standing one each month. This eased the pressure on clinic funds. The doctor called several times during the year to encourage all of us and we were extremely grateful to him.

A very sad side to the story is the number of widows, widowers and orphans left behind. Pregnant women had delivered babies on the roadside as they ran for safety. Too weak to get up, more often than not they died. Somebody would take the tiny baby and continue to run. Many of these babies survived, saved by the milk and food given at the clinic.

The Kono area, much fought over because of its diamond reserves, was eventually declared safe and people began to return home. In truth, for many there was nothing left to go home to. Houses had been burned to the ground, some with people in them. Now would come the heartbreak of looking for those who might never be seen again: husbands, wives, mothers, fathers, sons, daughters, brothers, sisters. Now more than ever, the people need support. They will continue to need material, spiritual, and psychological help.

Let us pray that a spirit of lasting peace, love and brotherhood will prevail in this beautiful land.

Sr Teresa McKeon is from Streamstown, Co. Westmeath. She went to Sierra Leone in 1954, before its independence, and has worked in various parts of the country and in Guinea. She is now in active retirement with the Kono people, with whom she worked in the refugee camps.

Guinea: life in a refugee camp

The decade-long (1991–2001) bloody civil war in Sierra Leone took its toll in every region of the country. The atrocities by the rebels forced thousands either into displacement in other war-torn areas of the country, or to seek refuge in the neighbouring Republic of Guinea. 300,000 Sierra Leonean refugees found themselves in Guinea, where they lodged in numerous camps.

In 1995, the Sisters of St Joseph of Cluny were forced to leave Sierra Leone, along with other missionary congregations. It was the first time in 129 years that there were no Cluny Sisters in the country. Some of the nuns, rather than returning home, went to Guinea, where they lived in the refugee camps, helping the most vulnerable groups – women and children. For five years they worked there in various camps, until Guinea itself, the host country, came under several rebel attacks in the year 2000.

Once again, the refugees were forced to flee. Many of them were able to return to their homes, but the eastern region, a diamondiferous area, was still unsafe. The Konos, who came from this region, had to live in internal displacement camps for a further two years. The following text is from a letter sent home to my friends in Ireland near the end of the war:

> Dear Sisters,
> A lot has happened since you last heard from us. We have moved from Fangamandou camp (Guinea) to a new camp, Kat Kama.
>
> We had spent three fruitful years living in Fangamandou camp, close to the border with Sierra Leone. However, 1999 began as a year of great uncertainty and insecurity, with threats of rebel attacks on our camp. The United Nations High Commission for Refugees (UNHCR) decided to move the camp further inland, but many of the refugees were reluctant to leave, since they had lived there since 1991. To add to the tension, the local citizens did not want them to move either, since they were benefiting from the refugee supplies! And nobody seemed to know when the move was going to happen.
>
> It's no easy achievement to move thousands of refugees, so for months we were in a kind of limbo, not knowing when or where we were going. Meanwhile, the roads out of the camps were fast becoming impassable since the rains came earlier than usual and we Sisters feared we would be cut off from Guechedou (the provincial HQ), as happened last year. To make the 64km journey to Guechedou to get provisions, etc., was a real feat – one needed all the blessings of Allah to get there safely.
>
> New sites were being prepared by UNHCR along the main road to Conakry, to accommodate the refugees who would be moving. Huge plastic-covered dormitories would receive them until they were able to build their own mud booths. One can just imagine the heat inside these shelters, exposed as they are to the burning sun without an atom of shade, since all of the trees had to be cut down to make room for them. We identified one of the largest of these sites to pitch our own tent. By June many of the camps surrounding Fangamandou

were on the move, as was the largest one in Fangamandou itself. By the beginning of July we ourselves were ready to move.

It was not easy to say farewell to the beneficiaries of our efforts, both refugees and citizens, with whom we had spent three happy years. All were so grateful for the training they had received. But it was the very old and the children that we felt we were abandoning, since they benefited from our material assistance. However, to our amazement, there was no groaning or moaning, only gratitude for all we had done for them, expressed in song and a strong belief that the God who had provided for them would continue to do so. A truly amazing people and for us a very humbling experience.

As I write this I am sitting here in our new camp, Kat Kama, in one of our training booths, a kind of makeshift shelter erected with bush sticks and a grass roof. No need for doors and windows as it is open all around. So it's gloriously cool – a welcome escape from the burning heat outside. Since we arrived here in September eight of these booths have been erected on a lovely site assigned to us by the UNHCR. The refugee men and women do all the work, the latter bringing all the sticks and grass from the surrounding bush, while the men folk do the construction work – a marvellous feat of engineering, since everything is done by hand, without any tools apart from a cutlass. To complete the picture, an office and all-purpose room have yet to be constructed – a somewhat more sophisticated building since it needs walls, doors and windows!

Since house construction is one of the skills the young women want to learn they have already begun the making of the mud blocks using the rich soil from the anthills around. So the site is a hive of activity with long lines of women carrying sticks, like a moving forest, while others carry the long grass for thatching on their heads, with babies, sometimes invisible under the grass, on their backs. In a corner, a small group of women are busy preparing and cooking the midday meal, a large pot of *bulghor* and palm oil sauce, a real treat for refugees. As one fellow said the other day, licking his fingers, 'This is citizen, not refugee, chop' (the host population are referred to as 'citizens').

Sr Maria McCarthy seems to have got a new lease of life in this new camp! She is out visiting the 'vulnerable', as they are called – the very old and the handicapped, many of whom are amputees, whose faces light up with her golden handshake. They are the most neglected in camp life. Some of these old women, recognising that they did not fit into any category for training, soon let us know their needs. Their occupation, back in Sierra Leone, had been spinning cotton, which they did in their own homes. They communicated their need for this work to Sister in sign language, miming the various movements of their skill. But there could be no spinning because there was no money to buy cotton, the raw material required.

Now Sr Maria is in the process of setting up a cotton industry for these old ladies. To confirm their eligibility for this business they take off their head-ties to show their grey hair! Sister is the buying agent for the cotton, which is grown in the area and which she will distribute to these women, who will then be happily occupied. They will get a market for their thread in our own project since weaving is one of the skills the younger women learn. We only hope the supplies will not exceed the demands.

So once again we begin anew, grateful to the good Lord for the health and energy to do so, while waiting for the peace agreement in Sierra Leone to take shape.

Fionnbarra Ó Cuilleanáin, from Cork, is a member of the Society of African Missions. He is currently living in Cork City. He originally wrote the following piece (here slightly abridged) from Rwanda for readers of the *Cork Holly Bough* in 1995.

Rwandan massacre: Munster's response

We have put behind us the most tragic year in the history of Central Africa. Ethnic wars raged in Rwanda and Burundi. A million people were massacred in a campaign of genocide all over Rwanda. The majority Hutu government, army and police planned to annihilate, once and for all, the minority Tutsis (only fifteen per cent of the population), who had kept them under subjection for centuries. They succeeded fairly well, killing even the smallest children and babies. *Dia idir sinn agus an t-olc.*

Many of the most educated and capable people from all sections of society were killed – teachers, lawyers, business people, politicians, military officers, professors, farmers, doctors, nurses, and community leaders. There was no distinction made – all Tutsis were to be killed. All the churches suffered big losses of personnel. Among those killed in the Catholic Church were 4 bishops, 115 priests, 130 sisters, 60 brothers and 86 seminarians.

During the massacres, a well-trained Tutsi army was advancing from Uganda. Young men, who had themselves gone as refugees to Uganda a generation before, were now returning, well armed, to retake control of the country. Fearing retaliation by the Tutsi army, about two million Hutus fled Rwanda into neighbouring Tanzania and Zaire. In one day alone, a quarter of a million people crossed the Rusumo Bridge into Tanzania. It was the quickest exodus of that size ever witnessed, and overnight Banaco Camp became the second largest city in Tanzania and the biggest refugee camp in the world.

Setting up a city nearly twice the size of Cork is a major task. The new refugee camps had no roads, no houses, no water supply, no food, no toilets. There was absolutely no infrastructure, just hundreds of thousands of people resting in a safe place in the bush after escaping with their lives.

Concern and GOAL were in the forefront of the aid programme in Ngara and the people of Ireland responded with their traditional generosity. NGOs from all continents set up their camps, roads were built, and thousands of tents were erected, as well as tented hospitals and schools. Pit-toilets were dug by the refugees themselves, bore-holes were drilled, and a water supply was installed. Now there are six camps in the Ngara district of Tanzania, with a total of about 400,000 refugees.

While the refugees were still coming in their thousands, the Church in Tanzania appealed for priests to minister in the camps. Without hesitation, Fr Tony Gill (SMA) from Dublin, packed his jeep and set out for the refugee camps, a two-day journey from his mission in Kilulu near Lake Victoria. That was the beginning of the SMA Rwanda-Burundi refugee mission. Now in its second year (in 1995), the mission is well-established and serving three camps with a population of about 100,000 people. I moved to the refugee mission in early June to replace Fr Dan Cashman (SMA), who was going home to Millstreet for a well-earned holiday after spending several months living in a tent among the refugees.

Life in the refugee camps goes on just as in any other African village. The children are out playing as if nothing happened. But many of the adults and youths have still not gotten over the trauma. I usually spend the afternoons strolling around from tent to tent, visiting a different road each day. Everywhere I go, crowds of children and adults run to welcome me, shake hands and invite me into their tents, which are just shelters from the sun and the rain. We have many nice friendly chats there. They ask me to bless the old people, the sick, and those troubled by evil spirits. Malaria is the most common disease here among young and old, and even the Padre gets it occasionally.

Since I came here I have seen no rain. The camps are full of dust from all the UN water tankers, and Red Cross and other NGO vehicles speeding by all day. Many people suffer from throat and lung infections. In mid-August we were invaded by millions of ugly bluebottle flies. They are everywhere and it is a constant battle to keep them off the food. Small babies on their mothers' backs are particularly vulnerable, with flies landing on their eyes, ears, mouth and nose.

When travelling around the camps I visit the Irish volunteers working with Concern and GOAL. The door is always open; there is always a *céad mile fáilte*. Ireland can be proud of the wonderful work they are doing for the refugees. Kitali Camp has nearly 70,000 refugees and is run by a dynamic GOAL team. The camp manager is Niall O'Keeffe, from Newmarket. Other Munster volunteers in Kitali are Charlie Moore (Midleton), Michael Doyle (Youghal), Ann Hodnet (Ballymacoda), Helen Geraghty (Limerick) and Brian Kavanagh from my own parish of Ballinlough in Cork. Any time I pass the GOAL base I call in to read 'de paper'. With so many Munster people working there, the *Examiner* arrives frequently. It is a great thrill to get all the news from home.

Fifty kilometres away from Kitali is Lumasi Camp, where Anthony Coleman (Kilmeady, Co. Limerick) works with Concern in distributing food. In Rwanda I met John 'Ginger' O'Leary (Cork), who is on leave from the army at Collins Barracks to serve in Rwanda. With him is Michael Williams (Glandore). Both of them work with Trócaire in Gikongoro, together with many other Irish volunteers involved in the recovery and development of Rwanda.

We expect the SMA refugee mission to be here for many years. Rwanda and Burundi are still in the grip of extreme ethnic tensions. Recently, I visited the village of Ntarama in Central Rwanda, where one of the many massacres occurred last year. Five hundred Tutsis took refuge in the church; they were all killed, as were five hundred more outside. Their bodies were still lying on the church floor. Some were hanging over seats, their clothes stained with dried blood. Children and small babies had had their skulls smashed open. School children's exercise books were scattered among the bodies. The stench of death and decaying human flesh was everywhere.

After I left the church, the awful smell remained in my nostrils and on my hands for the whole day. It was the most horrifying experience I had in my twenty-seven years as a missionary in Africa.

CHAPTER SIX

Epiphanies – Moments of Joy, Moments of Sorrow

Fr Sean O'Leary served with the Spiritans in Taiwan from 1997 to 2008, and speaks fluent Chinese. Prior to that he lived in Kenya. Orginally from Cork, he now resides in Dublin.

Christmas Day, 1993

As part of my formation with the Spiritans (Holy Ghost Fathers), I was sent to Kenya for two years of overseas training. The mission was situated in East Pokot, which is in northern Kenya, and I lived and shared the life of the Pokot people. The area is a semi-arid region and the Pokot people are semi-nomadic pastoralists. Their lives revolve around the keeping of livestock: cows, sheep, goats and camels. They roam the land in search of grazing and water for the animals and consequently their homes are always temporary dwellings made of sticks, mud and grass. The staple food of the people is milk mixed with blood from the animals, as well as some wild vegetables. The cow is very precious in Pokot as their very lives depend on their livestock; each one had a name, and the children would sing songs to the cows while herding them at night.

The environment is very harsh and prone to drought. My first year in Pokot was a drought year and it was heart-breaking to see how the dams dried up, and there was no water or grass for the animals – and therefore no food for the people. It was a real struggle to survive, and many of the people did not make it through the drought season. But I was struck by their toughness, their vitality and their humour. They loved life and loved to celebrate. That which was most precarious was also most precious.

The day the rains finally arrived that first year, the heavens opened up and it rained and rained – for a full three days and three nights. The land was miraculously transformed almost overnight. After the first twenty-four hours of rain I came out of my room and looked down onto valleys of green shoots and waters tumbling down from the mountains. The land was transformed and the hearts of the people were also transformed – the drought was over, we had survived another year and it was time to party! The air was full of the sound of unconfined joy – singing, dancing and celebration.

I will never forget my first Christmas spent in Pokot. On Christmas Eve, a twelve-year-old shepherd boy, David, was brought to the clinic at the mission. Two nights previously, while he was out minding the cattle, a snake had bitten him and his friends had brought him in for treatment. They had walked many miles to reach us, and the time it took to treat the wound would prove to be very costly. We gave him our strongest medicine and hoped for the best. On Christmas morning, one of the workers informed me that David had died; the poison had already spread through his body and he was not strong enough to survive. On the day we celebrate the birth of the Good Shepherd into the world, a young shepherd sadly departed from it.

The Pokot are very superstitious concerning dead bodies and everyone quickly hurried away from the mission, leaving me and our cook to take the body and find a place to bury David. We drove up into the hills and found a suitable place for the burial. As the sun relentlessly bore down on us, we dug the hole which would be David's last resting place, and gently laid the young boy inside.

We had to find his family, and inform them of the tragic loss of their son. As we approached the compound I could hear the laughter and joy – the family were having a celebration, and I'm sure that they felt so happy and relieved that their boy David was in safe hands at the mission clinic. It was very difficult to break the news to his father, and as we left the compound we could hear the screams and cries of the women. Their laughter was suddenly turned into unbridled mourning.

That was my first Christmas Day in Kenya, and every Christmas I light a candle for David – buried in an anonymous grave in northern Kenya. I light a candle to remember that little shepherd boy and to celebrate his short life. In the Biblical tradition, to remember is to make present and I always feel that David's spirit is present with me on Christmas morning.

Sr Louise Shields is from Co. Antrim. She worked in Kenya for ten years, and is now living in Middlesex, England. She is a member of the Congregation of Our Lady of the Missions.

Njeri – aged five years
In the night time, in the early hours of darkness, there was a cry for help. '*Saidia! Saidia!*' These cries were followed by loud prolonged pounding on the

front door of our mission in Ruaraka, Kenya. On opening the door I found a small boy, about ten years old, tears streaming down his face, endlessly repeating in very swift Swahili: 'My little sister, she has died! She has died!' It was as if he was trying to convince himself as well as us of the terrible tragedy that had taken place some hours before. We brought the little lad inside and after calming him down, he was able to tell us the story.

Kariuki lived with his parents, a younger brother and two sisters in a large slum. Their home was a makeshift tin shack in the labyrinth of narrow squalid alleyways which were veined with open drains. People there live lives shaped by abject poverty, hunger, disease, desperation, violence … it is the survival of the fittest. To make life even more difficult, the rains had failed that year and the rivers dried up. There was no water.

One enterprising man, refusing to be beaten, started digging a bore-hole in the hope of finding water. He dug in an open area. He dug relentlessly for hours and after reaching a depth of six feet, he finally found some precious water. Off he hurried to find a container, but in his haste forgot to cover the hole. While he was away, a group of local children came to play in the open space. Among them was Njeri, the little sister of this boy. She was just five years old. Njeri is a Kikuyu name that means 'the jolly one'. She was indeed a very happy little girl, full of life, energy and fun. Whilst playing she accidentally fell into the uncovered bore-hole, banged her head and, in a tragic irony, drowned in a few inches of murky, muddy water.

In most parts of Kenya there are no undertakers. Responsibility for burying loved ones lies solely with the family. Every person who dies is taken to the city mortuary where a post-mortem is carried out. Being very poor, Njeri's family sent the little boy to the only place where help might be forthcoming – the mission.

After hearing his story and visiting the hovel they called home, we tried to do what we could. I remember going to a large fruit shop in Nairobi and begging for an empty orange box. I lined this with some old discarded vestments, complete with a little pillow. This would be little Njeri's coffin. Some time before, my mother had sent a First Communion dress from Ireland. I decided to dress Njeri in it. With the 'coffin' in the boot of the car and the family piled in beside me, we drove to the mortuary. A pall of silent sadness hung over the place, and etched on the faces of those who waited was the pain of loss, a sense of finality, hopelessness, and yes, defeat. Like so many other things in their lives, death was something over which they had no control.

After waiting for a very long time, our little group was allowed into a cold, dreary, and heartless room, where we found Njeri lying on a slab. After washing her tiny body, we dressed her, enfolding her with as much love and care as we could. I remember thinking that this was probably the best dress that little Njeri had ever worn. She looked like a little angel.

Her tiny body fitted perfectly into the converted orange box, so with the lid in place, the 'coffin' was put into the boot of my car. Usually the dead are buried near the home so that even in death their spirit is close to those whom they had loved in life. But this could not be done in the slum, so we buried her in the cemetery. A simple wooden cross, made by a local carver, marks the spot.

Timothy's story

'Of all days, the day in which one has not laughed (or smiled) is the one most surely wasted' – Sebastian Chamfort.

I agree with Chamfort's words. You probably do too. Regular laughter, or at least a smile, is essential for our physical and spiritual well-being. A day without laughter or a smile is a very anaemic one. It was through a smile that I first met Timothy.

I had just changed missions, moving from Ruaraka near Nairobi to a town called Machakos, about fifty miles south of the capital. I had moved from the lush, green and productive *shambas* of the Kikuyu people to where the Kamba tribe were trying to eke out a hopeless existence on land that was as dry, arid and as close to desert as you could get. Famine and drought were frequent visitors. My work in Machakos was to supervise the teaching of Religious Education in nearly three hundred primary schools that were scattered over a very wide area. Thus I was 'on safari' most of the time, trying to visit as many schools as possible.

Syanthi primary school was one of these. It took me a couple of hours to get there travelling over dusty 'roads' that were no more than dirt-tracks, often through dried up river beds. The school consisted of a row of sprawling corrugated-roofed buildings. The walls were built with local red mud bricks. There were holes in the walls where the doors and windows should have been. The floors were earthen, the 'desks' were rough makeshift benches and the only equipment or teaching aids in the classroom consisted of a blackboard and a piece of chalk: no pictures, no books, yet these children wanted to learn more than anything else in the world.

On arrival at Syanthi, I was shown into the head-teacher's office. He brought me to the top class (Standard Seven) to talk to the children. As I walked into the crowded classroom, my eyes were drawn to a young boy who was sitting in the second row. He had the largest, toothiest and happiest smile

I had ever seen. I went over to greet him and great was my surprise when I discovered that he was severely disabled. Where his legs should have been there were two malformed useless feet. He was perched on a roughly hewn bench and in spite of a precarious balancing act he was still smiling. This was Timothy.

The head-teacher explained that Timothy had had polio as a baby and his parents were too poor and too ashamed to get help. 'How long has he been coming to school?' I asked. 'Seven years', I was told. In other words, he had gone right through primary school with his disability, but the fact that he could not walk was a very minor problem for someone as determined as Timothy. In a place where there were no buses or any means of transport except perhaps an ox-cart, my next question was a natural one. 'How does Timothy get to school every day?'

The head-teacher answered by pointing to a rusty, battered old wheelbarrow in the corner of his office. Apparently he was pushed to school each day by his friends who also took care of all his needs. Timothy smiled through it all. His courage and determination amazed me and I wished that I could do something to help him.

I wrote home and Timothy's plight touched the hearts of some children in a small primary school in Crumlin, in Northern Ireland. They went without their lunches and donated the money raised towards the cost of a new wheelchair for Timothy. New horizons and opportunities opened up for him. He proved to be intelligent and a very good student. He finished his education and trained as a shoemaker. He now has his own business in Thika. I know for a fact he is still smiling!

Fr Denis O'Neill served with the Kiltegan Fathers in Kenya from the 1950s, at a time when it was still a British colony. He now lives in his native Dublin.

The call of duty: a day in the life of 'Onilu'

Today I went to a place called Miuuyuni, in the general direction of Kiio. I went by car, as there is a cattle path I can follow. Miuuyuni is one of the most remote places I have ever been to. I called to the school there and met the teachers.

At Miuuyuni I also met an elder called Ngui. His chest was covered with white hair, and scarred; it might have been smallpox. He told me he wanted to go to Sosoma. I knew there was a school there. So remote is Sosoma it is like the end of a long branch hanging over the edge of the world. Ngui told me there was a passable track to the place. On the spur of the moment I decided to take him; I must have been in an adventurous mood! I doubt if many Europeans have ever reached Sosoma. We talked as we went along. Ngui pointed out the abandoned site where he had lived as a child. The family had moved away because of the drought. There are still about forty families scattered over the wide area around Sosoma. As we approached the school I opened the window on Ngui's side, as a few delicate drops of rain fell. 'If this is rain', Ngui said, 'then truly God is here.' In fact it did not rain; at least, not when I was there. But for Ngui a few drops of rain were a blessing on his poor cattle.

The area around Sosoma is semi-desert. There are no roads, no public transport, few bicycles, no shops, no dispensary, no water. To buy salt you would have to walk to Ukasi through miles of bush. The local *shifta* (bandits) are armed with rifles, hand grenades and even machine guns. They are dangerous because they are desperate; there is so little food in the area where they operate.

A woman from Ukasi, which is on the main road between Nguni and Garissa, told me that at one time the bandits as a group walked into Ukasi – naked! They had nothing to eat. If they had come into Ukasi wearing their bandit gear they would have been riddled with arrows by the Wakamba. Appearing naked was evidence of peaceful intent.

Anyhow, I went to the school and chatted to the teachers for a while. There were about thirty or forty children. The schools all have a visitors' book, so I wrote my comments. It was not the kind of place that saw many visitors. I left Ngui in Sosoma and set out for Ukasi, following car tracks. At one point the tracks had been wiped out by a passing herd of cattle or goats and I knew I was off-course. I was not particularly worried because I knew I was in the general vicinity of Kiio. I stopped under a tree. I had a flask of tea with me, and sandwiches, and began to eat.

But you are never alone for long in Africa! Two young girls suddenly appeared, obviously herding. Life in Ukambani (the Wakamba tribal lands) revolves around herding. Youngsters, septuagenarians, octogenarians and nonagenarians, male and female, even tots, all have to herd. Goats and cattle are the only wealth here. Everyone has to tend the family wealth.

'Fathah', said one of the girls, 'have you lost your way?' It seemed she recognised me. Should I have recognised her?

'I remember meeting you before but I have forgotten your name.'

'I am called Kanini', she answered, 'and my friend is called Mwiyathi.'

'It's true', I answered. 'I have gone astray. I was following the car tracks but I lost them. I went to Sosoma with Ngui Malombe.'

'Oh', she said, 'the man with the scars. Has he gone to see his cattle?'

'Yes, Ngui has gone to see his cattle. I left him in Sosoma. You go to school, don't you?', I ventured.

'Yes', she answered, 'I go to school in Miuuyuni. I am in Standard Four class.'

'And your sister', I asked Kanini, 'does she go to school?' Mwiyathi answered, 'I do not go to school.' Kanini then said, accusingly, 'Fathah, you not come to pray with us in Kiio anymore.' I felt like Jonah before the accusing sailors.

'Kanini, I have been away', I answered, 'I went home to see my people but I have come back.' This was not the whole truth. A dose of malaria had laid me low and I had knocked Kiio off the itinerary. The journey there was taking too much out of me.

'And are you not coming to Kiio to pray with us anymore?', she asked.

'Kanini', I promised, 'I will come back to Kiio again.' She insisted, 'We will not believe you, we will think you are cheating us, unless you tell us the day you are coming.' I checked the calendar in my diary. This was becoming serious. 'I will come to Kiio on 3 November – at this time', I said, pointing, 'when the sun is there (about 4pm).'

There are no clocks or watches in Sosoma. Then she asked, 'And the grandmothers, are they to come?'

'Tell your *susu* to come', I said to her, 'the grandmothers above all are to come.'

I took out the sandwiches and gave Kanini and Mwiyathi and another herder who had appeared a piece of sandwich that they graciously accepted. We parted. They showed me the road I was to take and went away laughing and happy. Further on I came across a girl leading a donkey loaded with sacks. Seeing the car, the donkey shied; the loads fell off and became entangled with its legs. I stopped the car.

'Take it easy', I consoled the girl, who identified herself as Mbuthya. 'We will put everything back.' Two boys appeared. All three were neighbours of Kanini and Mwiyathi. 'It is Onilu!' the boys cried. They have difficulties with names ending in a consonant, names like Denis, so I tell everyone my name is 'Onilu'. Then they said, 'You do not come to pray with us anymore.' So I told them of the *kyathi*, the arrangement I had made with Kanini.

It does seem, doesn't it, that I will have to go to Kiio on 3 November!

Sr Mary Dillon is from Co. Clare. She worked as a Columban Sister for many years in hospitals in Korea, before specialising in HIV and moving to Myanmar (Burma), where she now lives.

You never get used to it

You never grow accustomed to the pain and distress, the unremitting sense of loss that is always present in people suffering and dying from AIDS. This is never more true than when the sufferer is a mother.

Lu Pa was one of the many mothers whom I look after daily on my rounds in Burma. I visit a wide area. Most are very poor; they have little to sustain them and oftentimes are bereft of family and friends. Lu Pa was one such woman. Broken-hearted, she had been abandoned by many of her family and friends.

Lu Pa was born where the northern highlands form part of the Himalayas, a place known as Ice Mountain. Beautiful it may be, but it was hard grind to eke out a living there, with days spent climbing steep hillsides looking for vegetables or gathering wood to make a fire. One of eight children, she had left home at thirteen to earn a pittance as a domestic helper in the gold mining area of Hpakant. At eighteen, full of dreams, she married and eventually saved enough to build a small home, and had the joy of giving birth to a son and daughter. Then, one day, her husband fell ill. He was diagnosed with HIV and tuberculosis. She spent their savings and borrowed to care for him. Then she found out that she too had HIV. Exhausted, she came seeking help from my health clinic.

I visited her in a ramshackle house with a leaking roof, holes in the wall and the bare minimum of comfort. Her hostile mother-in-law, with whom she now stayed, blamed her for her son's death. Her space in the house was a mat in the open area facing the entrance. This was her home for herself and her two children. Who can tell her anguish? Day after day I sat listening to her pain, hearing her hopes, and trying impossibly to halt the disease. Some days it was unbearable and she sank into a terrible darkness.

The doctors decided to give her antiretroviral drugs for AIDS. The initial surge of hope faded and she rapidly lost weight. How helpless I felt as we waited those last weeks. No one else came to visit her. In 2006 she died, alone, with only her four-year-old daughter near her. It is heart-breaking that this little girl and her brother are now orphans, left to fend for themselves in a harsh environment. Some months later, it was with a heavy heart I learned that the daughter had contracted HIV from her mother and was also HIV-positive.

No, you never really get used to it.

Doreen Boland (Society of the Sacred Heart) is originally from Blackrock, Dublin. She has spent thirty-two years in Uganda, over two spells. She now lives in France.

Demonstration for peace

During my latter years in Kampala, I belonged to an inter-religious/intercultural group for dialogue. It was when the NRA (National Resistance Army) war was at its height. Our group decided to have a demonstration for peace, in the central park, in the heart of the city, at rush hour one evening.

What kind of demonstration? A demonstration of shared prayer. But how, for example, to name 'God' among all the religions present, while keeping communion among us? We took the decision to have an hour of silent prayer, in full view of passers-by. The hour chosen was between six and seven o'clock in the evening. So we came with our candles.

At exactly 6pm, a little bell was rung. Silence immediately fell on the group of about one hundred participants. We sat down on the grass in a big circle, and each one entered into silent prayer. I was very impressed by the composition of the group, and the deep concentration of everyone. Facing me were two Egyptian Muslim men, and two Punjabi Sheiks in their large turbans, sitting in a yoga position. There were Mexican Indians; Africans – Christian and Muslim; young and old; Americans and Europeans of different denominations ... all deep in intense prayer.

By 6.30pm it was dark. Silently our candles were lit, and were placed on the grass in front of each of us. Since this was a 'demonstration', the police were present, but when they saw us all sitting down, they too sat down at a little distance from us, and they also received a lighted candle. They seemed to have joined in our prayer.

All of this, without a word, in complete silence. At exactly 7pm, the little bell was rung once more. We stood up and began to share with each other in a simple and friendly way. There was joy on everyone's face, and we all said: 'We must do this again.'

For me, this was one of the most precious experiences of shared prayer I have ever had. I wonder if one might say that this type of 'Demonstration for Peace' might be more efficacious as a form of dialogue for peace and communion than the more noisy and spectacular ones?

Mgr Killian Flynn (1905–72), from Donegal, was one of the first Irish Capuchin missionaries in the Western Province of Zambia, an area twice the size of Ireland, where the early missionaries had to walk everywhere or travel by barge on the River Zambezi. Fr Edwin Flynn (born 1927), from Cork, followed in his uncle's footsteps by joining the Capuchins and going to the same mission in Zambia. His special interest is in the history of African religion, and he taught at primary, secondary and tertiary levels. After fifty-five years in Zambia, he returned to Ireland in 2008, and now lives in the Capuchin Friary overlooking the River Lee in Cork. The following extract was sent by Fr Edwin.

Football under a Zambian moon – from Fr Killian's letter to his parents, October 1934

You remember how much I looked forward to boating and fishing around Glandore or Rosscarbery. It was the bright, sunny, summer days that I loved then. I never bothered about the moon or the stars at night. How things change! Now, here in Africa, I am very conscious of the moon and all its phases. With no clouds in the sky, it is spectacular to see the moon lighting up the countryside, and you feel like going out for a breath of cool air after the furnace-like heat of the day. When there's no moon, you can see all the stars, but it is too dark to venture out, so 'tis not surprising that people here count the days from one full moon to the next.

Well, two moons ago it was full and I looked out on an enchanted garden, the thatched roofs glistening like frost, the sand like snow in the cold light. All down the valley was silvery, while two miles away a bonfire in a village glowed orange and gold. Who said we have no colours at night?

It was also a full moon the night our two fellow Capuchins, Fr Casimir and Fr Chris, came to visit the three of us here in Loanja, Zambia, our first mission station. If you can imagine what life is like without newspapers or a radio, you will understand how we in the bush look forward to visitors coming from the town. Fr Seraphin had finished building the small church and Fr Phelim was back from a week-long tour of the schools. We had lots of news to share. It felt like a celebration.

All five of us were sitting outside, talking and smoking in the moonlight, when I got restless for a kick of a football. In the moonlight the world seemed as bright as day!

'What! Are you mad?' said one.

'Sit down, you eejit!'

'Clown! Stop him!' … and such remarks from all of them.

However, I got the ball and gave it a mighty kick straight up – and with that didn't the whole lot of them give a war-whoop and off like madmen we ran after that there ball. Such shouldering and scrums you never beheld! And old Fr Casimir was the maddest of all! And the yells! To my horror it brought the Africans from the nearby villages to stand and gaze at us running about like lunatics. But we played away regardless – and Casimir kicking as forcefully as any of us. He said it was twenty years since he last played.

Well, we found it was not really as bright as day – and Casimir, with one almighty kick, hit the cross on top of the church and sent it flying! Sacrilege! The four of us bolted like schoolboys, leaving poor Fr Seraphin gazing sorrowfully at the remains of his handiwork. However, next day we fixed it up again with no sign of damage. But then they all started blaming me, saying I was the madman who had started the shindy!

Well, I have never laughed so much as that night. The memory of five friars in white habits chasing around – and the shadow of a ball whizzing past in the moonlight! Then all of us after it again, shoving and pushing and shouting! And next day, despite our prophecies, Casimir wasn't a bit stiff. But that moment of tension as the ball hit the cross – and Casimir exclaiming, 'Oh my God!' – and turning tail and bolting, was the funniest thing I had witnessed for years!

Now I am away on a two-week safari trying to get to know the people and the area around our mission. But when the moon lights up the night and there's no one to kick a ball with … I feel lonely.

Fr Richard Griffin was a native of Salthill, Galway, and a Kiltegan Father. He was ordained in 1972 and appointed to Nakuru, in the Great Rift Valley of Kenya. He worked there from 1973 to 1980, returned to Ireland to take up the post of vocations director in Kiltegan from 1980 to 1986, and then returned to Kenya. He remained there until 2005, when ill-health forced him to return to Ireland. He died at Kiltegan on 25 October 2006. Fr Griffin wrote the following piece for the Kiltegans' *Africa* magazine.

Significant people

In the course of a lifetime there are people and occasions that we never forget. They influence the rest of our lives. I would like to tell you about some people I met, some experiences I had during my early years as a missionary in northern Kenya.

Living is not easy in the Turkana Desert where I ministered. Growth of any kind is sparse. That desert is home to 300,000 nomads. One little inhabitant I had the privilege of meeting was a young girl of somewhere between six and eight years of age. Akukuut stood out among the other children. She was small, had very thin legs and arms, and always wore a small cloth cap that covered a birthmark. Her eyes were her special feature. She wasn't able to join in the antics of her playmates, but she watched with glee as they jumped around.

From her I learnt a lot about generosity. She and her friends regularly congregated around our mission house, hoping for some small gift, perhaps a few sweets. I remember one Christmas giving her some extra sweets. What I noticed about my young friend was that, as soon as she got the extra portion, she went about sharing it with her friends. Her gesture was for me a profound lesson in sharing.

The old man, Lomokirion, also came to mind. He and his extended family lived about 3km from the mission house. Their home was a series of igloo-shaped huts; branches covered with skins and pieces of plastic. I frequently went on my motorbike to visit them. We would sit and chat and pray a little. The thrill for the children was a quick ride on the motorbike around the compound.

Lomokirion had an important function to perform in our main parish church on Sundays and major feast days, as he would also be invited to bless the people. This he did with real gusto, calling down in his own native language the blessings of God and of their ancestors on all the people and their animals. The blessing took the form of a chant and response, the whole congregation playing their part. He reminded me of an Old Testament, Moses-type figure. I will always remember his faith, his leadership, and his love of his people.

Many images remain with me from those old days in Turkana. I remember seeing a young child wheeling his grandmother to the local hospital in a wheelbarrow! The hospital, such as it was, had no doctor or state registered nurse. It was run by medical orderlies. Serious cases were transferred to the district hospital in the main town of Lodwar, some four hours drive away.

I once got a call from the hospital to collect the body of a dead woman and bring it for burial. A few young people from the parish came with me to the mortuary, which was a galvanised iron-sheet hut at the back of the hospital. The remains were wrapped in a green plastic sheet. There was no coffin. After the burial, but before filling in the grave, the hospital orderly, who had accompanied us, asked that we retrieve the green plastic sheet. The sheet would be used for the next remains to be brought to the mortuary.

I remember, too, the parents who stayed close to their sick child at the hospital. I recall one mother who was nursing her very sick daughter. They were sitting on the hospital steps, availing of the sun's warmth. But the frail and wasted body of the girl was still shivering with fever. Then it struck me. Christ came that we may have life and live it to the full. How distant some of our sisters and brothers are from that fullness.

There are occasions, there are people that we never forget, that we cannot forget. I remember those people who have influenced me greatly, and I am thankful for that.

Heather Martin (née Evans) comes from Greystones. The following stories are from her time working as a maternity nurse in Tanzania with the lay Anglican organisation BCMS (now Crosslinks). Heather and her husband, David, now live in the greater London area.

Triplet joy in the maternity ward

I worked for two years for the diocese of Central Tanganyika (as it was then) as a nurse-midwife, having trained in Dublin at the Adelaide for my general training and at the National Maternity Hospital on Holles Street.

I was put in charge of a new children's ward and tried to pick up Swahili and a few greetings in Cigogo, the language of the Wagogo tribe who were my patients. I shared a house with Bessie, the nurse tutor, and Joan, the matron – two Australians who helped me with Swahili and taught me many of the local customs. Needless to say I made many mistakes but the Africans were happy to laugh with me, not at me.

The marks of the tribe were a mark in the centre of the forehead, extended ear lobes, and a middle tooth missing from the bottom of the lower teeth. Soon after I arrived at Mvumi Hospital, twenty-five miles from Dodoma, I broke the denture I wear on my lower set of teeth. Nobody could fix it so I just had to go on duty without it. Next morning I went in to the ward and greeted the women in Cigogo. Then one said in Swahili, *'Huyu ni Mgogo'*. This means 'She is Mgogo' – a local name. I replied that I was indeed one of them and showed them the missing tooth. They just laughed and laughed and called others in to see my missing tooth! It was great fun as it really allowed me to share good times with them and their children.

There was great excitement one morning when a woman named Mama Violet gave birth to triplets. As far as we know, they were the first to be born in Kilimatinde Hospital. Mama already had five children. When I told Ernest, our cook, about the triplets, he asked, 'How can Mama feed three babies? She only has two breasts!'

My husband, David, who was visiting the hospital, took a photo of Mama and her husband, Pastor Yohana. I sent a copy of the photo to the national newspaper and they published it, as triplets were so rare! I also sent a copy of the photo to Nestlé, who kindly sent us free Nan milk for a whole year to help Mama feed her babies. She had to spoon-feed the Nan milk, as there was no way of sterilising a bottle. So Mama got into a routine of breastfeeding two babies and spoon-feeding the third. She did it on rotation, and wonderfully the triplets survived. To get them to the clinic at the hospital after they were discharged, two of the older girls in the family had to take a day off school. It was wonderful to see Mama and the girls arriving by bus, each with a baby tied on her back.

Br Liam McCarthy is a Dubliner and a member of the Franciscan Order. He has lived and worked in Zimbabwe since 2001.

Farewell to Teresa

Under the shadow of Mutemwa Mountain the little procession made its way from the chapel to the cemetery. It was a Sunday morning at Mother of Peace Orphanage, near Mutoko, in Zimbabwe. I had just celebrated Mass for the orphans and staff. Stella, who, with her sister Gene, takes care of the orphans, whispered to me: 'There's a funeral today – a little orphan has died – nine months old.'

Two chairs were placed in front of the altar and the small hardboard box was reverently carried and placed on them. All knelt for the prayers, the sprinkling of holy water – and then we all set off for the cemetery: the adults, and little groups of bare-foot children clutching bunches of flowers and greenery, holding hands. Some came and held my hand as we accompanied baby Teresa on her final journey. The little infant had come to the orphanage with the name 'Fortune' – and at baptism had received the name Teresa.

Arriving at the graveside the little coffin was placed beside the open grave. I continued the prayers – *May the Angels and Saints welcome you, Teresa – May all your ancestors welcome you – your grandparents, your great-grandparents – all your family who have gone before you – May they welcome you into Paradise.*

The little box was placed in the grave with great dignity, holy water sprinkled, and the grave carefully filled with clay. Then it was neatly finished off with a border of stones, marking the spot where Teresa was laid to rest.

It was then that an unforgettable image was imprinted upon my memory. The little ones clutching greenery and flowers were asked to now play their part. They rushed to the grave, climbed up on the clay mound, and for a few moments seemed totally engaged in the task they had to perform. Then, together, at a given signal, they all withdrew from the grave – and behold, it was a garden of flowers, beautifully planted. There was no more clay to be seen, only a blaze of colour. Little Teresa had gone home, surrounded by the love of her orphan friends – and flowers, planted by tiny hands, to say farewell.

Br Vianney Kerr, from Derry, is a St Joseph's Brother. After studying in Cork he worked as a nurse in London. Qualified in tropical nursing, he moved to Nigeria in 1967. He now works at a drop-in centre in Dublin.

Two deliveries – worlds apart

On the morning of 21 September 1967, our plane from London touched down at Kano Airport, Nigeria. Three of us were to set up a rural maternity health centre – two as nurses with training in tropical nursing, and a third Brother to build the centre. Headed for a remote area in the north-west region, it was our religious congregation's first foreign mission. It was also my thirty-third birthday.

We flew from Kano to Kaduna, then travelled by car to the central mission in the town of Minna, about 240 miles away. The following morning we set off for our final destination in a remote bush area, Kafin Koro, fifty-four miles east of Minna. There we met our mentor and chaplain, Fr Jerry Kiely, now deceased. Over the years there were many happy and successful engagements with the indigenous tribes, and there were also many sad and unsuccessful outcomes. The following tale falls into the latter category.

Usually, if someone was ill at a distance from our village, an 'intercessor' arrived to ask a villager of the same tribe to come to our Centre and intercede on the sick person's behalf. I was awakened one morning about 1am by two men knocking on my bedroom door. I should mention that all rooms in our residence had doors opening on to our veranda, both back and front. A woman of the Koro tribe was having difficulty giving birth. Would I come? She lived about eight miles away in the bush.

The man from the village, his 'intercessor' and myself set off in our car, and I drove for three or four miles before the bush track ended. We then set off on foot carrying our lighted lanterns and the medical bag. We lived in the savannah grasslands, with few trees, and giant grasses that grew to a height of about twenty-five feet by the end of the rainy season. It is customary and safer to walk 'crocodile fashion' – each person about three feet apart. This allows any snakes to pass uninterrupted! I dispensed with the lantern because of the thousands of insects drawn to the light, and to my arms and legs. Not very comfortable when being attacked on all sides by mosquitoes, flying ants and flying cockroaches – though the locals didn't seem to mind one bit.

We eventually arrived in the village, and in the quiet of the night we heard the 'keeners'. Yes, the keeners, just as in Ireland years ago. This was not a good sign. The village was small, each family having its own compound. A compound was a circle of single-room mud huts, each made of 'bricks' of compressed mud and grass (shades of W.B. Yeats and 'of clay and wattles made').

We entered the compound and into one of the mud dwellings. The sight was unforgettable. Several women, all crying (the keeners), the mother sitting, supported by another woman, a dead foetus on the floor, a pig, two goats and blood. Burning embers created eye-smarting smoke – this was their method of dispelling the myriad of insects. After getting the women to wash the mother I gave her injections and medication with instructions to her husband. He was to bring his wife to the clinic in four days. It was all I could do. We returned home.

Next day I had to travel to our nearest market town, a distance of fifty-five miles, to get some items and collect mail. The latter included my local paper, the *Derry Journal*, a few weeks out of date as usual. Returning to our residence I sat down in the evening to catch up with all my Derry news. A headline in large lettering caught my attention: 'Taxi Driver Delivers Baby'. Evidently, an expectant mother was being driven to hospital in the early hours and did not quite make it. The taxi driver stopped in John Street, called a young woman passing, who happened to be a nurse, and between them they delivered the baby in the taxi.

While the mother in my case lost her baby in horrendous conditions, a Derry baby was born in a reasonably comfortable situation under the care of a nurse. One made headlines, the other did not. I sat down on our veranda in the heat of the setting sun, and cried.

Anne-Marie Brennan is a member of the Sisters of St Joseph of Cluny. After many years as a nurse and midwife in Sierra Leone, she had a spell administering the Sisters' work in West Africa (Sierra Leone, Gambia and Ghana), and is now missioned to Ireland and Great Britain. She sends the following piece about a colleague.

Minding 'Muddah'

The paraffin-filled storm lantern could be seen from a distance, snaking its way through the trees and shrubs in the middle of the night. Many an animal would be disturbed in its natural habitat as the small group stumbled along through the dense greenery. Word had gone ahead, and in a clearing some way off, an old woman breathed a deep sigh of relief as she sat on a low stool outside the mud hut. Inside there was much wailing. The old woman called through the door that everything would be okay – 'Muddah' was coming.

Muddah – Sr Oliver Cronin, a native of Co. Cork – was doing her usual rounds, ever at the beck and call of all those in need of a nurse and midwife. Before dawn had broken, a little, healthy, safely-delivered baby girl was lying sleeping beside her exhausted young African mother. The fearful wailing had given way to great rejoicing! Sr Oliver, smiling with satisfaction, then began her long trek back to the convent. Along the bush path she'd walk, her mind already engaged on another busy day's work ahead of her.

I got to know Sr Oliver when she was in her seventies and eighties. Anyone else of similar vintage in Co. Cork would have been long retired – not Sr Oliver. A tiny wisp of a woman, weighing perhaps 38kgs, she was a well-known and well-loved figure in Sierra Leone. A dedicated nursing Sister, she remained in harness to the day she died. I was a young nursing Sister and loved the people, the country and my work with a passion. But now and then, as I climbed under the mosquito net at night, I'd say: 'Lord, just for tonight, keep everyone healthy.' One full night's sleep was always a wonderful bonus. I doubt if Sr Oliver ever said a prayer like that. Being called out day or night or both was fine with her. By 8am her clinic at base would be opened and when it closed in the evening, she was free for 'call-outs', or for writing the innumerable letters she sent to charities, seeking aid for her patients, most of whom were the poorest of the poor.

As often as not there would be no electricity in the evenings or at night and Sr Oliver would scare us to death with her perilous routine of writing those all-important letters at night – when she had time on her hands. Because the mosquitoes had rested all day, they were full of energy as darkness approached, probably lined up as the sun went down to enjoy a few vampire-like sorties. They were vicious creatures. Sr Oliver would get under her net, sit up in the bed with pen and paper at the ready and her lighted candle balanced precariously on the mattress beside her. One or other of the Sisters in the house would act in conjunction with Sr Oliver's guardian angel and keep a look-out for the inevitable moment when the pen would slip out of her hand and the head would bow with exhaustion. The candle would be snuffed out before there was a conflagration, and the house would settle down in darkness for the night.

How long did the sleep of the just last for Sr Oliver? Probably not for very long, because when we'd meet for breakfast in the morning the letter would be lying on the table, addressed and stamped and ready for the day's post. These letters would go out to the ends of the earth as she appealed for her beloved patients to have a wee share in just a little of the riches of the planet.

Sr Oliver lived for decades on the West Coast of Africa, the 'white man's grave', as it was called. She had survived many illnesses, some of them serious. Some of her years were spent on an island off the coast of Freetown, the capital, and if there were no small planes flying (which was frequently), then travellers had to go on a tortuous journey of several hours by road, usually by lorry, and then take a boat down the river, which could be accomplished in six hours on a good day – or anything up to twenty-four hours. And I'm talking about a small boat with an out-board engine.

Any nun travelling back to Bonthe Island after a trip to Freetown would bring back as many essential items as possible since there was an extremely limited supply of goods available on the island. As 'Muddah' would pack her small box of groceries under the benches along the sides of the boat, she would tell the boatman that she had breakables in the box. Thus, any time the boat went out of control and crashed into the banks of the river – which was a frequent occurrence – the boatman would yell: 'Mind the Mother's eggs!'; this, of course, while African mothers would be screaming and snatching their kids from falling over the sides. However, as the years passed and Sr Oliver was aboard when collisions occurred, the boatman would yell: 'Mind Muddah'! In his eyes she was now much more fragile than a dozen eggs.

In spite of her frailty, Sr Oliver lived to a ripe, happy and active old age. One morning the Sisters in her community were surprised when Sr Oliver did not appear for early morning prayer, Mass and breakfast, as was her wont; they were happy to think she was taking a rest. However, even as they were talking, her soul was winging its way to her Maker whom she had served so faithfully and purposefully. The Sisters found her a short while later: she was sitting in a chair and had obviously been getting ready for another day's work when the Lord called. Her memory lives on.

CHAPTER SEVEN

Development Projects, Great and Small

Fr Shay Cullen is a Columban Father and the founder of PREDA, a foundation that works to rescue vulnerable women and children in the Philippines from sexual abuse and exploitation. He has received several human rights awards and has been nominated on three occasions for the Nobel Peace Prize. He has testified before the US Congress and the Philippine Senate, and is a well-known speaker and facilitator at international conferences. The following abridged extracts are from *Passion and power*, Fr Shay's account of his work in the Philippines, where he has been living since 1969.

Defending the 'Untouchables'

I am fortunate to count the Irish-American actor Martin Sheen as a close friend. As well as being the hero of the *West Wing* television series (in which he portrays a liberal Democratic US president), he is also renowned for his famous role in *Apocalypse Now* and many more great films. Martin is well known for his Christian activism for justice in the US and is proud to say that he has been arrested more than fifty times for taking a stand for peace and human rights, mostly in front of the US Congress.

He came to visit me in the early 1990s when he was playing a small role in a war film that was being shot at the nearby Subic Bay, a former military base. Martin came to PREDA and joined the children at the Sunday Mass, and then came again in November 1997 to support the urban poor and their campaign for social justice in Manila.

Alex Hermoso, Martin and myself went to the Payatas garbage dump to campaign for help and support for the redevelopment of the area as it was deadly and dangerous for the hundreds of people living and working there in sub-human conditions. Payatas is a giant heap of putrid stinking garbage where the poor suffer endlessly. The men, women and above all, the children, spend their lives scratching the garbage for scraps to live on. The acrid smoke that covers the dump comes from the smouldering toxic waste. It causes lung diseases and asthma and endless ill health.

Martin trudged silently through the garbage tip of hopelessness, surveying the depths of human misery. The people were covered with the filth, smoke and smell of the garbage. Martin's face expressed feelings of pain and frustration that humans should be forced into such inhuman conditions. To the world of the well-off these people are outcasts, lepers, untouchables.

After his visit to the Philippines Martin became more committed to the peace movement and joined more campaigns for human rights and social justice. All we could do was support the campaign of the people's organisations at the Payatas dump for the huge mountain of rubbish to be flattened and the site redeveloped, and a decent life to be given to the hundreds of poor. This went unheeded – despite the publicity Martin's visit brought. This trip was organised by Dennis Murphy and Ed Gerlock, two former priests who have dedicated their lives to helping empower the poor and elderly in Metro Manila. The people's concerns were well-founded and they needed the publicity to get the government attention. The government ignored them.

Then, three years later, in 2000, after a week of torrential rain, the great mount of garbage was saturated and began to move. Slowly at first, and then with unstoppable force, a million tonnes of compressed garbage came avalanching into the village of scavengers squatting at its base. More than 500 garbage pickers were buried alive under the decomposing stinking mass. Only 150 bodies were recovered, the rest left buried under the mountain where they had had to struggle daily for food to hold on to the barest thread of life.

The 'death squads'

It was a letter dated 19 August 1999 that started another campaign to help endangered children.

> Dear Father Cullen,
> A death threat looms over our children and youths in the streets of Davao City. The deliverer of doom is called a death squad disguised as a group of vigilante citizens who promote peace and order. Some of our children and youth, considered an unsightly nuisance to our community, have been killed in mysterious circumstances and this has endangered the lives of their friends.
>
> We need your support to stop these senseless deaths and the harassment inflicted on our children and youth in the streets of this so-called Child Friendly City. Please express your urgent concern by sending letters of protest to the City Mayor through this address: Hon. Mayor de Guzman, City Mayor, 8000 Davao City, Philippines.

We call on you to urgently respond to this situation. We believe that it is only through our concerted actions that we can ensure the protection of the rights of our children and youth.

The letter was signed by a very courageous leader of a children's rights group in Davao City, Pilgrim Bliss Gayo-Guasa. Death squads are not new to the city of Davao. There is a history of such violent groups in the Philippines going back to the Alsa Masa and other anti-communist groups that unleashed a reign of terror on the city residents in 1988.

Davao is a wealthy city in Southern Mindanao, the second largest island of the Philippines. It has thriving fruit and tourism industries. The majority of the residents are impoverished, however, having fled there from the countryside. Government statistics showed that in 2006, Davao Del Sure had 24.2 per cent of families below the poverty line. Hundreds of hungry street children scrape a living from collecting recyclable junk from the garbage dumps and around the city streets. Their emaciated, scarred and unwashed bodies, gaunt faces and tattered clothes are silent condemnations of the selfishness of those who have it all.

Now the children were being targeted by an assassination squad, out to cleanse the streets of their unwelcome presence. Their existence was a living reminder that the power- and property-grabbing families that make up the oligarchy, about two hundred of them, have much to answer for. Their domination of politics and the economy is the root cause of poverty and rebellion. Government resources and the opportunities of power enlarge their personal fortunes and keep them in control. The opposition is another group of jealous clans seeking the top posts for themselves. The dispossessed and landless are left to live and die in disease-ridden slums.

By branding the street children as drug addicts and criminals the oligarchy can justify the killings and make them appear as necessary to maintain law and order. They present the executions as an exercise in civil virtue.

On 6 July 1999, two men in dark clothes riding on motor bikes without plate numbers, equipped with radios and guns, pulled up at the Galaxy cinema and levelled their weapons at two street kids. Two shots rang out, killing both. Another boy, Roger, ran as fast as he could and escaped into the crowds. He had recognised one of the killers. Many more youths had been shot, threatened and intimidated and a cloud of fear hung over the hundreds of street children. Two weeks later, on 19 July, a group of eleven children went with social workers to the City Hall to report the harassment and threats. Standing near the Mayor's office was one of the hitmen who had killed Royroy and

Mamay. Terrified, the children fled and hid. According to the human rights workers there was a total of 104 children murdered on the streets since 1998. In 2002, the figure had risen to forty-six assassinated that one year.

I wrote a letter, dated 8 September 1999, to the Mayor, describing the killings and quoted a national newspaper article which said Mayor Benjamin de Guzman supported 'secret marshals'. I was leaving for abroad and arranged with the PREDA staff that the letter be sent a few days after I left. My letter explained:

> This shooting and harassment of street children must stop. It is a direct violation of Philippine law, international law and the Convention on the Rights of the Child. As City Mayor you will be held responsible before the international community for these atrocities against children. It is for this very reason that in my keynote speech before the World Forum on Children's Rights this September 5th (in Stockholm) I am calling for the establishment of an International Court of Children's Rights. Like the officials who allow, order or approve, by act or omission, the violation of human rights, and are brought to trial at the International Court of Human Rights in the Hague, Netherlands, likewise, higher leaders and civil authorities who cause, allow or approve the execution of impoverished street children by hit squads must be brought to trial.
>
> I am appealing to the international community and the presidential committee for the protection of children for direct action to stop these murders since you are unable to do so. I appeal to the world community of child advocates to demand the killers be brought to trial.
>
> They are known and have been identified; it is your duty to bring them to justice for the murders of these children. Denial and claims of ignorance about these murders have no credibility. The evidence is clear; children are being murdered on the streets by an organised squad of motorcycle riding gunmen.
>
> If this is a method of curbing crime in your city then it is the most cowardly and dastardly action ever heard of. Picking on malnourished, abandoned, vulnerable and defenceless children, is the worst of crimes.
>
> Sincerely, Fr Shay Cullen.

When I was in Stockholm that September at an International Conference on Children's Rights, I presented a paper at the World Forum calling for a special court to bring to justice those responsible for the mass killing, torture, and abuse of children. My letter became part of our international letter-writing campaign that asked our friends and supporters to write to the Mayor. Many quoted my letter and apparently this infuriated him. He set up a special response desk to answer the hundreds of letters pouring in and promptly sued me and the Child Advocacy Team of PREDA for libel.

Mayor De Guzman claimed that my letter was defamatory and said:

> ... the whole scope and apparent object or motive of respondents – is that I, as Mayor of Davao City, harbour vigilantes out to murder street children, and that the killing of malnourished, abandoned, vulnerable and defenceless street children by organised crime or motorcycle riding gunmen is a daily occurrence in Davao City under my administration.

Of course I had made no such accusation, but just pointed out the reality and the need for him, as the Mayor and most authoritative person, to protect the children and bring the criminals to justice. Perhaps painful to the Mayor was the statement I made saying that all high officials who allow the abuses ought to be accountable to the international court of human rights. I had never said that he had actually allowed or was behind the death squads.

Like most of the fifty-four or more court cases filed against me and the PREDA human rights advocates, I answered this myself point by point in a long counter-affidavit. I couldn't afford to hire a lawyer then. What I had written was not libellous; it was a letter challenging the city official to do his duty or be held accountable. Many newspaper articles had reported the killings by the death squad. Most kids had been shot in the head with the same .45 calibre weapon.

One point was that, should a libel case like this be sent to court for trial, the law would be used as a weapon to instil fear in critics. It would restrain and inhibit the constitutional right to speak out and would silence the voice of the innocent who cry out for justice. This was especially true for advocates and defenders of children's rights. And, according to Philippine court procedure, an arrest warrant can be issued at once. The accused has to pay bail or go to jail and await trial. With a death squad around me, I paid the bail.

With the help of Robert Garcia – our paralegal officer at PREDA – and Alex Hermoso, I appealed the resolution of the prosecutor all the way to the Department of Justice in Manila. Before that office gave an answer it was already February 2001 and the case had to be called in the Davao regional court where I was to be arraigned. We couldn't have it postponed any longer. I flew to Davao City wondering if the death squad would meet me at the airport and get it over with. I had been warned.

There was a welcome committee all right but it was a big group of children with welcoming banners and placards calling for justice for children. As I was about to board a *jeepney*, I noticed a huge billboard announcing Davao as the winner of *The Most Child Friendly City* in the Philippines. I should have known. I stayed as a guest of the Maryknoll Fathers who were very supportive and encouraging. They too had been active behind the scenes, working with Fr Pete Lamata and Fr Paul Cunanan of the diocesan justice and peace group to reach some kind of compromise.

The Mayor wanted a public apology from me and the PREDA team, which would have been tantamount to an admission of guilt. That I could never agree to. Once you stand up for something it's not wise to sit down again just because of threats. I told Frs Paul and Pete that there would be no apology and if convicted of libel for standing for children's rights, so be it, I would serve my sentence. I had no defence lawyer in Davao other than hiring a lawyer to file motions and get copies of court documents.

On the day of the arraignment, 14 February 2001, the pavements were packed with street kids, supporters and well-wishers – all making their silent protest against the death squad. The courtroom was packed with media people. The heat was stifling and there were just two lazy fans churning the humid air. I sat with one of the Maryknoll Fathers – no Columban could make it, to my disappointment. The tension mounted as the time came to call the case and still the Mayor didn't show up. I felt there was a chance he would drop it and admit we were right.

Suddenly, there was a commotion by the door, and the crowds parted as Mayor de Guzman's lawyer walked in. He was the Mayor's private prosecutor. The judge ordered the case to be called: *The People of the Philippines versus Fr Shay Cullen.*

The lawyer for the Mayor stood up and passed a letter to the clerk of court. The judge read it and gave it back. Everybody was straining to hear, microphones were outstretched, and tape recorders were piled in front of the clerk as he began to read. The cameras were clicking and video cameras zooming to catch every movement and facial expression. The clerk of the court stood and read the following:

Heeding the appeal of the religious led by archbishop of Davao, Fernando R. Capalla, thru his emissaries, Fr Pete Lamata and Fr Paul

Cunanan, and other Non-Governmental Organisations and well meaning Davaoenos, Mayor Benjamin C. De Guzman, in the spirit of genuine reconciliation and unity, has decided to forego the prosecution of Fr Shay Cullen and place all issues to rest so that he can attend to more pressing demands of the City. With this, Davaoenos can move on and look forward to a better and more meaningful life ahead of them.

The media people exploded – some rushed out, talking to their mobile phones as cameras flashed. Applause was heard out in the corridor as the magic word spread: *withdraw*. Judge Robillo banged his gavel for order and ordered the clerk to continue. He looked very relieved. I was quietly delighted and quickly sent a text message to Alex and the team back at PREDA. We had won.

Judge Robillo gave his decision dismissing the case outright. Several months later the Department of Justice also ruled in our favour, recognising the validity and correctness of our legal arguments. We, the children and the brave social workers of Davao got more publicity for the cause than we had ever dreamed of.

Mayor de Guzman lost the next election and his rival, Rodrigo Duterte, was elected. The death squad became more active and the killings increased. President Gloria Macapagal Arroyo appointed Duterte as crisis manager for Southern and Central Mindanao; a crisis allegedly created by the killings – for which no one was arrested or brought to justice.

David Deegan is a Dubliner. He works with communities in Guatamala, educating teenagers academically and in Mayan traditions and values. He has been in Guatamala since 1998. The following excerpts come from his newsletter, which he sends home to Ireland.

Down-to-earth solutions in Guatamala

I suppose the biggest news on the projects front is that we have received funds to start a lemon tree orchard. We have called the project 'Roy' in honour of the sponsor's late husband. Work has already started, and in May we will plant about 150 trees. We will also be experimenting with some different types of trees to see if they grow well on our land. In three years the lemons should bring in a very welcome income to the project, as well as offering employment and lots of vitamin C for the teenagers. We have been investigating this project for over a year, and all the experts we have contacted have been very encouraging.

Our biggest struggle will be the watering of the trees. So, we are now deepening our wells. We are always trying to improve things. With the water shortage everywhere in the world today we feel we should be using the rainwater in our daily lives – if we could only capture it. It always breaks my heart to see so much water running away during heavy rain when we have a huge need for it in the dry season. We have six tanks that can hold a total of 20,000 litres, and these can fill in one afternoon when there is a heavy rainfall. Our plans are to construct a tank that will hold at least 100,000 litres. We are working on our proposal and I hope we can find a grant to build it. We will be looking for some donors to help with this.

I mentioned in previous editions that we have started a rabbit project. We would like to feed the rabbits well but at no expense – they are almost worse than teenagers to keep in food! So we have an arrangement with people in the market to give us left-over leaves from vegetables. In a sense we pay for the leaves by buying all our vegetables from this one vendor ... and we eat lots of vegetables. The rabbits, being rabbits, have blessed us with over twenty offspring from the four small ones we started with (some have died and a couple have escaped). We feel there will be a reasonable market for them.

About a year ago we started a wormery, which we hope will give us good fertiliser. There is not a lot of work to it – just give them scraps and keep them watered. Because I was away for a while they were not well cared for, and even when I returned I have to admit I forgot about them myself. So, many disappeared, but now they are starting to increase. Unlike the rabbits these are not very nice to pick up and cuddle!

Our turkeys are still moving along nicely. We sell the turkeys when they are still small. This saves on feed and gives us a small income. We also rent the male turkey out. This also brings in some income and keeps the turkey very happy!

In May of last year, the confirmation class of the primary school I went to (just a few years ago) donated funds which we used to buy a *molino*, or corn grinder. This may not seem like anything great to you, but to us it is a major change to our lives. Before, the kids had to walk to the nearest *molino* every day, or at best every second day. Although it is only about an eight or ten minute walk away, they had to carry a heavy basin of corn that distance. Many times the *molino* was closed and they would have to go to one further away. Sometimes I would have to take them into the city to have the corn ground there.

Now we don't have to worry about not having dough to make tortillas. Without tortillas we would starve to death. They are the most important thing in the indigenous diet. Everyone is so thrilled with this machine. Now we can have freshly ground flour to make our delicious tortillas, and our kids can have more time to play or study or just be kids.

Sr Patricia McMenamin is from Rathmullan, Co. Donegal. In her time with the Sisters of Our Lady of Apostles, she has worked in Ghana (twice), Zambia, Italy, and Argentina, and is currently living in Ireland. She recounts the following experiences from her last station.

Resilience amid recession in Argentina

'The little things that make life great' – a line by the Chilean poet Pablo Neruda – is quoted by Teresita Durkan in her book *Ó Mhuigheo go Valparaiso*. It sums up for me the years I spent in Argentina. A new world had opened for me in 2001 when I arrived in Córdoba fresh from a language school in Bolivia. With my very limited Spanish I was in at the deep end. We were four Sisters of Our Lady of Apostles forming an international community: we were from France, Argentina, Nigeria and Ireland. Our common language was Spanish!

Argentina was going through a serious recession that had started in the late 1990s. At its peak, banks were closed and people lost their life savings. Many lost their jobs, and they took to the streets in protest, banging bin lids and chanting slogans. At times there was violence and in Buenos Aires a number of people lost their lives.

Many people were hungry, so we opened two centres with a view to initiating some little craft work – and indeed the Argentinean women proved to be very gifted with their hands. Barter was introduced and each day there was an exchange of food: sugar for milk, for example, or potatoes for other vegetables. Meat, which Argentineans love, was beyond buying for quite a time. Yet in the midst of these troubles I was very impressed by the poor who shared whatever little they had with those who were worse off.

I moved to Buenos Aires and one of my involvements was with the children in Chakarita – really a space taken over by families who came down to the capital from the north to try to find a better way of living. With a few of the women in our parish we went in the evenings to bring a *cuppa de leche* to the children when they returned from school – usually it was just some hot chocolate and bread and whatever else we could bring them. There was only one small hall that was also used as a classroom, chapel and a shelter for children to do some homework at times.

After enquiring about the possibility of getting funds for another small building I discovered that funds would never come when we had no evidence of ownership of the land. We found an alternative! It came in the form of a haulage container paid for by the then IMRS (Irish Missionary Resource Services). It was a great gift.

One day I met an artist friend and told her about our new 'classroom'. She immediately decided to bring a few friends and let the children do murals on it. They had been colouring pictures which I photocopied each week for them, but now all their artistic skills came to the fore and we had a very colourful *casita* (little house)! Another gift came from some doctors, who volunteered to come to the *casita* to tend to the children and the sick of the area. That was wonderful.

Fr Michael Crowley grew up in west Cork. After his ordination as a Sacred Heart Missionary in 1958, he lived for forty-five years in South Africa, throughout the period of apartheid and the eventual transition to black majority rule. In 2008, he published his memoirs, *To Cape Town and back*. He is now living in Co. Cork.

Tshabalala's women

In 1968, because of the scarcity of local medical services – the nearest hospital was 40km away at Elim – the nuns set up a day clinic and a small children's hospital. They ran a busy and highly regarded place of healing and comfort, especially as a maternity home.

The *sangoma* – witchdoctor – also played a big part in the life of rural South Africa. His or her intervention was sought especially in time of sickness, severe drought, tragic accident or theft. The *sangoma* was both revered and feared in the community.

On their way to St Brendan's Clinic, the pregnant mothers would pass through Ha-Pasha village where Tshabalala, a *sangoma* of great stature, resided. As was the custom in olden times, he would perform some kind of ritual on the pregnant women and demand a fee – after all, he had twenty-two wives to support, as well as his children. The mothers were extremely poor, and when they got to our clinic sometimes the *sangoma* had relieved them of their few rands. The mothers were never refused help, but we had to survive also. There were no grants or subsidies, and wages had to be found, so we expected some small remuneration.

We called Tshabalala to a meeting on the *stoep*; there was an air of expectancy throughout the mission. The African nuns stood in a half circle fingering their beads, praying that their priest would not be turned into a goat! Strong opinions were voiced. Thankfully, the problems were resolved amicably. Tshabalala would desist from his ministrations to the Christian mothers on their way to the clinic. He was happy that some of his wives would continue to be employed at the mission, and that many of his children – now Catholics – were attending our school.

The Irish nuns staffed the clinic until its closure in 1995, replaced by a government clinic. The closure was regretted by the people of the neighbourhood, where so many of their children had been born.

Hilary Lyons is a Mayo woman, born in 1924, the eldest in a family of nine. A member of the Holy Rosary Sisters, she was sent to study medicine in UCD, graduating in 1952. In 1953 she started her long life as a nun and a doctor in Sierra Leone. She has described many of her experiences in two books – *Old watering holes* (2001) and *Where memories gather* (2009). She loved Sierra Leone and its people, and all the time she spent there. Now retired, she lives in Dartry in Dublin.

Re-defining mission

Recently, I came upon a book, *Into Africa*, by Martin Dugard. I was astonished at the incursion of traders and explorers who went into the continent of Africa in the nineteenth century. Explorers competed to be the first to reach various locations, to describe the geography, people, flora, and fauna – and to plant their flags. Thus they acquired the celebrity status of their day. What we know of many of these incursions has come from the pens of the explorers.

We, the missionaries, arrived in Africa at the time of the colonial expansion at the end of the nineteenth and beginning of the twentieth centuries. There is little indication of what the indigenous people thought of all these foreigners. One anecdotal comment has come down to us: during a rebellion against imposed taxes in Sierra Leone at the end of the nineteenth century, one chief decided to spare the missionaries, saying, 'we do not know what good they do, but they certainly do no harm'!

All that was very far from my mind as I arrived in Freetown, Sierra Leone in February 1953, having celebrated my twenty-ninth birthday on board the merchant vessel *Tamele*. At nineteen I had chosen to enter a missionary congregation in order to go to Africa to help those in need. Ten years later, having trained as a nun and a doctor, I had refined my mission a little: I was to bring Christianity and health to those who needed it. As a religious, I was to be a woman of faith, strengthened by the study and practice of the Christian message.

Whilst taking my medicine degree in UCD I had assumed that hospital-based care was the model that would best change health patterns in Sierra Leone. I was to find out that hospital care without a community base was totally inadequate.

The Mende tribe who live where I worked are a farming community engaged in the production of rice as a main staple. The experience of growing up the eldest of nine on a farm in Mayo gave me a good comprehension of the vicissitudes of farming life. But the method of farming was very different to anything I knew. Typically, trees were cut down, burnt, and the rice planted with the tree stumps still in place. Inevitably, the yield was poor, creating serious nutrition problems for health care workers.

One of the complications of severe malnutrition was the dreaded *kwashi-orkor* in children between two and five years. Their bodies swelled up, they became anaemic and their mouths sometimes ulcerated. I have a memory of a small boy, maybe three; he was bright as a button but his mouth was so ulcerated he could not tolerate anything by mouth. A naso-gastric tube was inserted, strapped to his cheek, the open end of it sticking out somewhere near his ear. He was fed a smoothie of peanut paste, beans, rice flour, fish and a little milk from a large syringe. The nurse called me from outpatients one day to see, as she said, 'a wonderful thing'. She was cooling the mixture by spooning it up and letting it dribble back into the cup in front of the child. It was tantalising. He sat up rocking back and forth in a misery of hunger and waiting. As soon as the nurse produced the syringe he lay down fast, tube side up and pointed his finger to the open end of the tube! This way for dinner please!

He left the hospital fit and well and I figured he would do well in life. I never knew. That was a sad aspect of health care in Africa. Lack of communications made follow-up impossible. Now, I am told, the mobile phone has transformed life for millions in Africa, their families and carers. Thank God for that.

As for health problems when I arrived in Africa, there were conditions appearing daily that were not in my medical texts, and surprise surprise, I was the only doctor in the area. So I did surgical, medical, and obstetric interventions with improvisations that would be hair-raising for professors in Ireland. For example, ruptured Fallopian tubes in early pregnancy were common. Patients came in with racing pulse and disappearing blood pressure. There was no blood donor scheme at that time. So we learned to use a pre-sterilised bottle containing anticoagulant, collect the blood from the belly, pour it into the bottle and give it directly into the vein of the patient. It worked marvellously.

There were shoals of taboos, such as that eating fish during pregnancy would result in gills or fissures in the baby's neck; if the baby at the breast got diarrhoea or if the labour was prolonged the mother was believed to be having an affair. This last was particularly disastrous, as the woman would be kept in labour until she confessed. Often this delay caused rupture of the uterus and death. At the beginning we wrestled with these beliefs; later we came to respect them and dialogue with those concerned.

One of the greatest of our accomplishments in my experience was the training of three categories of nurses: State Registered, State Enrolled Community Health Officers, and our pride and joy, the granny midwives in the bush. The latter probably did more to reduce the maternal mortality rate than any other category. When war drove us out of the country the training left behind was our greatest comfort. Knowledge shared directly with people is a self-perpetuating gift.

Preaching the Gospel was more of a soul-expanding experience for me. I found that the people had their own experience and perception of God. They believed devoutly in a Supreme Being who more or less rewarded the good and punished the wicked. In this belief they had woven together a system of rites and rituals to engage with mystery/worship. Faced with the advent of two major religions, Christianity and Islam, many chose one or the other and combined it with their original beliefs. It was often a confusing picture. For example, persons in polygamous unions were not given full membership of the Church. There did not seem to me to be adequate study by theologians of the situation.

In the event I was unable, due to sheer volume of health work, to do direct pastoral work, choosing instead to witness the Gospel of love for one another in health care. This was common to all religions and I learned a lot, including a deepening of my own faith. For this I bless the people of Sierra Leone.

After a lifetime there, leaving Sierra Leone, where so many of my yesterdays lie buried, was truly heartbreaking. During the war that erupted in the 1990s we were obliged to leave hurriedly. The practical affairs of packing, organising flights and last minute arrangements blanketed any feelings at the time. The grief rose up inside me later.

One evening I met a friend, Peter Michael, here in Ireland, in whose garage our vehicle repairs were done in Bo. I met him coming out of the National Concert Hall and suddenly a picture rose of the garage, his mother's house, and the corner where I always parked. In that swift moment I could *see* the place, I could *feel* the heat, *smell* the exhaust fumes and the coffee – and I was taken back to where Peter and myself enjoyed a cup of Lebanese coffee and settled world affairs in agreeable discourse. In that same moment I knew I would never see that place again. The tears came quietly flowing down my embarrassed face. This was a common occurrence in the two years that followed.

This sense of loss is common for all missionaries of the 'long haul era', who had spent up to fifty years in a country where they worked so closely with people that had become dear to them. It is often poignantly expressed in quiet chats as they share memories of their missionary days: 'I was fifty years there and loved every day of it'; 'We were thirty years there – the day we left it was a beautiful spring day'; 'We left the sanctuary lamp burning…'

But there is a sense, too, that nothing is lost, nothing has died. Something was planted in the living hearts of the communities we loved. Many women now read and write and many are teachers or academics. Many women no longer fear illness or even death just by having a baby, because missionaries were there. Thousands of religious men and women have been trained to take up the baton.

I wish that old rebel chief who spared the early missionaries was still alive – I would ask him if he would reconsider his assessment of missionaries now. How about: 'We do not know what problems they might cause, but they certainly do an awful lot of good'!

Sr Catherine (Kay) Connolly was born in Buncrana, Co. Donegal, but spent most of her childhood in Letterkenny. She entered the Good Shepherd Congregation in the 1950s, and subsequently lived in France, Sri Lanka, Sudan, Pakistan, Egypt and Guam. She is now living in Derry.

Development in Sri Lanka: a worm's eye view!

I had celebrated my twenty-second birthday just before arriving in Sri Lanka in 1957. At that time we all believed that our adopted country would be the land where our bodies would be laid to rest, as were those of the many Good Shepherd missionaries before us. Little did I know that my missionary life would take me on to Pakistan, Egypt, Sudan and Guam.

My first fifteen years were spent as housemother to a group of between sixty and eighty girls in St Joseph's House of Children in Nayakakande (*Nayakakande* means 'Hill of Snakes'). At that time, being orphans or children born out of wedlock, the children were stigmatised by society – hence the need for a special school. In the fifteen years I spent there I played the role of mother, tutor, nurse, peacemaker, PT instructress, Brownie and Girl Guide leader, choir mistress, job hunter/provider and matchmaker! It all came to an end when I was told by my Provincial that I was to go to Italy to do a crash course in sericulture (the breeding of silk worms). Needless to say, parting from the girls was painful for me, and also for them. We had bonded as a family and despite the fact that we were always over sixty in number, the girls had created a true family spirit and I learned much from them. Although many are scattered over different parts of the world today we keep in contact and manage to have get-togethers every now and then.

The 1960s and 70s were troubled times in Sri Lanka. Sinhalese was made the official language of the island and, as the majority of the middle class and the elite were educated in English and spoke little Sinhalese, there began a steady exodus to Canada, England, Australia and elsewhere. Sri Lanka was greatly impoverished by this brain drain. There was a lot of unemployment, including among university graduates. Adding to the unrest, the government had banned the importation of many essential commodities and people were dying of hunger.

Our Provincial Superior, Sr Good Counsel (Eileen) Mills – who hailed from Tramore, Co. Waterford – was a woman of great zeal and vision. She was to leave a lasting mark on the economic and social development of the whole of this beautiful island. In her great wisdom, she saw the tragedy that was about to engulf the poor and especially the youth of the island and decided to take action. With the help of CEBEMO, MISEREOR and other international funding bodies, she started sending Sisters to different parts of the world for training in agriculture, dairy farming, sericulture, handloom weaving, batik and handicrafts of all kinds, with a view to starting development projects which would be labour intensive and viable on a tropical island.

Selling some property belonging to the congregation in 1965, she bought an estate in Hanwella, 30km outside Colombo, and started a training centre there for boys and girls in agriculture and animal husbandry. This project was to encourage the youth of the country to turn to the land and become self-sufficient in essential food commodities. Boys and girls from all over the island availed of this training. With the aid of a revolving loan many started their own farms or went home to help their parents on existing farms, using their new skills and expertise.

Another development project – called the Mahalpe Sericulture Farm – had already been established three years when I joined it at the end of 1972. The site chosen was a small village eleven miles from Kandy in Mid-country, where the inhabitants were all Buddhist and unemployment was high. Twenty-three acres of mulberry had been planted and were being tended by twenty-one men who were responsible for the pruning, leaf-picking for the worms and general well-being of the trees. Two girls were employed in the scientific breeding of the worms (we had forty-six pure breeds of silk worm!) and another twelve-to-fifteen girls were involved in the rearing of the worms. All our employees, both men and girls, were from the village.

The project was thriving and government officials as well as visitors from the World Bank, FAO, and other international organisations visited our farm to evaluate the feasibility and success of the project.

There were three phases to this project: one in Mid-country, one in South Rural and the third in Nayakakande, close to the capital, Colombo. With the financial help of our Sisters in the Provinces of New York, Australia and Japan, silk-reeling equipment such as dryers, boilers and twisting machines had been purchased and installed in our provincial grounds in Nayakakande. Here, a group of our young unmarried mothers were trained and employed.

By 1975, as the demand for our silk products was increasing, it was decided to plant eleven acres of mulberry trees on the Hanwella estate and start silk-worm rearing there too. I was named as project manager for this venture. I spent many hours on the plantation with the workers who had to be introduced to the planting and maintenance of the mulberry trees, as well as taught what leaves the worms ate at the different stages of their development. The leaves were handpicked and as the worms came close to their spinning stage they ate voraciously. It was certainly labour intensive, both on the field and in the rearing rooms. For the rearing of the worms I had a few trained girls from the Mahalpe silkfarm. These were a great help, and trained and supervised our new recruits from the surrounding villages.

I spent three very busy and rewarding years in this historic, adventurous period of our Good Shepherd mission in Sri Lanka. My next posting was to Karachi in Pakistan … but that's another story.

Sr Louis Marie O'Connor was born in Kanturk, Co. Cork. She worked for more than forty years in Sierra Leone, as a teacher and in organising projects and supports for local women. She has been in Ireland since the mid-1990s.

Our students making a difference: Christiana Thorpe

More than sixty years ago, Sr Teresa McKeon and I were professed on the same day, and on that same day were handed slips telling us: 'Obedience sends you to Sierra Leone'. Neither of us was entirely sure where it was. We were expecting to baptise all the 'black babies', but the ensuing decades turned out to be quite different.

We worked as teachers in a school for girls. Sierra Leone was a British colony at the time. Issues of independence, human rights and national development seemed a long way off. Among our pupils was a young girl who would grow up to play a major part in the country's painful struggle: Christiana

Thorpe became the country's first female minister for education, and is now a leading human rights activist. She credits her early years in our convent in Freetown with shaping the values that have informed all of her convictions and achievements. Sr Teresa formed a particularly close relationship with her.

While Christiana was studying as a novice at UCD in Ireland, Sierra Leone was in turmoil. A succession of coups after independence brought a breakdown of normal life, and all the Irish Sisters' expectations of their future role were turned on their heads. In a sense we were arrogant, really – we had all the answers. The arrival of Sierra Leonean Sisters, such as Christiana, forced us to review our role. We realised we'd have to look more deeply into their culture.

After twenty years as a nun, Christiana began to question her vocation. She left the convent, sensing there was more she could do to help her country, and in particular its women, to give them the opportunities she'd had. In her lay role she remained committed to the values acquired in the convent. She now set about improving the education system in Sierra Leone, and her expertise was sorely needed. When she was appointed minister for education we worried for her safety. I knew her life could be in danger in that troubled land. (More recently she has taken on a potentially more dangerous role as national elections commissioner.)

While in office and before another coup brought yet another change of government, Christiana introduced many measures which have made a big impact on the emancipation of women in Sierra Leone. To take just one example: she legislated to ensure that pregnant girls are no longer obliged to leave school. In recognition of her achievements in the area of human and women's rights, she was declared runner-up to the African Woman of the Year in 2009.

Our role in Africa certainly turned out differently from what we expected when we arrived, back in 1948!

Fr Gerry Clenaghan, of the Oblate Order, moved to work in Canada in the 1940s. For many years he was heavily involved with the 'Frontier Apostles' lay missionary movement. He later ministered in Alaska, where he worked with the local Inuit population, and, more recently, in California. He now lives in Dublin.

Bishop O'Grady's dream: the 'Frontier Apostles'
He was born in Canada, but was always proud to say his grandparents came from Ireland, from Clare and Tipperary, which explains the name: John Fergus O'Grady. He was known simply as 'Fergus'. Ordained an Oblate priest in 1934,

he spent many years as a teacher and administrator in the missionary schools, eventually becoming provincial of St Peter's Province, home to the English-speaking Oblates of Canada. At that time, the province stretched from sea to sea, 4000 miles, all the way from Newfoundland to British Columbia.

He was installed as bishop in Prince Rupert in 1956. His territory, later to be known as the diocese of Prince George, covered an area four times the size of Ireland. We had about two dozen priests and Brothers then, many living in very isolated locations. The older priests were from France, and among the younger men were eleven of us from Ireland and seven or eight from Canada. The two largest towns, Prince Rupert on the Pacific coast, and Prince George, 500 miles inland, each had a population of 3000–4000, and each had a Catholic school. In the hinterland we had about thirty-five smaller villages and missions, many accessible only by riverboat or bush plane. Truly, the Frontier.

There was great delight at the announcement that 'Fergus' was to be our new chief pastor. But when he told us what his plans were, he really took us all by surprise. Because of his experience over the years in the field of education and especially his work with the native peoples, he stressed that our most urgent priority would be to provide a dozen new Catholic schools throughout the diocese. We were dubious! While we took delight in the friendly, persuasive and totally sincere way in which he made his apparently grandiose proposals, we also felt that realism may not have been his strong suit. To our expressions of doubt, however, his recurring response was, very simply: 'If God wants it, we can do it.'

We soon came to realise that Fergus the dreamer was also Fergus the inspirer, the animator. He certainly had a deep and abiding trust in God. But what was probably as impressive was his unshakable trust in the goodness and generosity of people. When we told him that with no financial support from the government of British Columbia it would be impossible to pay teachers, he replied: 'That's OK. We'll go to the universities and training schools and ask young men and women, when they graduate, to donate the first year or two of their career to the missions.'

We objected: 'But we won't be able to collect enough to pay for materials and labour to build the schools.' Answer: 'That's OK, too. I'll go to the lumber mills and the hardware suppliers and ask them to donate materials.' He proposed to get other young men to volunteer as builders, drivers, plumbers, and electricians. 'With all those guys giving their time, and with the Lord's help, we can do it.'

I'm afraid, in 1956, I was rather naive, and still had a lot to learn from this man of God who spiritually and intellectually towered head and shoulders above the average mortal. I came to know him, to love and respect him, as a gentle giant whose faith and sheer personality could move all obstacles whenever it was a matter of 'building the kingdom of God'. Among those obstacles in March 1956 was me!

When I told him I thought the plan was a great idea, but it wouldn't work, he immediately changed the subject and said: 'You've been nine years here on the missions without a holiday in Ireland. I want you to go home to visit your family. Take a few months … and, while you're there, see if you can find a few teachers and others to come out and help us.' So, that's how I got a job that lasted for nineteen years: he had just appointed me director of the volunteer project.

I must admit I really welcomed the idea of a holiday. It had indeed been a long nine years. That summer, five young ladies volunteered to give up their jobs and come out to British Columbia. Even without school buildings, the bishop had decided to go ahead and begin classes in church halls and other temporary accommodations. Thus began the project known worldwide as the Frontier Apostolate, one of the most successful lay volunteer programmes in the modern history of the Church. And all this was prior to Vatican II.

Our five young trailblazers from Ireland were Catherine Sheehan from Waterford; Peg Hyland from Clonmel; Ann McAteer from Tyrone; Theresa Lally from Dublin; and a cousin of mine from Co. Antrim, Rita Clenaghan, who taught at Lejac Indian School. We owe a great debt of gratitude to these and all the pioneers who placed their trust in God and in the missionary bishop, Fergus O'Grady.

He had the ability to involve all the Oblates in various aspects of the great dream. Fr Joe Bogues, from Belfast, was given the task of planning, and then implementing, the huge building programme. By intuition, the bishop had recognised his many talents in this area and Joe responded with his whole heart. Just four years later, in 1960, while he was in the process of building five schools throughout the diocese, he was killed in a tragic car accident at the early age of thirty-six. His passing was a tremendous loss to the bishop and to the diocese, but from that day on we knew we had a special intercessor in heaven.

Fr John Vincent O'Reilly, from Co. Kildare, was given the responsibility of dealing with the federal government in Ottawa, and the provincial government in Victoria. His effective public relations work led eventually to the province of British Columbia granting a measure of support to all private schools, Catholic and otherwise. Thanks to his untiring efforts these schools today receive grants covering just over fifty per cent of their operating costs.

Others in those early years who recruited volunteers to work in the new schools to be built in their parishes were Fr Kevin Silke, from Roscommon, and Fr Tom Shiel, from Mountrath. They too gave wholeheartedly to the cause of Catholic education in our vast mission territory.

Bishop Fergus himself went to Ireland to visit many convents, inviting the Sisters to come and manage his new schools. He made arrangements with the Sisters of Mercy in Callan to send five nuns to begin a missionary project that eventually led to about twenty-five of their members coming over to teach in our schools. They too have been an answer to prayer, and have served in faith and joy over these past forty years.

As the years went on, the word got around. More and more interest was expressed in the role of temporary lay missionaries in the Church at large. Volunteers came from Ireland and Britain, from Canada and the States, from Europe and Australia, from New Zealand, Hong Kong and even Nigeria. Twelve primary schools and one secondary school (today well known in Prince George as O'Grady High School) were built with the help of hundreds of volunteer tradesmen and labourers, each contributing their talent and time to this worthy cause. The bishop's dream turned out to be no mere flight of fancy, but a practical, down-to-earth reality.

In the thirty years that the Frontier Apostolate movement was in operation, just over 3,500 volunteers gave a year or more to this missionary endeavour. We benefited hugely from their efforts. But they benefited too, returning home with a new vision, a new understanding. There is a new and deeper meaning to the words: 'Whatsoever you do to the least of my brothers and sisters, you do unto me.' And a sizable percentage of volunteers received a very special 'bonus'. It was through their service in the Frontier Apostolate that many found their lifelong soul-mate, and married! I could name a few names!

After thirty years of service as head of the diocese of Prince George, Bishop O'Grady retired in 1986. That same year the University of British Columbia awarded him an honorary degree in recognition of his great achievements. On 3 March 1998, John Fergus O'Grady was called home to God. His funeral Mass was attended by representatives of the various other churches, government and civic leaders, and a large congregation. His mortal remains were laid to rest in the Oblate cemetery in Mission City, not far from Vancouver, where he had begun his priestly work sixty-four years earlier.

But why should such a wonderful idea, and such a fine programme, come to an end after thirty years of success? The answer lies simply in one word: success. The schools have been so successful that it finally became possible to obtain funding from the government of British Columbia to partially offset actual operating costs. Also, as time passed, the diocese could no longer be seen as 'Frontierland'. Prince George is no longer a town of 3,000 people; it is now a city of about 120,000. Work on a voluntary basis here is no longer necessary while there are so many who are much more in need in other parts of the world today. Indeed, we thank God that in recent years many young people from our own diocese have heard the same call that motivated an earlier generation, and have gone as volunteers to Africa and other developing countries where the need is as great as ever.

Catherine Veale, from Dunhill, Co. Waterford, joined the Good Shepherd Congregation in 1950. Her first mission was to Sri Lanka in 1951, where she taught in a collegiate school in Colombo for twelve years and spent much of the rest of her time engaged in social work with the Good Shepherd ministries. In 1979, she pioneered a new foundation in Madagascar. She served there until 2000, when the young Malagasy Sisters took over the work. She went to work in Ethiopia, but returned to Madagascar for a further year. She is now retired in her native county.

Madagascar: carried on eagles' wings

After spending six years working with rural folk in Sandrandahy, Madagascar, our congregation was urged to open an apostolate in the capital, Antananarivo. Things were rough there at that time. The episcopal secretary who had been handling the purchase of a suitable property for us, Frère Roy, was murdered in his office on 28 May 1984.

The Sisters named for the foundation arrived on 16 January 1985. The beginnings, like so many other beginnings, were a series of crosses and miracles. Looking back I can only say we were carried on eagles' wings. Our house was situated in the city centre but there was no room for expansion; however, today we have a spacious social centre thanks to a chance meeting with a generous donor.

The meeting went like this: that year Madagascar had been invited to host the summit of Non-Aligned Nations, and, to clear the capital of beggars, the government had ordered the refuse vans to collect all beggars from the streets and dump them outside the city. As I was coming home from shopping one day, I found many women and children waiting at our door looking for food. Just as we were talking, the refuse van drove up and the driver began manhandling the women and children. I intervened: 'Excuse me, but I am looking after these women!' He went away disgruntled, telling me in no uncertain terms: 'You look after them, then!'

Now, what was I to do? Our house was in the heart of the city and the Sisters were all foreigners, but these women and children needed help! Fortunately, the parish priest listened to my story and gave us the use of an old dilapidated building close to the church. It wasn't adequate and needed urgent repairs.

Shortly afterwards, as I was walking towards our house one day, a young foreigner came along jogging, and stopped to ask for directions. He asked me what I was doing in Madagascar. I replied by inviting him to come and see, which he did. What he saw was the inadequate building the nuns were using and the crowds that were being ministered to.

It turned out that this man was from Holland and was working in the United Nations in New York; he was just spending a short holiday in Madagascar. As we were going round he asked what plans we had in mind for the building. I did some quick thinking. The site provided by the parish was suitable from every point of view, but neither the land nor building was ours. Nevertheless, I knew at once that if we could knock down that building and build a suitable social centre, it would be wonderful.

The Dutchman asked if I knew any organisations in Holland. Fortunately, while in Sri Lanka, I had worked with CEBEMO, the Dutch international development organisation, and personally knew the man in charge. Our new friend suggested: 'We will ask CEBEMO to help'. He promised that if I prepared the plans, he would do the typing and photocopying. I consulted the cardinal on matters relating to Church property, and, fortunately, he agreed with our plans.

Our first request for aid met with a refusal; they claimed our plans were too ambitious. Later, however, I got a letter saying that if our first request was really essential, they would seek help from another organisation. This they did and Caritas Holland agreed to share the expenses. What a miracle! God wanted to raise these people up, and we were simply instruments in His hands.

The social centre is now a three-storey building; the ground floor provides food and health care for malnourished children, the first floor for early school leavers, and the top floor for women whose lives have been changed through meaningful work. Who can say that God does not care?

Noreen Foley was born in Co. Kerry. She joined the Sisters of Mercy in Tralee, trained as a teacher, and taught in Colaiste Íde in Dingle. She then moved to Kenya for ten years, returning to Dublin in 1994. She also worked in Nigeria for a number of years, and now lives in Mallow, Co. Cork.

Small beginnings

The one thing that bothered us as Sisters of Mercy in Kipkelion District in Kenya was that the poorest girls in the village could not avail of the academic course we were providing. A critical need requiring our attention was 'technical education'. However, we had neither the facilities nor the equipment. Neither had we teachers qualified in relevant subject areas. But the time arrived when we could wait no longer; we abandoned ourselves to God and decided to go for it. Our own teachers responded with generosity and even excitement: 'I'll teach agriculture!'... 'I'll do business studies!'... 'I'll teach mathematics!'...

In no time, all the subjects were covered. An old store was emptied of garden tools and made ready with benches and chairs. Later that first weekend I remarked to another Sister that I would love to know where Jane M. was now. Jane was a past student whom we had sponsored for training in dressmaking – just the sort of person we needed. We had no clue where she might have gone at this stage.

That very weekend the assistant priest arrived back from Nakuru town. He pulled up to our house and began to offload huge cardboard boxes all bearing my name. We opened them excitedly to find nine sewing machines! As I read the enclosed letter I remembered that a woman called Sylvia had passed through the mission the year before and heard me remark that one day we hoped to start a course in dressmaking. On her return home, she mustered the help of her friends, managed to get nine sewing machines in good working condition, and went to great trouble to get the consignment to us, along with some agricultural tools for ourselves and for the Patrician Brothers in Iten. I was gobsmacked and kept muttering like someone drunk: 'God bless her! God bless her!'

On Monday morning, I arrived at the school to see someone dressed in immaculate white – like an angel. I gasped in amazement: it was Jane. 'I have just completed my course', she explained, 'and yesterday my mother said to me, "Jane, it's high time you went to see Sister!"' I was speechless. As were the other Sisters and the staff. Word went fast through the village: *Mercy Technical is opening!*

Within a day or two, we had a rush of eager applicants for places. By the end of the week an excited bunch had started the first course in dressmaking. Under Jane's expert guidance, local girls and boys got an opportunity to train in dressmaking, and later in tailoring, arts and crafts, mathematics, business studies and agriculture. They even opened their own school shop, running it as a business enterprise. As numbers increased and their skills developed, they supplied top quality uniforms, crafts and clothes to schools and shops in the locality – our own secondary school included. This boosted their morale and encouraged many to set up their own private dressmaking and tailoring businesses later. It created a new kind of school complex too ... one we never envisaged.

Agents of liberation

After more than a decade in Kenya I returned to the home mission in Ireland in 1994. Since then I have had the great joy of visiting Kipkelion again on two occasions. On my last visit, my feelings were mixed. It was sad for me to see beautiful Kipkelion and its surrounds look so dismal. Just when they were recovering from the tribal clashes of 1991 and 1992, they were plunged into great suffering all over again during the troubles of 2008. Their lives under threat, many people were forced to leave. Our beloved Cistercian monks, who lived some 20km away from us, have had to say goodbye to their monastery and head for Uganda and elsewhere.

Yet through these dark times, life in Mercy Girls goes on. Our schools and clinics are thriving now under the management of a local congregation. They still employ Jane to run the technical school. These Sisters have added greatly to the schools and built a new clinic with a beautiful laboratory. God blessed us in our coming and in our going. As university and college graduates, many of our past students are, in their turn, preparing the next generation to serve as teachers, doctors, nurses or nuns. Others again run their own private businesses or agricultural programmes.

Through patience and perseverance, attitudes are gradually changing. The girls are sent to school now. Because they have been so downtrodden, historically, some let themselves be taken as a second or third wife. For the most part that has changed now, except in the interior, in the remote bush areas. In addition, the women have an increasing sense of their own dignity and value their own wisdom and giftedness. They all know how to cook, sew and knit.

My greatest joy was to hear a young woman say to me: 'Sister, I have a little money in my own pocket now, because I can sell my own knitted goods.' I could have cried for joy for her. She felt so proud of herself! I hope that the cycle of female exploitation will continue to be broken, as African women become active agents of their own liberation at every level. *Moladh go deo le Dia!*

Sr Mary Hudson, SSpS (Missionary Sisters Servants of the Holy Spirit), spent twenty years working in Papua New Guinea, mainly in communications – training and working with radio and television producers for many Pacific Island nations. She currently lives in Bristol, England. The following piece comes from her experience in Ethiopia as part of the Misean Cara team.

Water projects in Ethiopia

In February 2010, I was privileged to spend three weeks with our Sisters in Ethiopia. I was there on behalf of Misean Cara, an Irish funding agency, to monitor a water rehabilitation project being implemented by the Women Centre in Badessa headed by Sr Maria Jerly Renacia (SSpS).

What struck me forcibly about our Sisters' work in Ethiopia, especially in Badessa, was the integration of the different aspects of human development. In Badessa itself we have the Women Centre which oversees rural development projects, such as agricultural improvements, as well as numerous programmes that address issues like women's literacy, gender equality, skills training, income generating, upgrading of education for teenage girls, nutrition, health and HIV/AIDS; the centre also provides a kindergarten. This integration of development projects is also seen in Gulcha Sake, where four of the surrounding villages have access to a wide range of services. Sr Isabel from Brazil oversees the education programmes and Sr Florence from Papua New Guinea the health programmes.

Water – a commodity that is under-appreciated in rain-sodden Ireland – is of critical importance for many of these development programmes. The water rehabilitation project aims to provide clean water to three villages and a government health centre. The villagers are active participants in the project and have already provided some funds towards its realisation. Also, in each village, there are water committees who will receive management training so that they can eventually take over the responsibility of managing the water sources themselves.

Of course, not everything runs smoothly, and much patience is needed to deal with delays which seem unavoidable when dealing with government bureaucracy. Equipment and materials are not always readily available and much needs to be done before the rainy season makes travel and working conditions difficult. In the midst of all this is a human dynamo, Sr Jerly, who tries to keep everything moving in spite of obstacles.

I enjoyed visiting the different communities and seeing the nuns at work among the people and particularly meeting up with Sisters who had spent time in England and Ireland. I was very impressed by the fact that they had all struggled to learn Amharic, which is a difficult language with a completely different alphabet.

Br Colm O'Connell, from Co. Cork, was for many years the principal of a secondary school in the Rift Valley in Kenya. A Patrician Brother, he has over the years been a coach and mentor to many world-famous Kenyan athletes. Though he would be too modest to agree, he has helped to revolutionise middle- and long-distance running, and in the process brought respect, dignity and self-worth to the athletes and their communities. The following piece is adapted from a column he wrote for *Africa* magazine in 2004.

Taking on the world

Before many African countries gained independence, there must have been a burning ambition among its young men and women to gain immortality in the greatest of arenas, the Olympic games. But it was only a dream until Abebe Bikila of Ethiopia crossed the finishing line, barefooted, on that memorable night in Rome in 1960 – a victory in the marathon that opened the floodgates not only for his native country, but also for the whole continent. Few athletic enthusiasts realised at the time that a force was about to be released onto the world of middle- and long-distance running that would from then on leave a mark that no other continent could match.

Although Bikila was to provide the inspiration to Africa as a continent, it was the athletes from a smaller area in the western highlands of Kenya who were to capitalise on it. Winning their first medal in Tokyo in 1964, the Kenyan team left an indelible mark in Mexico City four years later and gave the world notice of their arrival. Who can forget that tactical win by Kipchoge Keino over the favourite, Jim Ryan, in the 1500m, or Naftali Temu's victory over the great Ron Clarke of Australia and Mama Woldre of Ethiopia in the 10,000m?

Walking around some of the rural villages in the western highlands of Kenya, one can come across world and Olympic champions strolling along the street or taking a cup of tea in one of the local restaurants. It may be difficult to imagine, yet it has become part of life here. Village after village in this area has such champions, either made or in the making. World-beaters, and yet they are treated as ordinary human beings at home. They, therefore, feel free among their familiar surroundings of open spaces and undulating hills.

When they speak of Kenya, many people visualise young kids running long distances barefooted to school, along dirt-roads and grassy fields. This is still a familiar sight in rural areas. It is a natural and effective environment for athletic development. There are those that even say that contact between bare feet and the natural ground is a source of inspiration. There are, of course, other theories put forward as to why Kenyans are such good runners – from lifestyle to diet, from altitude to genetics, from the hardship of the environment to the possibilities of wealth and fame. And the honour and glory of the little village.

The Western world tends to over-analyse things, always looking for perfect solutions and methods. It is not so in Kenya where people have a greater level of acceptance of life, taking it as it comes. Participation is often more important than results. And is this not the true spirit of the Olympic movement? Do Kenyans want to win? Yes. But I think that they have a good perspective on things and this is reflected in their attitude to winning and losing. Go to your local schools athletics competition and you will invariably notice the enthusiasm, interest and fun. Excessive demands and expectations in competitions can often take from the level of enjoyment, especially among the young. Do we place too much emphasis on winning?

It has taken time for society here to accept that running can be a career for women and that it can be successfully combined with marriage, but athletes such as Catherine Ndereba and Edith Masai have achieved great success. Years ago in Kenya, running had been considered a sport for girls, but not for women, and there is a clear social distinction between the two in Africa. We have come a long way since then.

Mary Lavelle, a Sister of Mercy, grew up in the 1940s in a family of eight children just outside Castlebar, Co. Mayo. She has lived in Kenya almost all of her adult life. She thinks that her happy childhood summers working on the home farm and saving the turf made the transition to Kenya smoother – when Kenyans remarked 'Sister, you don't understand' about their deprivation, she felt like replying, 'well, if you only knew!' She continues to learn a great deal from Africans and their way of life.

A community growing alongside a nation

'Sisters of Mercy to pioneer in troubled Kenya.' This was the eye-catching headline in the *Irish Catholic* in early 1956. It caught my eye and, above all, it took hold in my heart. By March, the first Mercy nuns had set sail from Dun Laoghaire to set up a Mater Misericordiae Hospital in Nairobi.

The 1950s in Kenya were years of the Mau Mau troubles with Jomo Kenyatta and his insurgents determined to free Kenya of colonial domination. This was the Kenya the nuns arrived into, via Mombasa, in March 1956. By September that year, after my Leaving Cert, I entered the novitiate of the Sisters of Mercy in Blackrock, Co. Dublin to start my religious and professional training.

On the stroke of midnight on 12 December 1963, the Union Jack was lowered in Nairobi, and Kenya had become an independent state. Ten months later, having trained in Dublin and London as a midwife, I arrived in Nairobi Airport. My heart was set on a missionary life.

The Mater Misericordiae Hospital had opened its doors in 1962. At the end of 1964, when I arrived, it was functioning well. The medical and surgical wards were busy. My first assignment was in the operating theatre. Instead of female theatre nurses swirling efficiently around, the staff comprised three African males. Our visiting surgeons and anaesthetists were of European and Indian nationality. It would be some years before there was a trickle of Kenyan doctors returning home following training in Makerere University in Uganda.

English was the language spoken throughout the hospital but at times people lapsed into their mother tongue, Kiswahili, or one of the many other languages of Kenya. I picked it up as I went along, but was not always quick enough to save being caught out. Once during an abdominal operation, as assistant to the surgeon, my role was to anticipate his surgical requirements from the instrument table. His hand was outstretched as he gently said '*Kisu*', meaning knife in Kiswahili. I hesitated, and he said, 'Oh sorry Sister, knife please'… before mischievously adding, 'Did you think I said "kiss you"?'

Altogether we were eight Sisters in the community, covering two wards (one medical, one surgical) and a kitchen. The laundry, maintenance department, and the boiler house all came under the watchful eye of the administrator who happened to be the Mother Superior.

It was a time of great change, growth and development. Kenya was growing as a young nation. We felt, as a Mercy Community, we were growing alongside and into the nation. There was pride and challenge in *Mzee* Jomo Kenyatta's motto and clarion call of *Harambee*, meaning 'Let us pull together'. When he waved his flywhisk aloft on national days the celebrations commenced and the park erupted in song and cheers. Our role as missionary Sisters to the people of Kenya became clearer and more joyful as we settled in our new homeland. Our inspiration came from our community's constitution, which reminds us of our 'preferential love for the poor'.

Sadness descended on Kenya in August 1978 with the death of Mzee Kenyatta. State House and its environs offered a scene of uncontrolled grief as we filed past his body lying in state. The state funeral was one of pomp and ceremony befitting the dignity of the man. His mausoleum is one of Nairobi's landmarks. His successor as president, Daniel Arap Moi, visited the hospital on a number of occasions while his son Jonathan was a patient. He appreciated the service given and hoped that there would be extension of the facilities.

His hopes and ours were realised in the coming years as land was made available and the site prepared. Eventually, the bed capacity was increased to 130. Residential accommodation was provided for staff. Ancillary services were modernised and improved to meet the ever-increasing demand. We owe a deep debt of gratitude to our donors who throughout the years have assisted us in carrying out our mission, especially to the poor of society.

In August 1982, there was an attempted *coup d'état*. Fortunately, forces loyal to the government succeeded in bringing the situation under control, but not before there was a trail of havoc and destruction. At the hospital, orders were given not to treat the 'rebels'. It was my first experience of fear since arriving in Nairobi. How was I to distinguish, I asked the three officials who came to deliver the order. Check their military affiliation! A person seriously injured, maybe on the point of death! This would shatter all of our policies with regard to care of the needy in critical circumstances.

I thought and prayed, then rang Cardinal Otunga for guidance. Normally a man of gentle disposition, the anger came across in his voice: 'Sister, treat any person who is injured, as you and the staff deem necessary.' He took the issue further. Within two hours, there was a directive from the Department of Health to each hospital in the city: *All injured persons to be treated regardless of affiliation.* It took some months before peace was fully restored.

As the years rolled by and I started counting not in years anymore but in decades I came to realise my classification as a *shosho* (elderly woman or grandmother in Kiswahili) was accurate. I thank God for having assumed a less physically demanding but equally enjoyable role as assistant librarian in our Catherine McAuley School of Nursing. It is an exhilarating experience to work with young Kenyan students, so keen to acquire knowledge by energetically availing of all resources at hand. It is a blessing and privilege that Kenyans have taken their rightful place in our institutions as well as in the public service. Of the 500 staff employed here there are currently just five Sisters of Mercy, three of whom are Kenyans.

Sometimes I am asked when will I return and retire at home – meaning Ireland. The fact is, home for me has been in Kenya for the past four and a half decades. I love my Sisters and family members in Ireland but, if God so wills, may the Kenyan soil rest gently o'er my grave.

Aisling Foley, a solicitor from Co. Cork, went to Cape Town, South Africa as a lay missionary in 2009.

Where there is hope

If someone had told me three years ago that I would go from working as a solicitor in a large Dublin office to working in a children's home in South Africa, I would have thought they were crazy! Maybe it's a testament to the human character that we are capable of adapting to different environments much more than we think.

Home of Hope was opened by a South African couple five years ago in response to the increase in violence against children in South Africa. Some statistics to put this into perspective: a child is abused every eight minutes in South Africa, a child is assaulted every fourteen minutes in South Africa, and a child is raped every twenty-four minutes in South Africa. Frightening statistics that I got to see first hand in the babies I cared for in *Home of Hope*, all of whom had been abandoned, abused or neglected. One child had even been raped at twelve months old.

Home of Hope was delighted when I joined them as they had many projects with which they needed help. My initial role was to train staff and volunteers on good child care techniques; help with caring for the babies; counsel the abused teenagers; and generally assist with the running of the home.

Using research skills I had acquired as a lawyer, I embarked on researching one of the main conditions affecting about fifty per cent of the children in our care. This condition is known as Foetal Alcohol Spectrum Disorders (FASD). About 72,000 children a year are born in South Africa suffering from FASD. FASD is a series of conditions affecting children whose mothers drank heavily during their pregnancy. The effect is that the children are born with permanent brain damage which is displayed in their behaviour, being typically labelled as hyperactive, difficult, slow, aggressive and undisciplined. Naturally, they don't do well at school and so, typically, drop out early and get into trouble with the law.

The Western Cape of South Africa, where Cape Town is situated, has the highest rate of FASD in the world. Despite the massive number of children suffering from this condition, very few people (including the parents of these children) know much about FASD or how to bring up children with the condition. Very few of the children are diagnosed and practically no support is offered to their care-givers. My research developed into a booklet explaining the condition and containing practical ways to deal with and care for these children. We hope to distribute this widely throughout the community to help care-givers and teachers to better understand these children and their unique needs.

As time went on it became apparent, through observing the children in our care, that most children suffering from FASD are incapable of succeeding in mainstream schools, and so, in 2010, *Home of Hope* made the decision to take on the pioneering project of opening a school specifically for FASD children. This will be the first school of its kind on the African continent and as project manager I feel honoured to be involved in such a pioneering project that is going to change the lives of so many children.

Living in a different country far away from family and friends comes with its challenges, but even on 'bad' days you know that the work you're doing is making a difference. It's easy to get trapped into a cycle of materialism – making sure that you have the latest car, clothes and other mod cons that we convince ourselves we need. Those of us who were lucky to be born into caring families and to get a good education sometimes have a unique opportunity to 'give something back', and when we see that opportunity we must grab it if we can.

Fr Seán Mullin (CSSp) is a Galwayman from just outside Tuam. He is a parish priest in Durban, South Africa. Here he tells of his experience of the 2010 World Cup.

Learning together

We have a small, inner-city, non-residential parish which draws people from all over Durban. Football-loving parishioners follow the English Premier League week after week, and Manchester United and Liverpool are especially big here.

On World Cup Sunday we had eighteen teams participating in a World Cup parish programme, which started immediately after Mass. There was a great sense of joy and unity on that day when people stayed right to the end. Most wore football jerseys, and we had banners for the different countries, and so on. Since mid-May, we have had the flags of the countries participating in the World Cup flying high, with the South African flag at the entrance to welcome visitors.

At our two schools, St Anthony's and St Augustine's primary schools, each class adopted a World Cup team, but something far greater developed from this. It became a history and geography lesson on the countries concerned – pupils researched population figures, the different ethnic groups, the climate, the major cities, and so on. Classroom windows and walls were filled with material. The teachers and principals took all of this on board wonderfully.

At every lunch break mini-World Cup tournaments, with pupils togged out in the featured teams' colours, were played, and vuvuzelas were blown at full blast. The whole World Cup experience has promoted a tremendous sense of joy and enthusiasm which has radiated right through the parish and schools. The challenge from now on, hopefully, is to keep this experience going, at community level and throughout the country.

I see sport as a great unifier of people. I see a great sense of national pride in South Africa in being able to pull off an event on such a scale. It showed the potential of building a nation with no reservations in their shared joy, and in which race and colour are left behind. And it revealed what great things might be achieved by coming together in unity and joy. It is *ubuntu* – the wonderful Africa concept of respect and kindness, and connection with others.

Fr Jack Finucane's involvement with Concern dates back to its founding in 1968 in Nigeria/Biafra, where he was a Spiritan missionary. He served for many years as country director in Ethiopia and in Bangladesh and later served as regional director for the Horn and Central Africa. He has had a long and distinguished career in the development field. After he officially retired in 2002, he continued to undertake special assignments in Sudan, Ethiopia, Sri Lanka and Haiti on behalf of Concern. He continues to sit on the board of Concern US.

A most ambitious project

Concern Worldwide began in 1968 as a response of the people of Ireland to famine in Biafra, the breakaway eastern region of Nigeria. Efforts to reintegrate the oil rich breakaway state had been stubbornly resisted. As Biafran territory shrank before the advance of the vastly greater Nigerian forces, famine and internal displacement of population escalated.

The area that was Biafra had huge associations with Ireland through the activity of missionaries. There were more than 700 priests, nuns and brothers from Ireland in Biafra. Associated with them in schools, hospitals and community work were numerous young Irish teachers, nurses, doctors and social workers, including many Irish Protestant missionaries. Irish Methodist missionaries were particularly well-established in several places.

It was little wonder that the story of the mounting disasters in Biafra found a sympathetic audience in homes throughout Ireland. Television, newly installed in so many homes in the 1960s, played an important role in fanning this wave of sympathy. There was an outpouring of caring and generosity. Countless fund-raising efforts, great and small, got under way.

One initiative, Africa Concern, was later described as 'the most ambitious relief project ever mounted in Ireland ... nothing less than a national crusade began with a few people who believed in lighting one candle rather than cursing the darkness.' It was in the home of Kay and John O'Loughlin Kennedy on 19 March 1968 that a group of people decided to organise more formally, and chose the name 'Africa Concern' for their organisation. From the beginning, the Holy Ghost Fathers were involved and played a very significant role in the development of the organisation. Some were involved for a few years, others for many years – like Frs Raymond Kennedy, Mick Doheny, Aengus Finucane and myself.

Concern purchased a 600-ton vessel, now named the *Columcille*, which delivered its first cargo of relief supplies to the island of São Tomé on 29 September 1968. From this Portuguese island off the coast of Nigeria, relief supplies took off nightly for Uli in Biafra. These flights over Nigerian-held areas, and often through gunfire, provided the last link in the relief chain to Biafra. In October 1968, it was resolved 'that the sending and financing of specialist teams to help with relief work or rehabilitation or development of underprivileged countries was, in principle, an appropriate activity for Africa Concern'. The organisation was broadening its support base as well as spreading in West Africa. It would grow to be the largest NGO in Ireland and a significant player on the international scene. Forty years after its inception, Concern has more than 3,200 staff and workers in thirty countries.

In February 1969, Africa Concern began to operate charter flights from Liberville in Gabon. And when a second plane joined the operation, flights averaged fifteen per week. In the first year Africa Concern despatched five shiploads of relief supplies to Biafra, as well as operating an airlift from Liberville and being part of the huge Joint Church Aid airlift operating from São Tomé. The organisation had volunteers in Nigeria, Gabon, Ivory Coast and São Tomé.

It was at Ihioma Catholic mission on 10 January 1970, where I was then parish priest and Caritas co-ordinator, that the advancing Nigerian forces met a Biafran delegation and began to negotiate the surrender. Several missionaries were arrested and imprisoned following the surrender. Ihioma mission had been the distribution centre for the vast amounts of airlifted life-saving supplies which were filtered to village level through the mission network during the war.

When the hostilities in Biafra ended in January 1970, the board of Africa Concern met to plan future policy (Africa Concern's strong pro-Biafran stance was anything but popular with the Irish government!). Africa Concern made the *Columcille* available to UNICEF for use between Lagos and the famine areas along the coast. For eighteen months work continued in Gabon, caring for many stranded Biafran families, and facilitating the return to Nigeria of some thousands of children who had been flown to Liberville on returning relief planes. They were given intensive care in special camps.

Any doubts about there being an ongoing role for the organisation were dispelled when the world was alerted to staggering needs in East Pakistan at the end of 1970. A massive cyclone from the Bay of Bengal swept through the low-lying delta region in November of that year. On the heels of this disaster came the civil war which resulted in the creation of the independent state of Bangladesh. This war created a huge refugee problem in Calcutta.

The name 'Africa Concern' gave way to 'Concern' when the organisation sent a medical and engineering team to Calcutta in June 1971 to help cope with the more than three million refugees who had poured into the region. Concern's work in Asia thus began at Salt Lake refugee camp in Calcutta, India. In February 1972, Concern sent its first team to Bangladesh. It was in Bangladesh that Concern first operated with a large team of volunteers and it was there that the guidelines for volunteering with Concern were developed and standardised.

It was in Bangladesh also that Concern moved beyond emergency response to rehabilitation and development programmes. In 1975, there were fifty-five volunteers engaged in a wide variety of projects, each with a rehabilitation and training component, and they were working hand-in-hand with a growing number of committed and skilled Bangladeshi staff. At this time several Holy Ghost Fathers were involved. Raymond Kennedy was CEO, based in Dublin; Aengus Finucane was director in Bangladesh; I was director in Ethiopia; Michael Brosnan replaced Jimmy O'Toole, who died in Yemen; and Mick Doheny had a roving brief. There is no doubt but that the ethos of the Holy Ghost Fathers was passed on to Concern.

Fr Aengus was to continue working with Concern until his death in 2009. In the early 1980s, he became CEO and continued in that role until his 'retirement' in 1997, when he became honorary president of Concern US. For forty years he was the driving force behind Concern.

Concern has been involved in every emergency since 1968 in Africa, Asia and the Caribbean and it has gone from strength to strength since those early days in Biafra. Our motto is:

> *Do as much as you can,*
> *as well as you can,*
> *for as long as you can,*
> *for as many as you can.*

Glossary of Terms

Blackwater fever	a serious complication of malaria
Catechist	a trainer of catechumens (see *Catechumen*)
Catechumen	an adult receiving instruction in the principles of Christianity, with a view to eventual baptism
Duik duik	a type of small antelope
Hakuna matata	a Swahili phrase, meaning 'all will be well'
Hodi	in Swahili, a greeting meaning 'may I come in?'
Jembe	a hoe, in Swahili
Kiswahili	see *Swahili* below
Meitheal	in Irish, a work group composed of neighbours and friends
Murram	a dirt-track
Mzungu/wazungu	white person
Novitiate/postulancy	the periods of training or preparation undertaken by a novice member of a religious order before taking vows
Piki piki	the Swahili term for a scooter
Shamba	a field used for growing crops
Swahili	(or, in Swahili, *Kiswahili*) a Bantu language widely spoken in East Africa

The Irish Missionary Union Survey

Fr Eamon Aylward (SS.CC) is the executive secretary of the Irish Missionary Union (IMU). The IMU is an umbrella group representing eighty-three lay and religious Catholic missionary organisations. The Association of Missionary Societies (AMS) fulfils a similar function for Church of Ireland missionary societies. The IMU kindly provide the following survey on Ireland's current missionary activity.

Survey of Irish personnel overseas, 2008

The survey of Irish missionary and volunteer personnel working overseas has again been revised by the Irish Missionary Union. This edition represents the figures as of December 2008.

This survey provides the reader with statistical information regarding the number of missionaries and their associates in various countries throughout the developing world. In particular, the major part of the survey deals with the numbers of Irish-born missionaries, linking them with their organisations and the countries where they serve. If you are interested in knowing the type of work our Irish missionaries are involved in, go to our IMU website at www.imu.ie and click on 'Irish Missionaries Worldwide'.

Undoubtedly, there are other Irish-born missionaries at work in the developing world who are not included in this survey. Some of these may belong to orders with whom we at the IMU have no contact, because they are not members or they may be missionaries who joined a religious order in the US or in one of the other European countries. Despite these limitations and the mobility of missionary personnel, you can regard this survey as a reasonably accurate picture of the number of Irish-born missionaries serving overseas.

Once again in this survey we have attempted to provide missionary numbers from Europe, from mission areas and the total numbers in congregations that have a base in Ireland. The figures for the overall totals are not accurate as some groups were unable to access the information covering their international operations.

Currently there are approximately 1,969 Roman Catholic missionaries from Ireland working in eighty-six countries in Africa (1,199), Asia/Oceania

(385), Latin America and Caribbean (349), the Middle East and Eastern Europe (36). There are 182 missionaries from other Christian churches on mission in various parts of the developing world. The overall figure of 2,151 Irish missionaries for 2008 represents an 11.04% decrease from our survey in 2006.

My sincere thanks to all who submitted statistics for this survey. My thanks also to Karen Whelan at our IMU office, for compiling these statistics into a usable format.

NUMBER OF IRISH CATHOLIC MISSIONARIES PER COUNTRY OF ASSIGNMENT

Africa

Algeria	2
Angola	2
Botswana	8
Cameroon	15
Egypt	10
Ethiopia	13
The Gambia	10
Ghana	19
Kenya	213
Lesotho	2
Liberia	5
Malawi	20
Mauritius	10
Morocco	3
Mozambique	2
Nigeria	122
Senegal	2
Seychelles	4
Sierra Leone	9
South Africa	412
Sudan	16
Swaziland	6
Tanzania	49
Uganda	48
Zambia	142
Zimbabwe	55
Total:	**1199**

Asia/Oceania

American Samoa	1
Bangladesh	1
Cambodia	2
China	15
Fiji	20
Hong Kong	25
India	52
Indonesia	3
Japan	23
Korea	50
Macao	1
Malaysia	11
Myanmar	5
Pakistan	57
Papua New Guinea	7
Philippines	93
Siberia	1
Singapore	6
Solomon Islands	2
Sri Lanka	1
Taiwan	5
Thailand	4
Total:	**385**

Latin America/Caribbean

Argentina	18
Bahamas	1
Belize	1
Bolivia	6
Brazil	114
Chile	27
Colombia	2
Costa Rica	1
Cuba	1
Ecuador	17
El Salvador	7
Grenada	10
Guatemala	8
Haiti	5
Honduras	5
Mexico	8
Nicaragua	6
Paraguay	6
Peru	63
St. Lucia	4
St. Vincent	2
Surinam	1
Trinidad & Tobago	22
Uruguay	3
Venezuela	15
Total:	**356**

Middle East and Eastern Europe

Bosnia-Herzegovina	2
Czech Republic	1
Iraq/Jordan	1
Israel	8
Lebanon	1
Poland	1
Romania	6
Russia	2
Slovakia	9
Syria	1
Ukraine	1
West Bank	3
Total:	**36**

Missionaries	
Africa	1199
Asia-Oceania	385
Latin America-Caribbean	356
Middle East & E. Europe	36
Total:	**1976**

Countries	
Africa	26
Asia-Oceania	22
Latin American-Caribbean	26
Middle East & E. Europe	12
Total:	**86**

IRISH MISSIONARIES FROM OTHER CHRISTIAN CHURCHES AND
LAY MISSIONARY GROUPS

Asia (Central)	5	Germany	2	Paraguay	5
Asia (South)	1	Ghana	3	Peru	3
Asia (South East)	3	India	1	Philippines	8
Bangladesh	4	Indonesia	4	Romania	4
Benin	1	Jamaica	1	Singapore	1
Brazil	2	Japan	7	South Africa	1
Britain & Ireland	27	Kenya	10	Spain	2
Burkina Faso	4	Madagascar	1	Taiwan	1
Burundi	1	Malawi	11	Tanzania	2
Cameroon	3	Malaysia	2	Thailand	4
China	5	Mali	2	Tonga	1
D. R. Congo	1	Middle East	2	Uganda	10
East Africa	1	Morocco	1	Zambia	5
Egypt	2	Nepal	15	In Training, etc.	2
Ethiopia	3	Nigeria	4	**Total:**	**182**
Eurasia	2	Pakistan	2		

IRISH DEVELOPMENT AND RELIEF WORKERS

Afghanistan	2	Korea (North)	2	Sierra Leone	5
Angola	3	Kosovo	1	Somalia	1
Bangladesh	2	Laos	4	Sri Lanka	1
Bolivia	1	Lesotho	3	Sudan – North	9
Cambodia	5	Liberia	8	Sudan – South	14
Chad	5	Malawi	5	Tanzania	4
China	12	Malaysia	1	Timor Leste	1
D.R. Congo	5	Mozambique	6	Uganda	10
Ethiopia	8	Nepal	1	Ukraine	1
Haiti	1	Niger	5	Vietnam	1
Honduras	2	Nigeria	1	Zimbabwe	3
India	2	Pakistan	4	Roving Volunteers	6
Indonesia	3	Philippines	1		
Kenya	11	Rwanda	1	**Total:**	**161**

IRISH CATHOLIC MISSIONARIES OVERSEAS IN 2008

Continent	Priests	Sisters	Brothers	Laity	Total
Africa	482	594	59	64	1199
Asia-Oceania	212	132	38	3	385
Latin America/					
Caribbean	180	129	19	21	349
Middle East/					
Eastern Europe	7	29	–	–	36
Totals	**881**	**884**	**116**	**88**	**1969**

IRISH MISSIONARIES FROM OTHER CHRISTIAN CHURCHES

Continent	2004	2006	2008	Difference	% Difference
Africa	84	88	66	-22	-25%
Asia/Oceania	67	66	65	-1	-1.51%
Latin America/					
Caribbean	15	8	12	+4	+50%
Other Countries &					
In Training, etc.	49	49	39	-10	-20.40%
Totals	**215**	**211**	**182**	**-29**	**-13.74%**

TOTALS FOR ALL MISSIONARY SOCIETIES

Africa	**1265**
Asia/Oceania	**450**
Latin America/Caribbean	**361**
Other Countries/In Training, etc.	**75**
	2151[1]

1 This figure, 2151, represents a decrease of 11.04% since 2006. The figures **exclude** missionaries with whom the IMU has no contact, such as those working in industrialised nations (e.g. Canada, USA, New Zealand).

The following are the organisations included in the IMU survey:

CONGREGATIONS OF SISTERS
Sisters of Bon Secours
Brigidine Sisters
Carmelite Sisters
Columban Sisters
Congregation of the Sisters of Nazareth
Cross & Passion Sisters
Daughters of Charity of St Vincent de Paul
Daughters of the Holy Spirit
Daughters of Mary & Joseph
Daughters of Our Lady of the Sacred Heart
Dominican Sisters
Dominican Congregation of St Catherine of Siena
Faithful Companions of Jesus
Franciscan Missionaries of Divine Motherhood
Franciscan Missionaries of Mary
Franciscan Missionaries of St Joseph
Franciscan Missionary Sisters for Africa
Franciscan Sisters of the Immaculate Conception
Good Shepherd Sisters
Handmaids of the Sacred Heart of Jesus
Holy Cross Sisters
Holy Faith Sisters
Institute of Our Lady of Mercy
La Retraite Sisters
La Sainte Union Sisters
Little Company of Mary
Little Sisters of the Assumption
Little Sisters of the Poor
Loreto Sisters
Marist Sisters
Medical Missionaries of Mary

Mercy Sisters
Missionary Franciscan Sisters of the Immaculate Conception
Missionary Sisters of the Assumption
Missionary Sisters of the Holy Rosary
Missionary Sisters Servants of the Holy Spirit
Missionary Sisters of Our Lady of Apostles
Poor Servants of the Mother of God
Presentation Sisters
Religious of Jesus and Mary
Religious of the Sacred Heart of Mary
Religious Sisters of Charity
Rosminian Sisters of Providence
Sisters of the Sacred Hearts of Jesus & Mary
Sacred Hearts Sisters
Salesian Sisters
St John of God Sisters
St Joseph of Annecy Sisters
St Joseph of Chambery Sisters
Sisters of St Joseph of Cluny
St Louis Sisters
Sisters of Charity of the Incarnate Word
Sisters of Charity of St Paul the Apostle
Sisters of Our Lady of Charity
Sisters of Our Lady of the Missions
Sisters of Sion
Sisters of St Clare (Generalate)
Sisters of St Joseph of the Apparition
Sisters of the Infant Jesus
Society of the Sacred Heart
Ursuline Sisters

SOCIETIES OF PRIESTS
Augustinian Fathers
Capuchin Franciscan Order

Carmelites
Columban Missionaries
Comboni Missionaries
Divine Word Missionaries
Dominican Fathers
Franciscan Friars
Holy Spirit Congregation
Jesuits
Marianist Community
Marist Fathers
Mill Hill Missionaries
Missionaries of Africa (White Fathers)
Missionaries of the Sacred Heart
Oblates of Mary Immaculate
Order of St Camillus
Pallotines
Passionists
Redemptorist Community Ligouri
Rosminian Fathers
Sacred Hearts Community
Salesian Fathers Provincial Office
Servite Community
Society of African Missions
Society of St James the Apostle
Society of Jesus
St Patrick's Missionary Society
Vincentians

SOCIETY OF BROTHERS
Christian Brothers Province Centre
De La Salle Brothers
Franciscan Brothers

Hospitaller Order of St John of God
Patrician Brothers
Presentation Brothers

LAY MISSIONARY SOCIETIES
Viatores Christi
Volunteer Missionary Movement

ASSOCIATE MEMBERS OF THE IMU
Aid to the Church in Need
Apostolic Work
Pontifical Mission Societies
Church Missionary Society Ireland
Crosslinks
International Service Fellowship
Methodist Missionary Society (Ireland)
Overseas Missionary Fellowship
Presbyterian Church in Ireland
Serving in Mission Ireland
South American Missionary Society
Wycliffe Bible Translators

DEVELOPMENT AND RELIEF
  AGENCIES
Association for International Teaching
Childfund Ireland
Concern
GOAL
Irish Aid
Irish Red Cross
Plan Ireland
Trócaire

No hurry in Africa is Brendan Clerkin's engrossing and often hilarious account of his gap year in East Africa. He takes the reader on a roller-coaster ride from the slums of Nairobi to the snow-capped summit of Mount Kilimanjaro, and from the Turkana Desert to exotic Zanzibar (for further information, see www.originalwriting.ie).